D0078834

The Baltimore Book: New Views of Local History

YES, WE HAVE NO PAJAMAS TODAY
KAYLON'S ON STRIKE

SHIRTMAKERS UNION · A.C.W.A.

KAYLON WORKERS —ASK FOR— DECENT WAGES, HOURS of WORK and Working Conditions

SHIRTMAKERS UNION · A.C.W.A.

Critical Perspectives on the Past   A series edited by Susan Porter Benson, Stephen Brier, and Roy Rosenzweig

The Baltimore Book

New Views of Local History

Edited by Elizabeth Fee, Linda Shopes,

Linda Zeidman

Temple University Press: Philadelphia

975.26
B1971

Temple University Press, Philadelphia 19122

Copyright © 1991 by Temple University.

All rights reserved. Published 1991

Printed in the United States of America

The paper used in this publication is acid

free for greater permanence.

Library of Congress Cataloging in Publication Data

The Baltimore book : new views

of local history / edited by Elizabeth Fee,

Linda Shopes, Linda Zeidman. p. cm. –

(Critical perspectives on the past). Includes

bibliographical references and index.

ISBN 0-87722-817-5 – ISBN 0-87722-823-X (pb.)

1. Baltimore (Md.) – History. 2. Baltimore

(Md.) – Description – Tours. 3. Working

class – Maryland – Baltimore – History.

4. Baltimore (Md.) – Industries – History.

I. Fee, Elizabeth. II. Shopes, Linda.

III. Zeidman, Linda. IV. Series.

F189.B157B342 1991 975'.26–dc20 90-27469 CIP

The first two maps in Chapter 10 originally appeared

in the International Journal of Oral History

5, no.1 (February 1984):37. Copyright

© 1984 Meckler Publishing. They are

reprinted here with permission. The map

on page 216 originally appeared

in the Maryland Historical Magazine 80,

no.3 (Fall 1985): 205. Copyright © 1985

Maryland Historical Society, it is reprinted

with permission. The lines from

"Baltimore" by Randy Newman introducing

Chapter 11 are copyright © 1977

by Six Pictures Music. Used by permission.

All rights reserved.

TP

Contents

UNIVERSITY LIBRARIES
CARNEGIE-MELLON UNIVERSITY
PITTSBURGH, PENNSYLVANIA 15213

Introduction: Toward a New History of Baltimore

The Baltimore Book is a new kind of history of the working people of Baltimore—the activists who built organizations, unions, and working-class communities—and a tour guide of the places and events that mark their struggles and triumphs. The lives of these people—blacks and whites, men and women, Jews and gentiles, Irish, Germans, Poles, Italians, Finns, Greeks, and other immigrant groups—are celebrated here, some perhaps for the first time.

The history presented in this book, like the people whose history it is, has often been denied and devalued. Until recently, Baltimore has been a blue-collar city, a city of many laboring women and men and the few for whom they labored. Yet, with some welcome exceptions, its official history has been one of patriotism, war, and a few powerful white men. Most visitors and residents know about Fort McHenry, Francis Scott Key, and the "Star-Spangled Banner," but how many know about the mill villages of Hampden–Woodberry or the great railroad strike of 1877?

Baltimore has also been a racially divided city, one with deep racial antagonisms and a vital African-American community. How many city residents know that Frederick Douglass, the famous abolitionist, spent his early years as a slave in Fells Point? How many know the history of the civil rights struggle in Baltimore in the twentieth century?

This book is admittedly partisan. The authors were nurtured in the dissident politics of the 1960s and bring to their work both an appreciation for the dignity of working lives and a vision of social justice and equality. Our purpose is to look at the city in a new way so that visitors and those who live here can develop a deeper appreciation of the struggles of the people who came before us and built the city that we see today.

Each chapter in this book discusses the extraordinary history of some ordinary Baltimoreans and directs you to places where they tried, often under the most difficult circumstances, to create lives of meaning and purpose. You'll also meet people reflecting on their lives, explaining how they worked, with varying degrees of success, to make Baltimore a better place to live. Dozens of photographs bring the events and people to life and provide a firsthand look into the past.

For most of the Baltimoreans described in these pages, success has been measured in modest terms: buying a rowhouse in Old West Baltimore; working shorter hours; being able, as a black woman, to get a job at the telephone company; being able, as a white woman, to have a job as a cutter in a garment factory; managing, as a white man, to hold on to a job as a skilled can maker instead of being replaced by a machine; or, as a black man, being able to run for political office. Some have measured success by community achievements: saving a neighborhood from being destroyed by road building or redevelopment, having a voice in urban renewal, obtaining a better education for their children.

Working Baltimoreans, men and women without much power or status, often have taken great risks to achieve their goals. Many have risked their jobs and their homes to build a union or protest social injustice. These men and women have worked long and hard, on the job, at home, and in their communities. Where they have succeeded, they have done so against great odds, and their successes deserve to be celebrated.

The chapters in this book present a history of crisis, conflict, change, and failure to change, as those with little power over their lives have fought for more. People frequently think of success as getting ahead through individual effort, in competition with others. Yet some have sought to better their lives by group efforts to challenge basic inequalities. Their experiences suggest that they have been most successful when they were able to overcome the barriers of race, ethnicity, and gender and to act in unity.

Some of this book is about a history that many of us don't want to acknowledge or want to forget. It is also a history of people's frustrations, disappointments, crushed dreams, and anxieties to hold on to whatever security they have been able to achieve for themselves. These anxieties have sometimes been expressed as antagonism toward others, and racism is an especially tragic example, as this book shows.

The editors hope you will find these different discussions of the lives and work of ordinary Baltimoreans a welcome antidote to more familiar, sanitized views of the past. We hope, too, that some of these memories of an earlier Baltimore will strike a responsive chord and may provide insight into your own past.

How This Book Began
This book started as a series of presentations for the People's History Tour of Baltimore—a bus tour of places in the city that were important to labor, civil rights, and women's history. The initial tour in 1982 was one of several events celebrating the open-

ing of a center, created by a group of scholars, the Research Associates, for progressive organizations, offices, and events, and to house the Alternative Press Center, a day-care center, and a cooperative apartment. Research Associates bought and renovated an old library originally owned by the city, and in 1982 opened the Progressive Action Center at the corner of Gorsuch and Kirk Avenues in northeast Baltimore.

The three editors of this volume—Linda Zeidman, Linda Shopes, and Elizabeth Fee—agreed to put together a history tour of Baltimore. We pooled our knowledge, searched for new sources of information, and talked to professional historians and community residents who had researched aspects of local history. We looked for places and events to represent the city's major industries and reflect the lives of both white and black Baltimoreans.

The result was a five-hour tour stopping at a dozen sites. At each one, a local historian would meet the group, talk for 10 or 15 minutes, and answer questions. Many of the chapters in this book originated with those tour stops: Camden Station, Evergreen House, Hampden–Woodberry, Old West Baltimore, Fells Point, Sparrows Point, and Federal Hill.[1]

The People's History Tour clearly struck a responsive chord. Many residents, as well as visitors to Baltimore, wanted to hear about the issues and struggles dividing the city, rather than a romanticized version of the past. They were interested in the stories of ordinary people, not the famous few usually discussed in history books.

We soon found we could not fill all the requests for tours and decided we needed some way of helping people organize their own tours. We decided to turn our experience into a book, expanding the tour presentations, adding a few new ones, and illustrating them with photographs and maps. We also added interviews with some of the people who have actively participated in making the history of the city.

How to Use This Book
Since *The Baltimore Book* is both a history and a tour

1. Elizabeth Fee, Sylvia Gillett, Linda Shopes, and Linda Zeidman, "Baltimore by Bus: Steering a New Course through the City's History," *Radical History Review* 28–30 (1984): 206–216.

guide, the chapters recommend places to visit and are accompanied by maps and photographs. We hope many readers will decide to visit the sites we discuss in each chapter, both to discover new parts of Baltimore and to look at familiar places from a new perspective. Those with lively historical imaginations will be able to see the striking clothing workers picketing the garment factories on Redwood Street, the Fifth Regiment of the Maryland militia marching from its armory along Eutaw Street to Camden Station in 1877, and the civil rights leaders meeting at the home of Lillie Carroll Jackson on Eutaw Street in the 1950s.

Most of the chapters describe an area in which interesting sites are close enough to be visited in a walking tour or short car trip. Some of the original buildings have been torn down, and you will see how the cityscape represents layers of Baltimore's history.

A complete tour of all of the sites mentioned in the book will take at least a full day. A city outline map with each chapter map shows the general area discussed in each so that you can locate these areas in relation to the whole and plan a trip accordingly.

We have arranged the chapters partly to show relationships in subject matter and partly to follow a geographically logical route, starting and ending at the Inner Harbor. Because each chapter is a substantive historical essay on some aspect of local history, you can also follow your interests and read them in any order.

The Tour

The tour starts downtown at the Baltimore and Ohio Railroad Station at Camden Yards, site of a massive uprising in the great railroad strike of 1877 and soon to be the home of Baltimore's new stadium. The railroad was key to Baltimore's success as a center for trade and commerce in the nineteenth century; our first two essays deal with different aspects of the railroad's history.

We begin with the railroad workers. Sylvia Gillett describes the desperation of Baltimore's working class in the depression of the 1870s as they were subjected to wage cuts, unemployment, and homelessness. The strike of 1877 started in Martinsburg,

West Virginia, and spread along the railroad lines to Cumberland, Maryland.

When Governor John Carroll called out the Maryland National Guard to quell the strike, Baltimore's workers and citizens gathered at Camden Yards in angry opposition. Thousands of the railroad workers' wives, children, and neighbors, in "the fiercest mob ever known in Baltimore," joined the demonstration against the regiments of soldiers. So began the largest single industrial uprising in U.S. history.

We then travel north to Evergreen House, one of the homes owned by John Work Garrett, who was president of the Baltimore and Ohio Railroad during the 1877 strike. This mansion displays the wealth and luxury enjoyed by those who owned the railroads and factories and who profited from Baltimore's early industrial development. It thus dramatically illustrates the distinction between those who controlled and those who worked in the new industrial order.

Elizabeth Fee introduces us to John Work Garrett and discusses the economic and political importance of the railroads to Baltimore, Maryland, and the nation. She also notes that Garrett's daughter, Mary Elizabeth, was an early feminist who used some of her family's fortune to fund the Bryn Mawr School for Girls, the Johns Hopkins Medical School, and Bryn Mawr College—all to provide better educational opportunities for women.

Following the Evergreen House essay are two interviews excerpted from the Maryland group of ex-slave narratives collected by the Works Progress Administration (WPA) in the 1930s. On the eve of the Civil War, Baltimore had the largest free black population of any city in the country, and after emancipation, many former slaves left rural Maryland and came to Baltimore.

Caroline Hammond explains how she, her mother, and her father escaped from slavery in Anne Arundel County along the Underground Railroad and were sheltered in Baltimore on their way to Pennsylvania. They later returned to Baltimore where Hammond worked as a cook.

Richard Macks describes what it was like growing up as a slave on a tobacco plantation in Charles County, Maryland. After emancipation, Macks came to Baltimore and worked as a waiter and coachman;

later he became head butler to Robert Garrett, the son of John Work Garrett, who succeeded his father as president of the Baltimore and Ohio Railroad. Eventually, Macks opened a catering business and became a prominent member of the local African-American community.

From Evergreen House, we move to the working-class community of Hampden–Woodberry, which grew up around the cotton textile industry in the mid nineteenth century. Hampden–Woodberry was essentially a company town built around the cotton mills, with company housing, a company store, company-sponsored recreational activities, and company-financed churches.

Bill Harvey tells us about the people who left their farms in rural Maryland and Virginia to work in Hampden's cotton mills and who built a distinctive and distinctly white community, isolated from the rest of Baltimore. Life in Hampden was relatively comfortable until the decline in demand for cotton goods after World War I brought longer working hours and reduced wages. The workers struck, unsuccessfully, in 1923; Harvey describes how, as the industry declined and the mills were sold off, the tight community of mill workers began to erode. You can still see the remnants of the culture of the old mill town in Hampden–Woodberry, as residents work together to maintain their neighborhood and struggle to find their place in the economy and politics of the city.

As Hampden–Woodberry was a center for white migrants, so was Old West Baltimore for blacks. Racial segregation both shaped this community and maintained its boundaries. People of different class and income levels, excluded from other parts of the city, shared a common experience of racial discrimination. Beginning in the late nineteenth century, Old West Baltimore formed the center of both commerce and culture for the African-American community. Karen Olson discusses the early history of this community and some of its representative institutions: Sharp Street Church, Frederick Douglass High School, and the Royal Theater. She tells us of the struggle against racial segregation mobilized by Lillie Carroll Jackson, head of the Baltimore chapter of the National Association for the Advance-

ment of Colored People (NAACP), and Carl Murphy, publisher of the *Afro-American* newspaper, in the 1930s; this was carried forward through a decades-long movement for racial justice that laid the basis for the better-known civil rights movement of the 1960s. This struggle continues today in the ongoing efforts of the African-American community to gain increased economic and political power.

Following the essay on Old West Baltimore are interviews with two of the many people who contributed to the earlier civil rights movement. John E. T. Camper was a prominent black physician, a founding member of the NAACP, and chairman of the Citizen's Committee for Justice, an activist organization of the 1940s. A tireless worker for racial justice, Camper walked picket lines, organized marches, raised money, and ran for political office on the Progressive party ticket.

J. Broadus Mitchell was an economics professor at Johns Hopkins University and a president of the interracial Baltimore Urban League in the 1920s. He ran for governor of Maryland on the Socialist party ticket in 1934, investigated lynching on Maryland's Eastern Shore in 1933, and led an effort to get an African-American student admitted to Johns Hopkins University.

From Old West Baltimore, we move south to the downtown garment district. For many decades, Baltimore was a center of the garment industry. During World War I, for example, the garment industry employed more workers than did Bethlehem Steel. The major employers were German Jews: Greif, Strouse, Schloss, Sonneborn, and Schoeneman; the workers, also predominantly Jewish, were Russian, Bohemian, and Lithuanian immigrants or children of immigrants. Many of them were young women.

Jo Ann Argersinger describes the sweatshops and the "skyscraping factories," details the workers' efforts to unionize and improve their pay and working conditions, and notes the attempts of women workers to form their own locals. She tells us also of the struggle between two rival unions, the Amalgamated Clothing Workers and the United Garment Workers, between the relatively skilled and well-paid craft workers and the less skilled majority.

In the next essay, Roderick Ryon discusses the

rich culture developed by local craft workers, Baltimore's aristocracy of labor, in the decades before World War I. He takes us to the craft workers' union halls and meeting rooms, which acted as centers for information, employment, and political activities. Here, craft workers could proclaim and maintain their relative independence from employers; they could share news, improve their skills, and organize. Privileged white men, these craft workers made only halting efforts to join with women and black workers. But by the early twentieth century, industrial technology and scientific management techniques had undercut many traditional skills and had thus eroded the basis of the craft workers' power. The old craft workers' unions would soon be replaced by a reorganized and more inclusive labor movement. In Baltimore's east side, however, we can still catch glimpses of the lives and culture of the craft workers in the heyday of their influence.

From the east-side union halls, we continue east and south to Fells Point where Linda Shopes introduces us to the seamen, cannery workers, merchants, carpenters, laborers, and slaves who once worked and lived here. Frederick Douglass, the area's most famous resident, was a house servant and then a ship caulker in Fells Point before his escape from slavery in 1838. In 1866, the black community established a ship building and repair company in Fells Point, almost unprecedented as a black-run business in the United States at that time.

The area was also home to many immigrants. Shopes tells us about the long, hard days of the cannery workers and about the stable communities established by Germans, Poles, Czechs, Ukrainians, and other ethnic groups. She ends by discussing the recent battles between longtime residents who want to protect their familiar community, historical preservationists who want to restore old buildings to their original styles, city officials wanting upscale development and an enlarged tax base, and developers who want the opportunity to make a profit through new businesses and expensive housing along the east-side waterfront.

Following this essay is a set of interviews with community activists who have worked on issues of education, housing, and poverty. Beryl Williams played a leading role in the desegregation of the Baltimore school system and built the adult and continuing education programs at Morgan State University to ease African-American students' access to higher education. Betty Hyatt, founder of Citizens for Washington Hill, explains how she used skills developed in church organizations to maintain attractive, affordable, and racially integrated housing in the East Baltimore neighborhood where she was raised.

Lucille Gorham, a community activist from East Baltimore, explains how, as chairwoman of Citizens for Fair Housing, she has worked with city government and community residents to build public housing, subsidized rental units, homeownership units, playgrounds, and parks, all in ways that try to support and develop existing communities. Finally, Willa Bickham and Brendan Walsh, the founders of Viva House, which provides food for the hungry and homeless, explain their commitment as Catholic Workers to serving the poor and articulating their needs through political activism.

Fells Point, now an area contested by developers and historic preservationists, was once the transient home for merchant seamen. Linda Zeidman and Eric Hallengren tell us about the life of the seamen in the 1930s when these "homeless, rootless and eternally unmoneyed" men organized to form the National Maritime Union. They show how Baltimore's seamen gained a reputation for radical and militant union activity. They also describe the ways in which divisions between black and white longshoremen undercut their success.

Linda Zeidman then takes us to Sparrows Point, home of Bethlehem Steel, to tell the story of the unionization of the steel industry in the 1940s. Like Hampden–Woodberry, Sparrows Point was a company town. The most privileged of the steelworkers lived in company housing at "the Point," while others lived in Dundalk, Highlandtown, and Old West Baltimore. Zeidman takes us to these communities, noting on the way O'Connor's Bar in Highlandtown, where the Steel Workers Organizing Committee of the Congress of Industrial Organizations (CIO) began the drive to organize. Foreign-born workers played a prominent role in union building, and the African-American community of Old West Baltimore, its churches and its newspaper, the *Afro-American*, mobilized to support the union drive, contributing to its success in 1941. Until the decline of the entire U.S. steel industry in the 1970s, the union meant well-paid jobs, family security, and stable communities for Baltimore's steelworkers.

The final set of interviews presents several people active in labor and political movements. George Meyers, now labor secretary for the Communist Party USA, discusses his life as a labor union organizer, including his leadership of sit-down strikes in the 1930s and the struggle to integrate African-American workers into industrial plants in the 1940s. Robert Moore, president of the Baltimore–Washington local of 1199E, the hospital workers' union, speaks of his early experiences with racial segregation, his activities in the civil rights movement, and his work in organizing the predominantly black, low-paid workers in Baltimore's hospitals.

Sirkka Tuomi Lee Holm, now retired as a secretary and actress but still active as historian of the Finnish community, talks about growing up in a progressive Finnish family, her activities in the Finnish Hall, and her experiences as a victim of the McCarthyite attacks of the 1950s. She is followed by two radicals of the 1960s: Dean Pappas explains how he became active in civil rights and then became a leader of the local antiwar movement; and Ann Gordon discusses her long involvement with feminist and lesbian politics in Baltimore.

The final two chapters examine relatively recent structural changes in Baltimore's economy and geography. W. Edward Orser takes us on a seven-mile trip along the west-side corridor to explore the way the twin processes of suburbanization and racial change have altered residential patterns since the early twentieth century. He tells us how builders developed the areas on the margins of the city, attracting moderate-income buyers to the new rowhouses. With each new wave of suburban settlers, rowhouse designs changed and improved, and to add to the attraction, developers introduced such innovations as the shopping center.

The first suburban communities were exclusively white. Only in the 1950s did black Baltimoreans with similar dreams of suburban homeownership begin to move out from West Baltimore. Orser traces the movement of African Americans to the suburbs in the 1950s and 1960s and explains the phenomena of block busting by real estate speculators and panicked white flight. He concludes with a picture of the west side today, as African Americans struggle, with fewer resources, to maintain a stable community and as whites continue to leave the city in search of ever farther suburban "havens."

The final essay takes us to the center of Baltimore's renaissance as seen from the top of Federal Hill, where David Harvey surveys the vista of Baltimore's banks and insurance companies, the Chesapeake Bay, and the new tourist attractions of the Inner Harbor. He also looks at the less celebrated parts of the city that seem meanwhile to have been abandoned to the poor. Harvey tells the story of Baltimore's redevelopment and shows how downtown urban renewal has been carried out by corporate interests fueled by public funds and tax concessions. He takes us through the civil disturbances in the wake of Martin Luther King's assassination, the creation of the City Fair, the recessions and deindustrialization of the 1970s and 1980s, and the consumer pleasures of Harborplace. Baltimore's renaissance through Harborplace he calls the strategy of bread and circuses, a distraction from, rather than a solution to, the city's continuing problems of unemployment, impoverishment, illiteracy, and social decay.

The chapters thus address many aspects of Baltimore's history and collectively provide a much broader vision than that found in many more traditional accounts focusing on famous men, social elites, or patriotic events. They are, however, fragments of a larger whole. Those unfamiliar with the general contours of Baltimore's history may want a more general historical context for understanding the specific events discussed in this book and may want to read some of the books, articles, and other sources noted in the final historiographical essay. Here, we provide a brief summary that may serve as a framework for reading the specific essays that follow.

A Brief Look at Baltimore's History

Baltimore was founded in 1729 and came of age as

a major commercial center during the Revolutionary War and the decades immediately following it. Baltimore merchants amassed fortunes, taking advantage of the British blockade of Philadelphia during the war and the disruption of traditional trade patterns caused by continuing European conflicts during the early nineteenth century. They exported grain and tobacco to the West Indies and Europe and imported sugar and coffee from the Caribbean and Latin America, then shipping it abroad. Much of their activity was carried out on the sleek and swift Baltimore clippers, in violation of international laws of trade. One historian commented that "Baltimore merchant morality appears to have been one of honor among thieves."[2]

Despite its commercial importance, Baltimore lagged behind Philadelphia and especially New York in the early nineteenth century; both are closer to important European ports. To retain a competitive position, Baltimore sought to take advantage of its proximity to inland markets. Private investors, with the aid of public funds from the city and state, embarked on a massive program of internal improvements, building roads, canals, and railroads.

The most important of these was the Baltimore and Ohio Railroad, chartered in 1827 and reaching the Ohio River 26 years later, thereby opening up the trans-Allegheny West to local merchants. Also important to Baltimore was the coastal trade developing with the South. While Southern planters cultivated cotton, tobacco, and rice, Baltimore merchants provided them with fertilizer and the processed food, drygoods, household items, and hardware necessary to sustain their plantations. Linked by its railroads, the city thus became a hub for connecting markets in the West and South and a distribution point for manufactured goods from the Northeast.

Although Baltimore has never been able to overtake its commercial rivals, it has remained nationally important as a trading center. The city has also sustained an important manufacturing sector. In the years before the Civil War, shipbuilding and related maritime trades served the merchant community, and craftsmen, including tailors, shoemakers, print-

ers, blacksmiths, and carpenters plied their trades. After the Civil War, Baltimore began to develop industrially: Merchants sought new outlets for their capital, and existing trade networks, including both markets and transportation lines, provided easy access to raw materials and a ready outlet for locally produced goods. From 1860 to the early twentieth century, the men's clothing industry and the canning of oysters, fruits, and vegetables dominated the city's industrial landscape.

By the late nineteenth century, heavy industry also came to play an important role in the city's economy, including foundries and machine shops, railroad construction and repair shops, and factories for the manufacture of tinware, copperware, and sheet ironware. Some employed hundreds, even thousands of workers, including plants then outside the city limits, such as the copper works in Canton and the Bethlehem Steel Company in Sparrows Point. But many more establishments employed far fewer workers. Hundreds of small shops turned out such items as cigars and ladies dresses, and neighborhoods were dotted with bakeries and shoe-repair shops employing only a handful of people.

As in its commercial activity, Baltimore never topped the charts as a national industrial center. Neither did Baltimore become a central office city, like New York, Chicago, and Pittsburgh. Instead, by the early twentieth century, local firms were frequently bought out by large corporations. The city became a branch town, with its financial fate tied to the interests of outside investors.

By the mid twentieth century, Baltimore was slipping in rank as both a port city and industrial center. Between 1970 and 1985, as David Harvey notes, the city lost 12,000 jobs in transportation, communication, and utilities; 17,000 in wholesale and retail trade; and 47,000, or almost half, of its manufacturing jobs. Recently, it has tried to recoup its standing in the national economic scene by promoting itself as a regional center for banking and finance, tourism, and international trade, and by expanding its professional service sector.

Social Relations in the City

Over the years, Baltimore's unique position as the

2. Sherry Olson, *Baltimore: The Building of an American City* (Baltimore: Johns Hopkins University Press, 1980), 27.

largest East Coast city south of the Mason–Dixon line has created a special set of social relationships. Until recently, Baltimore was a blue-collar city, with most of its population either engaged in manufacturing or financially dependent on those in blue-collar jobs. Their security was precarious, dependent on the vicissitudes of the economy and on forces outside their control. As early as the eighteenth century, journeymen in various trades were protesting their situation by striking against employers who were trying to erode their control over the work process and cut wages.

Conflict between the employing class and the employed was most powerfully expressed during the railroad strike of 1877. Less than a decade later, on May Day 1886, some 15,000 workers demonstrated along Baltimore Street in support of an eight-hour day, with banners proclaiming *Labor Creates All Wealth* and *An Honest Day's Pay for an Honest Day's Work*. A tradition of labor activism was carried forward by the local Federation of Labor, the Amalgamated Clothing Workers, the Congress of Industrial Organizations, and the National Maritime Union.

Labor activism, while energetic and sporadic, has been difficult to sustain over the long haul. Unlike some other cities, Baltimore has never been dominated by one industry or form of work; its labor force has been scattered over numerous work sites, often in small shops that have been difficult to organize. Working people have also sought satisfaction in the creation of stable communities and families, and in numerous social clubs and religious organizations. At times, these neighborhoods and community organizations have provided a bedrock of support as people have challenged the larger structures of inequality; at times, they have been ends in themselves, giving people a measure of autonomy and pride in the face of economic dependency.

Although there has always been a progressive or reform element in Baltimore's social and political life, this tradition has not been especially strong. As one recent analysis of the city noted, Baltimore has "a weak tradition of civic action."[3] In the provision of everything from public schools to public sewers to public housing, the city's leaders have been slow to act. "Old money" has created its own exclusive world of private schools, country clubs, and social activities. Baltimore's position as a branch town has tended to direct locally generated wealth away from local investment.

With some notable exceptions, race has been perhaps the most profoundly divisive force in Baltimore's history. Though the city's diverse ethnic communities have often been proudly promoted, African Americans have outnumbered any single immigrant group since at least 1870. Since 1900, they have outnumbered the total number of foreign-born residents in the city.

Slavery did not play a significant direct role in the city's development; at the onset of the Civil War, a scant 1 percent of the city's population were slaves. Baltimore was, however, in the words of one historian, the "nineteenth century black capital";[4] on the eve of the Civil War, it sustained the largest free black urban community in the country. Though at times black and white workers have competed for an economic niche in the city, and occasionally have cooperated to improve their collective lot, in general the two groups have operated in two separate labor markets.

Until very recently, and with the exception of a small group of black professionals primarily serving the African-American community, the majority of black men were restricted to laboring jobs and black women to domestic service. Racial divisions in the workplace were replicated by law and by custom in housing, schools, churches, and most other public and social institutions.

Recently, racial segregation on the job has been lessened at some middle and upper levels. But at the same time, Baltimore, like numerous other "rust belt" cities, has increasingly become home to a relatively poor, largely black population. By 1950, African Americans constituted just under 25 percent of the local population. Their numbers increased steadily in the ensuing decades so that by 1985, African Americans were 60 percent of those who called Baltimore home.

3. Peter Szanton, *Baltimore 2000: A Choice of Futures* (Baltimore: Morris Goldseker Foundation of Maryland, 1986), 11.

4. Leroy Graham, *Baltimore, The Nineteenth Century Black Capital* (Washington, D.C.: University Press of America, 1982).

During the same years, the overall number of city residents actually decreased as a result of the increasing suburbanization of the white and more prosperous population. Indeed, in 1985 the median income in the city was $16,700, a little less than one-half the amount for the surrounding counties. Twenty-four percent of the city's population fell below the poverty line. This puts Baltimore in a league with other major industrial cities in the United States with a declining tax base and a rising number of economic and social problems to solve.

Politics in Baltimore

The political life of Baltimore, the process of municipal governance, has paralleled the city's economic and social development, reflecting both its power alignments and underlying tensions. For most of its history, political power in Baltimore has been in the hands of a few relatively privileged white men; yet politics, like labor activism and social reform, has also provided an arena in which those of lesser privilege have sought influence and power. As early as the 1790s, some Baltimoreans were protesting the customary property requirements for voter eligibility, and by the early nineteenth century universal white male suffrage had become the law. The political process itself was hardly democratic. Graft and corruption characterized successive administrations, and elections were repeatedly punctuated by outbreaks of violence, often directed against immigrants, especially the Catholic Irish.

During the Civil War, Maryland remained officially within the Union camp. In Baltimore, some opposed slavery; more opposed secession. Yet sectional tensions in the city were high: They reached flash point on April 19, 1861, as local citizens assaulted Union troops passing through the city on their way south. This outbreak, coupled with Baltimore's strategic position near Washington, D.C., resulted in the city's occupation by federal troops for the duration of the war.

After the Civil War, the Democratic party capitalized on widespread bitterness at the federal occupation as well as on white fears of the newly freed slaves —freed by a Republican administration. Democrats gained control of the city, and to this day, Democratic power in Baltimore has rarely been successfully challenged. Though ethnic communities have never voted as a block—Germans and Jews, for example, were as likely to affiliate with the Republican as the Democratic party in the late nineteenth and early twentieth centuries—the Democrats, dominated by business and professional interests, nonetheless were able to forge an alliance with the majority of ethnic voters.

From 1871 to 1907, local politics was dominated by one man, Isaac Freeman Rasin, a classic big-city boss. Though his official position was clerk of the court of common pleas, Rasin wielded enormous behind-the-scenes power. He established policy, raised funds from those who did—or wished to do—business with the city, doled out city contracts, dispensed patronage, and most important, controlled elections. While some have argued that the boss system was an effective way to organize a heterogeneous voting population, the administration of civic affairs and the provision of city services took a decided back seat to exploiting opportunities for favoritism, personal gain, and fraud.

Upon Rasin's death in 1907, the city's Democratic party split into rival factions. Four times in this century, Republicans were able to take advantage of these splits and elect a Republican mayor, most notably the liberal Theodore Roosevelt McKeldin, who was elected in 1943 and again 20 years later in 1963. In between, he served two terms as governor of Maryland. By the end of World War II, machine politics was breaking down in Baltimore, its power to dispense welfare and jobs eroded by New Deal services and postwar prosperity, its social base weakened by the rush to the suburbs. Yet the 1970s and 1980s witnessed the machine's revival in a new form as William Donald Schaefer, mayor from 1971 through 1986 and master of what some have considered cooptive and paternalistic politics, turned neighborhood organizations into political clubs.[5]

Others beside the Republicans challenged Democratic party hegemony in the city. In the late nine-

5. Kevin O'Keeffe, *Baltimore Politics, 1971–1986: The Schaefer Years and the Struggle for Succession*, Georgetown Monograph in American Studies, No.3 (Washington, D.C.: Georgetown University Press, 1986), 11–12.

teenth century, groups of upper- and middle-class reformers, including some women beginning to define a role for themselves in the city's public life, along with labor groups, challenged the corrupt practices of the Rasin machine and attempted to improve municipal services, with some success. The Great Depression of the 1930s and the Roosevelt reforms of the New Deal, which were systematically denounced and stonewalled by old-guard party regulars in the city, nonetheless stimulated widespread political activism, both inside and outside the two-party system, among those traditionally alienated from political life—the poor, the unemployed, African Americans, and to a lesser extent, other ethnic groups. And since at least the 1960s, reform Democratic coalitions, often rooted in community groups and neighborhood struggles, have made inroads into city government. The activism of these groups, coinciding with the emergence of the contemporary women's movement, has been critical in opening up politics to women: Senator Barbara Mikulski was first elected to the Baltimore City Council in 1971; Mary Pat Clarke, a city councillor from 1975 to 1983, was elected president of the council in 1987. Both have had strong ties to neighborhood organizations.

Baltimore's African-American community has played a critical role in city politics since 1870, when the Fifteenth Amendment to the U.S. Constitution enfranchised black men. Most remained loyal to the Republican party—the party of Lincoln and emancipation—until the reform politics of Franklin Roosevelt and the New Deal gradually drew them into the Democratic party in the 1930s. Republicans, despite their lack of power in the city, nonetheless needed black votes in state elections. Hence the party tried to sustain black voters' loyalty, while granting them as few political rights as possible to avoid white reaction.

Though some African Americans argued for independent political action in the late nineteenth and early twentieth centuries, most worked within the Republican party for greater political rights. In 1890 the African-American community, centered in West Baltimore, elected its own representative to the City Council, Harry S. Cummings, and through 1931 at least one black representative sat on the coun-

cil. Yet following national trends, the political position of Baltimore's black citizens worsened in the late-nineteenth and early-twentieth centuries. For example, the state legislature passed amendments designed to disenfranchise blacks three times—in 1904, 1908, and 1910. Though these were all defeated by state referenda, blacks tended to withdraw from the political process until first the New Deal and then the civil rights movement opened up renewed possibilities for civic power.

In 1955 African Americans began to regain some power on the city council, and in 1970 Milton Allen, elected Baltimore's state's attorney, became the first black official elected citywide. Other African-American candidates ran for local, state, and national office from Baltimore. Some, most notably former U.S. Representative Parren Mitchell, were victorious. More lost, however, unable to rally the majority of black voters and sizable minority of white voters needed for a black candidate to win a citywide local election. Racist campaign tactics also took their toll. The powerful and popular Mayor Schaefer was able to retain his unique position as the only white mayor of a city of more than 100,000 with a black majority for four consecutive terms partly because of a divided black electorate and partly because he did reach out effectively to black voters. Most recently, of course, Kurt Schmoke, an African American, was able to unite blacks and appeal to whites, winning first the state's attorney's race in 1982 and, in 1987, with Schaefer ensconced in the governor's office, the mayoralty. While it is likely that the African-American majority will continue to choose elected officials from among its own, the larger economic and social significance of this voting power is yet to unfold.

A New History

In this book we have discussed several of Baltimore's most important economic activities: railroads, steel, textiles, shipping and the port. We have looked at several specific communities: Hampden, home of native-born whites; Fells Point, home to immigrants and seamen; and Old West Baltimore, a center of African-American politics and culture. Several chapters discuss specific labor struggles and several discuss the relations of race and class in communities and in the workplace. Several highlight the contributions of women to Baltimore's history and discuss the roles of women as workers and as community and political activists.

One book, of course, cannot cover everything. We have not detailed the power structure in Baltimore, although the relationship of wealth to power—themes addressed most directly in the chapters on Evergreen House and Federal Hill—are certainly implicit in the book as a whole. We have said relatively little about party politics and much more about the politics of work and community. We have discussed some selected neighborhoods but have by no means included all of Baltimore's neighborhoods and communities. We have analyzed several major industries and paid attention to aspects of the history of organized labor, but we have said little about those who work in health, education, or domestic services.

We have presented no comprehensive view of gender, which would have required an analysis of housework and child care. We have provided no comprehensive view of African-American history or of the contributions of any single ethnic group; certainly, much more needs to be researched and written on race and ethnicity in Baltimore. Our essays, in general, emphasize the history of organized labor; we provide a glimpse into the lives of the upper class, but little information, for example, about small businessmen, professionals, or the unemployed.

Our justification for these gaps and silences is that this is a first effort to recover the history of often uncelebrated lives; we do not claim to provide a complete account but to point readers in new directions and suggest aspects of our history that have hitherto received little attention. We hope that some will be provoked to further explorations of local history and that collectively we can continue to build a more complete understanding of the history of our city.

Acknowledgments

One of the pleasures of working on this book has been the help and cooperation we have received from numerous individuals and institutions over the years. Without them, our work would have been impossible; we hope they will be pleased with the results. Our special thanks go to Research Associates in Baltimore, especially Cliff DuRand, Ric Pfeffer, David Harvey, and Vicente Navarro, who initially proposed the idea of an alternative history tour to us, helped organize various incarnations of the tour in numerous ways, and generously provided a grant to help cover the costs of publication. Several friends have helped with tours over the years: the Reverend Marion Bascom, Lewis Delano, the Reverend Vernon Dobson, Sylvia Gillett, Eric Hallengren, Bill Harvey, David Harvey, Geoffrey Himes, Sirkka Holm, Dottye Burt Markowitz, Stan Markowitz, Juanita Jackson Mitchell, Karen Olson, Kathleen Ryan, Stelios Spiliadis, and Cliff Welsh. Sylvia Gillett also worked with us in the early stages of producing this book and has been a continuing source of moral support. Karen Olson has also helped move this project along over the years.

Two local institutions have been especially helpful in answering numerous inquiries and easing access to important resources: our thanks to the staff of the Maryland Room and Averil J. Kadis, public relations director, of the Enoch Pratt Free Library; and to Richard Flynt, Dean Krimmell, and Mary Markey of the Baltimore City Life Museums. We would also like to thank the staffs of numerous other repositories of Baltimore historical materials. The following list, in alphabetical order, shows the major repositories consulted and sources of the interviews and photographs contained in the book:

The *Afro-American* newspapers
The American Social History Project, Hunter
  College, City University of New York, especially
  Joshua Brown
B & O Railroad Museum
Baltimore City Department of Transportation
Baltimore Museum of Industry
Baltimore Sun, with special thanks to Fred
  Rasmussen and Tiffany House
Bryn Mawr College Archives
Bryn Mawr School Archives
Mrs. Florine Camper
Art Cohen
Oral History Research Office, Columbia University
Martin P. Catherwood Library, New York State

School of Industrial and Labor Relations, Cornell
University

Dundalk–Patapsco Neck Historical Society

Eleutherian Mills Library, Hagley Foundation

Baltimore Steelworkers History Project, Essex
Community College

Peggy Fox

Jean Hare

The Jewish Historical Society of Maryland

The Alan Mason Chesney Archives of the Johns
Hopkins Medical Institutions, especially Nancy
McCall, Gerard Shorb, and Anne Slakey

The Eisenhower Library and the Ferdinand
Hamberger Jr. Archives, Johns Hopkins
University

Jacques S. Kelly

David Lavine

Maryland Commission on Afro-American History
and Culture

Maryland Historical Society

Maryland State Archives, especially Mame Warren

Office of Barbara Mikulski

Juanita Jackon Mitchell

Amelia Bernadette Pulley-Pruitt

Charlotte Cannon Rhines

Special Collections and Archives, Rutgers
University Libraries

Saint Bernardine's Roman Catholic Church

Christian Penn Sauter

J. Brough Schamp

Smithsonian Institution

Burt Sparer

Special Collections, Langsdale Library, University
of Baltimore, especially Gerry Yeager

Albin O. Kuhn Library and Gallery, University of
Maryland Baltimore County, especially Tom Beck

George Vorth

Walter Reuther Library of Labor and Urban Affairs,
Wayne State University

For permission to reprint published materials, we
gratefully acknowledge the *Baltimore Afro-American*, the *Baltimore Sun* and *Evening Sun*, *Fells
Point Gazette*, International Publishers, Maryland
Historical Society, Meckler Publishing Company, the
National Association for the Advancement of Colored
People, and Six Pictures Music.

We also thank the institutions with which we are
or have been affiliated for various forms of aid: Essex
Community College, especially Gardner Pond and
Dot Jones; the Johns Hopkins University, especially
Anne Smith; the University of Maryland Baltimore
County, especially W. Edward Orser and Carolyn
Ferrigno of the American Studies Department; and
the Pennsylvania Historical and Museum Commission, especially Brent D. Glass, Harry E. Whipkey,
and Robert Weible.

For Temple University Press, Susan Porter Benson, Stephen Brier, and Roy Rosenzweig, editors of
the Critical Perspectives on the Past series, have
sustained us with their faith in this project. Janet
Francendese, senior acquisitions editor; Mary Denman Capouya, senior production editor; Irene Glynn,
copy editor; and Richard Eckersley, designer, transformed the disparate pieces of this book into a coherent whole. Don Keller ably prepared the maps.
Though production got a bit hairy at times, all have
been a pleasure to work with.

We each also have our personal acknowledgments.
Elizabeth Fee would like to thank Sirkka Holm and
all her other friends in Baltimore who introduced her
to the history of this city. Linda Shopes wishes to
thank her parents, Edward and Marianna Samorajczyk Shopes, who taught her not to forget where
she came from; and her husband, Ken Albright, who
always did his share of the dishes. Linda Zeidman
thanks her parents, Rose and Boris Gottlieb; her
comrades Gretchen and Kostis; and her daughter
Ann, who grew up with this project. And to Eddie,
a special note: Without you, none of this would have
been possible.

We save acknowledging our greatest debt for last.
Dot Sparer joined us at a critical point in the editorial
process. Her ability to transform the often encumbered prose of academic writers into more accessible
language in large measure accounts for what clarity
and directness this book possesses. There is hardly
an article, sidebar, or interview that has not been immeasurably improved by Dot's deft touch. To her our
enthusiastic thanks.

The Baltimore Book: New Views of Local History

In July 1877, as the Sixth
Regiment of the Maryland
National Guard marched from
their armory to Camden Station, soldiers opened fire
on the crowds at the corner
of Frederick and Baltimore
Streets.

Chapter 1

Camden Yards and the Strike of 1877

SYLVIA GILLETT

The feeling not only in Baltimore but all over Maryland was intensely bitter, and the sympathy of the greater part of the working people was with the strikers.
—Charles Malloy, Maryland National Guard, 1877

Clearly within view from the corner of Sharp and Camden Streets—former site of the old Camden Station (*site 1*)—are signs of the new Baltimore. Festival Hall stands just across Camden Street. Farther to the east, shoppers fill the boutiques, booths, and restaurants of the Inner Harbor.

Yet, a little over a century ago, in the summer of 1877, crowds gathered here to challenge the power of the nineteenth-century railroads. Here began a protest that signaled the start of one of the most significant strikes in U.S. history, an event that was to bring Baltimore and the country as close as they have ever come to a breakdown of the social order.

Hard Times

In 1877 the people of the United States found themselves in the midst of a severe depression. Hard times had come in the wake of the stock market collapse and the closing of the stock exchange in 1873—events caused at least partly by speculation in rail-road stock. Industry sought to weather the storm by cutting wages for workers by 25 percent (below subsistence in many cases) and by throwing an estimated 1 million people out of work.

In many key industries—furniture, millinery, shoe making, cake and cracker making—the introduction of machinery reduced the need for skilled workers and enabled owners to control more closely the terms of daily work. Such changes encountered fierce resistance from workers. Their opposition, however, was no match for management's determination. Throughout the 1870s, more and more skilled workers lost their jobs to machines or found themselves forced to labor at unskilled, low-paying jobs.

Working-class people grew increasingly desperate and angry, and nowhere more so than in Baltimore. Here, in the early summer of 1877, about 150 box makers and 700 can makers in the city's second-largest industry had gone out on strike. Their protest followed a severe winter in which numerous groups of workers demanded that Mayor Ferdinand Latrobe provide employment because their families lacked even bare necessities. Investigators confirmed that more than 200 families in northeastern Baltimore had little or no fuel and food. Worse yet, nearly 400 of the city's homeless sought shelter each night at the Baltimore Police Station. An uprising seemed almost

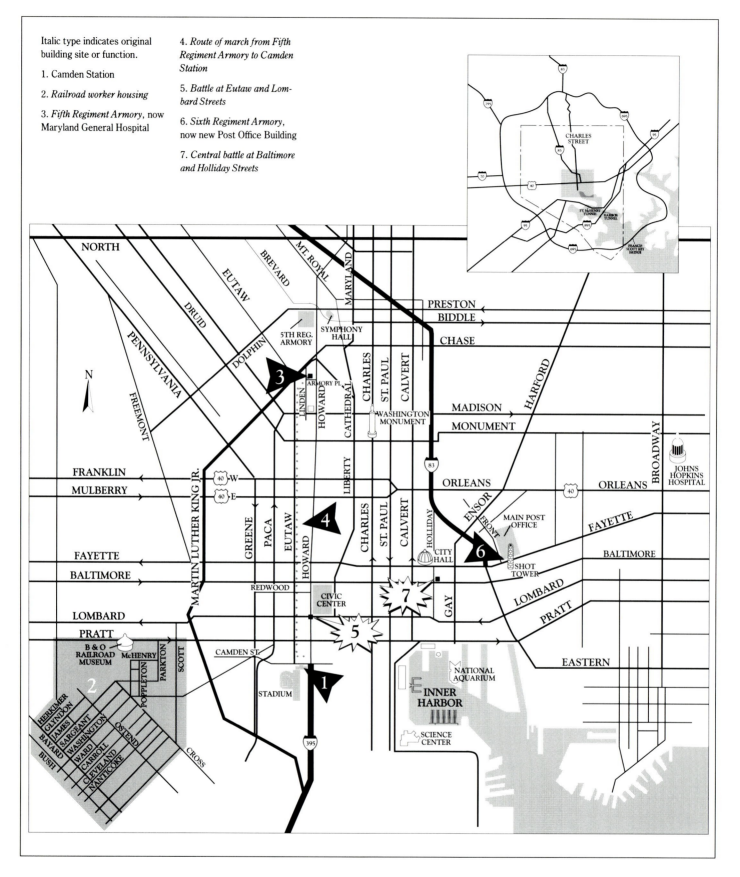

Italic type indicates original building site or function.

1. Camden Station

2. *Railroad worker housing*

3. *Fifth Regiment Armory*, now Maryland General Hospital

4. *Route of march from Fifth Regiment Armory to Camden Station*

5. *Battle at Eutaw and Lombard Streets*

6. *Sixth Regiment Armory,* now new Post Office Building

7. *Central battle at Baltimore and Holliday Streets*

Camden Station was mobbed and burned during clashes between protesters and the police and soldiers.

inevitable, since the families of workers as well as the unemployed suffered the effects of hard times.

Baltimore's citizens were no strangers to protest. Throughout the nineteenth century—in 1812, 1835, 1839, 1856, and 1861—there were riots in the city, some connected with local political developments, some with the larger issues of the Civil War. These unruly demonstrations earned the city a reputation as a "mob town."

Trouble on the Railroad

One of the city's and the nation's preeminent industries, the Baltimore and Ohio Railroad, was an obvious target for the resentments deepening in 1877.

Working conditions on the line were bad, even by industry (and depression) standards.

Wages for B & O workers averaged $400 a year, $200 less than the wages for workers on other railroads. Many workers received only two or three days' work per week, while short-handed crews handled the extra cars. Overtime pay had been eliminated. Furthermore, the railroad refused to allow workers who had ridden out as part of the train's crew to return home at the railroad's expense. Instead, they were forced to pay their own way back or remain many miles from home—also at their own expense—until they could find a job on a returning train.

Railroad cars were built at the Mt. Clare Shops on Pratt Street, one of the largest railroad shops in the world and one of the largest employers in Maryland in the nineteenth century.

Workers at the Mt. Clare Shops of the B & O Railroad, pre-1900.

Safety conditions on the B & O were woefully inadequate. The job of brakeman, for example, posed danger to life and limb. A worker running along the roof of a freight train in order to turn the brakes, car by car, might find his life suddenly ended by a low bridge, or he might catch his foot in a switch frog or in the open rail end of a switch and be drawn into the turning wheels of the train. So difficult were the link and pin couplings between cars that a brakeman was considered either exceptionally skillful or extremely lucky to keep both hands and all ten fingers for very long.

The Railroad Men

Who were the men who faced the difficulties of life on the railroads in the 1870s? Typically, they were men young enough to "bear fatigue and exposure," to quote John Work Garrett, president of the B & O. Doubtless some may have been young roustabouts attracted by the rootlessness and adventure of railway life. But married men constituted the majority because railroad managers believed family responsibilities made workers more likely to be stable, hardworking, and loyal.

Railroad men lived near their place of work. In Baltimore they clustered around the Camden Yards and Mt. Clare Shops in the area of South Poppleton, James, Ramsey, Amity, McHenry, Herkimer, and Glyndon Streets (*site 2*). They dominated their communities, socializing almost exclusively with one another, worshipping in the same churches, shopping in the same neighborhood stores, marrying each other's daughters, helping one another in times of need.

The saloon was the center of the railroader's social life. Railway men "would drink to soothe their grievances and demonstrate mutual sympathy; drink evil and bad luck to some obnoxious and tyrannical official and drink long life and continued prosperity to themselves," claimed an anonymous worker in the *Locomotive Engineer's Journal* in 1869. He maintained that, during their trips, "the fever of excitement was kept up by the influence of strong drink; and many a man had gained the reputation of being a swift runner, and making almost impossible time when he was half drunk." Later, "they would congregate in grog

shops and beer saloons to recount over their wonderful adventures on the road."

In more sober moments, however, the rigors of railway life frequently caused psychological problems and deep depression. A Baltimore newspaper account in the summer of 1877 made the following report: "In two instances, it is said, brakemen, after the loss of rest and under the depression of reduced wages, etc., have purposely thrown themselves under the wheels. Nearly all the men talked with said at one time and another when melancholy, they had meditated about stepping over the bumpers and meeting instant death."

The problems besetting the railroad men inevitably caused disruption to their families. The temporary consolation of drink, for example, frequently led to chronic alcoholism with its attendant domestic difficulties. Long trips away from home required wives to shoulder the burdens of the household alone. Periods of irregular employment or prolonged unemployment resulting from hiring conditions, illness, or accidents proved disastrous to family finances. Forced transfers meant dislocating entire households. In other cases, married men had to leave their families in search of work.

Sparking the Protest

As the economic situation worsened during the 1870s, problems of railroad workers and their families became increasingly acute. By 1877, only a spark was needed to ignite their grievances into protest. It came in July when John Garrett, B & O president, simultaneously increased stockholders' dividends 10 percent while cutting workers' wages by 10 percent—the second such cut within eight months. At the time, Baltimore's newspapers published glowing accounts of the railroad's actions, noting Garrett's hopes that workers would "cheerfully recognize the necessity of the reduction."

But workers' reactions failed to justify Garrett's optimism. On July 16, the day the pay reduction was to take effect, trainmen in Martinsburg, West Virginia, went out on strike, refusing to allow trains to leave their stations until Garrett rescinded the pay cut.

Almost the entire populace of this one-industry

town rallied to defy first the local strikebreakers, then the state militiamen from the Wheeling and Berkeley Light Brigades. Garrett responded by urging West Virginia's governor Henry M. Mathews to send for federal troops.

On Thursday, July 19, 300 federal soldiers arrived in Martinsburg to quell what the secretary of war had called an "insurrection." They enabled strikebreakers from Baltimore to get the freight trains out. In the meantime, however, the populace in communities along the line rallied in support of the Martinsburg action. The "communistic madness," as Allan Pinkerton, whose detective agency investigated the uprising, called it, was spreading.

In Cumberland, Maryland, a crowd of strikers and sympathizers—disgruntled miners, Chesapeake & Ohio canal men, unemployed and migrant workers, and young boys—gathered in support of the Martinsburg strike. Numbering 500 or 600 and allegedly armed with rude and improvised weapons, they succeeded in stopping virtually all trains en route to Baltimore.

Confronted with the growing success of the protest, President Garrett met with Governor John Carroll of Maryland at the Camden Street Station on Friday, July 20. Throughout the events of the next few hours and days, Garrett and Carroll were to act with a unanimity of purpose that demonstrated how state government served and protected private railroad interests.

Indeed, both the city and state governments had a financial stake in the B & O's success. Recognizing the railroad as key to the economic life of the region, both had given considerable amounts of public money and land to the railroad in an effort to encourage the development of Baltimore City. In addition, Mt. Clare Station and the Mt. Clare Shops just west of Camden Station were built on land that was part of the Carroll estate and was initially donated to the B & O by the Carroll family.

Thus, when the Cumberland blockade disrupted operation of the B & O, Governor Carroll needed little urging to call up the Fifth and Sixth Regiments of the Maryland National Guard in Baltimore under the command of General James R. Herbert. In issuing the call, Carroll seemed to anticipate citizen dis-

agreement with his view that what was good for private entrepreneurship was also good for the general public. In an interview in the *Baltimore Sun* in 1927, Charles Malloy, a former guardsman with the Fifth Regiment, recalled, "It had been easy to see that violence might and probably would grow out of the strike. The feeling not only in Baltimore but all over Maryland was intensely bitter and the sympathy of the greater part of the working people was with the strikers."

The Crowd Gathers

The mood was tense when Big Sam, a new riot alarm, sounded to call the troops to their armories at 6:35 P.M. on Friday, July 20. Governor Carroll had at first insisted that the alarm not be used for fear that it might incite the crowd to riot. But General Herbert, eager to try out the alarm and concerned that not enough militiamen could be summoned by courier, finally had his way.

When the 1-5-1 signal rang out at 6:35 P.M., the time could hardly have been more propitious for a spontaneous demonstration. City streets, the setting for much of working-class life during any hour of the day, were especially crowded in the early evening because many workers were just leaving the factories.

About an hour earlier, the evening newspapers had heralded the news of Governor Carroll's call-up, and a small crowd of strikers and sympathizers had already begun to gather at Camden Station. Within 15 minutes, thousands more joined them. Others gathered outside the Fifth and Sixth Regiment armories.

Among the throngs of angry and curious spectators were many of the railroad men's families and neighbors, who lived in the area around the station. The Mt. Clare Yards to the west also housed many railroad workers, particularly the Irish, whose homes lined Pratt and Lombard Streets. The staunch support of wives and mothers is described in this report from the *Baltimore Sun*: "They look famished and wild, and declare for starvation rather than have their people work the reduced wages. Better to starve outright, they say, than to die by slow starvation."

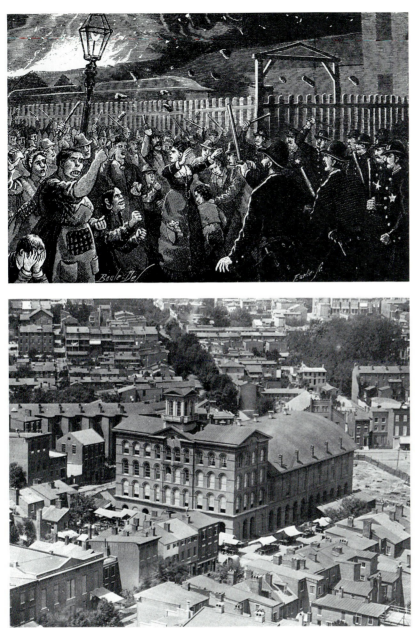

Women sympathetic to the striking railroad workers lead the crowd in a confrontation with the police. Note the emphasis on the fierceness of the women rioters, to the point of making them appear bestial.

In 1877, the armory of the Fifth Regiment of the Maryland National Guard was located on the second floor of the old Richmond Market, Linden and Read Streets. The militiamen gathered here before setting off for Camden Station.

Also among the crowds gathered in the streets on this balmy July evening were many of the neighborhood's small shopkeepers, as well as workers who hauled goods between the Baltimore port and the B & O lines. They, too, had grievances to express about the railroad.

Doubtless there were also others on the scene who fit the *Baltimore Evening Bulletin*'s description of "a rough element eager for disturbance; a proportion of mechanics either out of work or upon inadequate pay, whose sullen hearts rankled; and muttering and murmuring gangs of boys, almost outlaws, and ripe for any sort of disturbance."

In 1877 the Fifth Regiment Armory was located on the second floor of the old Richmond Market between Linden and Read Streets, current site of the buildings belonging to the Maryland General Hospital (*site 3*). Just across the street, present-day shoppers in the area peruse the many small stores of Howard Street's Antique Row.

On this summer evening in 1877, however, several thousand men, women, and children gathered in a spirit of excitement that at first appeared almost festive as troops from the armory began to march south on Eutaw Street toward the station. Some in the crowd broke into applause. But soon their good cheer changed to insults and verbal abuse.

Anger Deepens, Then Explodes

Today's Eutaw Street offers access to Lexington Market with its bright orange and red awnings and to a major Metro stop. It makes a gentle descent toward old Camden Station and the harbor area (*site 4*). Militiamen of the Fifth Regiment, beginning that descent, must have felt a simultaneous descent into the crowd's deepening anger.

When they got to the corner of Eutaw and Lombard Streets, they were bombarded with bricks and stones, many thrown from windows overhead (*site 5*). Even though 25 militiamen were injured by the crowd, the regiment maintained discipline until it arrived at its destination.

Meanwhile, the Sixth Regiment gathered at its armory on the second floor of a large building at the corner of Fayette and Front Streets (*site 6*). On that corner today stands the mammoth Central Post

A Letter to the Editor, July 21, 1877

The following letter to the editor appeared in the Baltimore American and Commercial Advertiser *on July 21, 1877, in response to an editorial two days before. While sympathetic to the plight of the railroad workers, the editorial had argued that the B & O's primary responsibility was to its stockholders, not its employees. Given the overall depressed state of the economy, the railroad was, according to the editorial, doing the best it could for its workers.*

Messers Editors of *The American*:

In your editorial in yesterday's paper, you say you see no reason for charging the Company with a disposition to oppress its employees. Please allow me to point out a few. You say it has tried to do something in the way of philanthropy by cutting down wages and dividing up the work of moving its trains among a great many people. I agree with you; they do employ a great many people, but it seems to me you should have left the philanthropy out. But before I proceed to tell you why, I will tell you something perhaps you did not know. They saw it would not do to cut and slash at the wages in a wholesale manner again, so they devised a plan that they thought would work—cutting the different positions up into classes—engineers four classes, conductors three, firemen and brakemen two each. The classes were all made, but there were no men to go into them, nearly all conductors and engineers being first-class men. Now, if there is any philanthropy about their mode of working, it may come in here. When a man's engine would go into the shop for repairs he would not be allowed to get on another one and run extra, if there was a chance, but a new man would be hired, of course into the lowest class, while the first-class man would often have to remain idle three and four weeks at a time, still always holding himself in readiness in case of emergency. When the new fireman gets out on the road, the engineer, as a general thing, either has to get down off his engine and fire it himself (and in doing so he is violating one of the Company's orders by leaving his throttle-valve) or get stalled on all the grades, throwing himself behind time, to be made up at double the speed required by book, or else back off for some other train, while if he meets with the slightest accident he is held personally responsible, taken before a court composed of five officers, given a poor man's trial (all law and no justice). The sentence of this court is never less than ten days' banishment, and sometimes thirty, or final discharge, with the privilege of coming back on fourth-class pay. Was it philanthropy and a desire to do what was just and fair, when they without any public notice, cut all train men in their service fifty cents per day regardless of rates received, and in a few weeks publicly announced in the papers that Mr. T. R. Sharp and J. C. Davis would be raised a couple of thousand per annum. Or, perhaps, it is upon those broad principles of justice they keep men lying in Martinsburg, Virginia, all night in hot and cold weather watching their engines, and tell them in the morning they are not wanted, and give them no pay for it? But they must be ready to take the first train down in the morning. I could cite you many instances of such philanthropy, but the reckoning would disgust you. But allow me to say, in conclusion, if the directors are in earnest about retrenchment, I think I can suggest to them a plan which would harmonize their men and save many dollars to the Company—let the Company look about then, and see the many little bosses and supervisors, who get large pay for little work, and discharge every man whose service could be done without.

Engineer, 1st Div. B. & O. R. R.

Office Building, across the street from the historic Baltimore Shot Tower. Not too much farther west, Baltimore's poorer citizens crowd into low-income housing in a neighborhood of squat brick buildings and littered sidewalks. To the east lies Baltimore Street with its strip joints and sex stores, next door to the Baltimore City Police Station.

Into this area in 1877 jammed an angry crowd of thousands. By coincidence, the streets were filled with loose bricks and cobblestones torn up for the laying of some gas pipe as part of a public works project. The crowd began to stone the armory, shouting "Hurray for the strikers!" By 8:00 P.M., they had broken every windowpane on the Front Street side of the armory.

Inside, officers made a fateful decision to lead separate companies out piecemeal along different routes toward the station. As three of the companies, fully armed and with bayonets fixed, left the armory, they were pelted with stones, brickbats, and pieces of iron. The soldiers fired into the air and then directly into the crowd. One man was killed and the crowd temporarily dispersed.

Troops marching toward Baltimore and Holliday Streets faced still further assaults, and the frightened militiamen began to fire indiscriminately into

Crowds gather outside Camden Station as flames shoot from the south end of the passenger platform.

the crowd (*site 7*). Nine civilians were killed and more than 20 were seriously injured. As the crowd continued its resistance, many of the troops fled from the scene in panic and changed to civilian clothing. Of the original 120 who set out from the armory, only 59 actually arrived at the station.

At the depot, a major confrontation was brewing. Inside the station were between 300 and 350 militiamen, city policemen, and a number of officials—among them General Herbert, Governor Carroll, Mayor Ferdinand Latrobe, members of the Board of Police Commissioners, and a vice-president of the railroad, John King, Jr. Outside stood a crowd estimated at 15,000, reaching from Camden Street on the north to Lee Street on the south.

The troops could not embark for Cumberland because the crowd had driven away the troop train's engineer and firemen. They had also torn up tracks. Three passenger cars and the south end of the pas-

senger platform were in flames. Firemen arriving at the scene were mobbed by the crowd—"the fiercest mob ever known in Baltimore," King called it.

Governor Carroll responded to events at the station by wiring President Rutherford B. Hayes to send the U.S. Army. He claimed that the rioters had "taken possession of the Baltimore & Ohio Railroad depot, set fire to the same, and driven off all firemen who attempted to extinguish flames."

Accounts by the press and eyewitnesses tell a different story. The press claimed that the militia and policemen "awed" the crowd and that firemen had, in fact, been able to put out the flames. By 3:00 A.M., less than five hours after the governor had appealed for federal troops, most of the mob had dispersed and order had been declared.

By this time, however, federal troops were already being summoned from Fort McHenry and from stations in the New York harbor. Carroll let his order

Baltimore City policemen battle angry protesters.

More than 100 people were killed and scores were wounded in the confrontations that took place in communities all along the nation's railroad lines.

stand, a decision no doubt reflecting a belief that federal troops were more reliable than the local militiamen who, as workingmen themselves, might harbor sympathies for the strikers. On Saturday afternoon President Hayes declared Maryland under martial law.

Saturday evening, July 21, brought another confrontation between strike supporters, the militiamen, and police. Militiaman Malloy described the scene as follows:

Late Saturday it was determined to make an effort to disperse the mob. We were thrown into formation at the corner of Camden and Eutaw Streets. Then we received and executed the command to load our guns. Scarcely were our pieces thus loaded when our ranks opened smartly, and a cordon of city police marched through toward the mob. They carried drawn pistols, and fired one volley into the air. Then each policeman charged the mob, seized the first man his hands came to and hauled him onto the station waiting room.

As soon as one rioter was secured, the policeman returned for another, until the station was packed with them. Had it not been for the militia, standing with loaded weapons ready for the command to fire, it is doubtful whether the police could have carried out the plan, for I don't think there were more than twenty-five of them.

But the plan was carried out and the backbone of the riot was broken, then and there.

The Battle Ends, the Protest Spreads

By Sunday, between 1,200 and 2,000 federal troops were stationed in the vicinity. The agitation in Baltimore had been quelled by a show of force designed to discourage further insurrections by workers. Sensing perhaps that events in Martinsburg and Baltimore might lead to widespread violence, public officials brought the full force of the government to bear against the strikers.

But despite Garrett's apparent victory in Baltimore, the protest spread to other cities and towns and to other railroad lines, as workers united in a struggle for better working conditions and higher wages. In some cases, their anger was fueled when frightened troops fired indiscriminately into the assembled crowds, killing more than 100 civilians and wounding scores of others. In other cases, local troops and police refused to oppose the protesters but instead disbanded and joined them.

In Pittsburgh, for example, members of the local militia and city police force joined the crowds in destroying locomotives, train cars, and railroad buildings and in routing the troops from Philadelphia who had fired on the crowd.

In the neighboring town of Allegheny, workers briefly took over management of the railroad line. Similar events occurred in Buffalo, Chicago, Scranton, Harrisburg, and Philadelphia, as well as dozens of smaller communities.

Perhaps the most successful strike took place in St. Louis, where workers from many industries formed an executive committee that closed down almost all the city's manufacturing operations. The strikers had the strength inherent in their numbers and in the fervor of their anger. Ultimately, however, they lacked the sustained organization to prevail against powerful companies backed by the state. By August, less than three weeks after it began, the largest single industrial uprising in U.S. history had ended.

The Strike's Legacy

The protest had forced public awareness of the grievances of railroad workers and the intransigence of Garrett's railroad. In Baltimore and elsewhere, an aroused public pleaded for reform of the industry and for government supervision. Perhaps in response to the strike and this public outcry, the B & O instituted a program of relief for its employees. In 1880, the company established the Baltimore and Ohio Employees' Relief Association.

Under this program, the B & O provided a large initial endowment and assumed all administrative costs. Employees were required to pay monthly premiums equivalent to a day's wages and, in return, received benefits commensurate with their contributions. Coverage included 52 weeks of sickness and indefinite time for recovery from accidents. In addition, employees were eligible for death benefits.

In 1884, the B & O also established the nation's first pension plan, which permitted men at the age

Joseph Thompson: Workingmen's Party Candidate for Mayor

One result of the railroad strike in Baltimore was the formation of a Workingmen's party that spoke to the interests of working people and waged a fall electoral campaign challenging local politicians and businessmen. Meeting on July 30 in Rechabite Hall only eight days after the strike was quelled, workers from around the city unanimously adopted a resolution that began with this accusation: "The authorities of the United States and several of the States have arrayed themselves on the side of capital against labor."

At a subsequent meeting on August 6 at the Maryland Institute, those present adopted an 11-point platform that included most of the labor demands of the late nineteenth century: the eight-hour day, improved living and working conditions, and the abolition of child labor. It concluded with the radical demand that all industrial enterprises "be placed under the control of the government as fast as practicable, and operated by free-cooperative trades unions for the good of the whole people."

Leading spokesman for the Workingmen's party and its candidate for mayor was Joseph Thompson, popularly known as the "Blacksmith of Old Town." A native Baltimorean, son of Irish immigrants, he and two of his brothers had formed the firm of Thompson Brothers on Centre Street to carry on the work of their father, a wheelwright and blacksmith.

Thompson had already achieved some prominence as one of the principal speakers at a labor meeting held by B & O railroad employees at Hollis Hall during the July strike. He was also recognized throughout the city as "a prominent champion of the working people," in the words of the Sun papers, particularly known for his opposition to prison contract labor.

Nominated as candidate for mayor by acclamation at the Workingmen's party meeting at Raine's Hall on September 6, Thompson opposed the powerful and corrupt Democratic machine. In the previous mayoral election of 1875, bossism and corruption had caused some Democrats to ally with the Republicans under a banner of reform. Their candidate, Henry Warfield, had run a strong but unsuccessful campaign against the Democratic candidate, Ferdinand C. Latrobe.

Warfield was again a candidate in 1877. Mayor Latrobe, however, had angered some of the party bosses, and this time around the party chose George P. Kane as their may-

oral candidate. The choice was a shrewd one because Kane had played a leading role in an earlier reform movement in 1860. In addition, he had become well respected as police marshal.

Thompson proved himself a formidable opponent to both candidates. He spoke frequently in almost every ward in the city to large and enthusiastic crowds. A speech given on September 14 at Hiawatha Hall is typical:

The principles upon which the workingmen's party is based . . . are enduring and vital. They are opposed to all class distinctions or class legislation. Whatsoever tends to make the rich man richer and the poor man poorer is wrong, and must be, if possible, blocked in its action. Land grants to corporations, subsidies and favoritism to railroad and steamship companies are not, except under extraordinary circumstances, conducive to the interests of the poorer classes, and it is impossible to decide when they should be permitted and when not. Therefore it is better to err on the side of safety, and allow none.

Desperate to discredit the popular candidate, his opposition labeled Thompson and the Workingmen's party communistic. Though disavowing communism, Thompson did believe, as he told an audience on October 15, in "law and property being respected, even to the extent of punishing the Mortons and Gilmans of society, where they defraud people of millions, as promptly and by the same mode as poor wretches who steal five dollars."

Despite his tireless efforts and evident popularity, Thompson finished second to Kane in the October 25 election. Official results gave Kane 33,188 votes, Thompson 17,367, and Warfield a mere 536.

Workingmen's party members and supporters around the city immediately cried fraud, claiming that Thompson's votes had been wrongly counted for Kane. Thompson himself said that he could not understand the small vote he received in some wards, given the extraordinary size of the turnouts for his speeches. Many citizens at the time and later historians as well have called the count fraudulent, but Thompson and his party lacked the funds to contest the results.

Although Thompson failed to bring the Workingmen's party to power in Baltimore, his campaign had gained working people's support for radical reforms and strengthened their class consciousness.

Built in 1856, the B & O Camden Station was the site of some of the worst rioting during the railroad strike of 1877.

of 65 who had worked for the railroad for at least 10 years to retire and receive benefits ranging from 20 to 35 percent of daily earnings. Both programs served as models for the industry.

In the broader political arena, agitation for reform led to significant public support throughout the country for reform and workingmen's candidates in the years following the strike. In Baltimore, for example, the Workingmen's party, formed as a result of the strike, received a third of the popular vote in the October 1877 mayoral election.

Even more important, the strike revealed the deep divisions between labor and capital and signaled a new era in labor–management relationships. The spontaneous uprising demonstrated labor's determination to say no to management and revealed labor's potential strength. Aware of that strength, Garrett showed his readiness to call for military force to crush the workers' protest. When it ended, he and others appealed to public officials for even more regiments and more armories to quell future disturbances.

Workers, too, had seen the strength inherent in a joining together of workers, the unemployed, and the community at large to express a shared sense of outrage. As a leader in the Baltimore strike declared,

The working people everywhere are with us. They know what it is to bring up a family on ninety cents a day, to live on beans and corn meal week in and week out, to run in debt at the stores until you cannot get trusted any longer, to see the wife breaking down under privation and distress and the children growing up sharp and fierce like wolves day after day because they don't get enough to eat.

In the years ahead, the site of the old Camden Station will be occupied by twin athletic stadiums. But the sense of class consciousness and potential for concerted action will live on as the greatest legacy of those who gathered there in 1877 to challenge the financial empire of the nineteenth-century railroads.

Acknowledgment: The author wishes to thank Ellen Smith for her assistance in preparing this chapter.

Built in the 1850s in classic revival style, Evergreen House was purchased in 1878 by John Work Garrett, president of the B & O Railroad. His son T. Harrison Garrett added a wing containing a billiard room, bowling alley, and gymnasium for his three sons. The eldest son, John Work, and his wife Alice later turned the bowling alley into an art gallery and converted the gymnasium into a private theater.

Chapter 2 Evergreen House and the Garrett Family: A Railroad Fortune

ELIZABETH FEE

. . . to the day of his death, the word of the president of the Baltimore and Ohio was law to governors, all state officials, including senators and members of the National House of Representatives.—1928 history of the Baltimore and Ohio Railroad

One of the most splendid and imposing houses in Baltimore, Evergreen House stands as a monument to the wealth and power enjoyed by members of Baltimore's upper class in the nineteenth century. Its massive fluted columns and terraces, its elaborately decorated interior filled with art treasures and rare books, its formal gardens, rolling lawns, and wooded hills demonstrate the elegance and opulence of Baltimore's wealthiest families (*site 1*).

Today you can stroll in the expansive gardens of Evergreen House or take one of the regularly scheduled guided tours of the interior. In 1942, John Work Garrett bequeathed the house to Johns Hopkins University, which now uses it as a rare book library and a setting for cultural, musical, and educational events.

It may help you to appreciate the magnificence of the house and its treasures if you understand the historic role of the first John Work Garrett, one of Baltimore's most wealthy, influential men. His whole life was tied to that main avenue of wealth and power in the city: the railroad. As president of the Baltimore and Ohio Railroad from 1858 to 1884, he influenced the lives of tens of thousands of men and women in Baltimore and across the country.

The Young Entrepreneur

Grandfather of the man who gave Evergreen House to Johns Hopkins University, Garrett was one of the most brilliant, most successful capitalists of the mid nineteenth century. Along with Johns Hopkins, the Baltimore merchant and financier, Garrett belonged to a small group of powerful men who guided the early industrial and financial development of Baltimore and made their personal fortunes in the process.

In 1832, John Work and his brother Henry inherited a small trading company worth less than $5,000 from their Northern Irish immigrant father Robert Garrett. By the Civil War, they had parlayed their inheritance into more than a million dollars— one of the greatest fortunes of the day. The brothers expanded the business into real estate development, shipping, stock speculation, and investment banking, participating in the dynamic growth of Baltimore City. While building their complex financial empire, they became directors of many local companies, including banks and insurance agencies.

But the Baltimore and Ohio Railroad was the most

profitable of all their enterprises. It was the key to Baltimore's economic expansion and energy. The railroad brought coal and agricultural raw materials to Baltimore for export, then carried back supplies of manufactured goods for farm families in the Southern and Western states.

Like most early railroads, the Baltimore and Ohio was financed by both private and public investors. The city of Baltimore and the state of Maryland provided much of the original capital because they believed the railroad would serve the economic interests of the city and state. It would encourage commerce, farming, and manufacturing; increase land values; help the import and export trade; and provide transportation.

But the combination of public and private stockholders in the Baltimore and Ohio led to conflicts of interest. Of 30 railroad directors, 12 were elected by private stockholders, 8 appointed by the Baltimore City Council, and 10 named by the state of Maryland. The public stockholders favored low transportation charges over profits and wanted improvements in services to be financed out of earnings. The private stockholders wanted profits and the payment of dividends on their initial investments.

In the 1850s, these conflicting interests escalated into a prolonged, complicated struggle between the public and private factions for control of the railroad. Led by Johns Hopkins, the prominent Baltimore merchant and banker, the private directors campaigned for a 30 percent dividend, saying that profits should be paid to stockholders instead of being spent on new construction. As Garrett rapidly emerged as the leader of the private stockholder interests, Hopkins nominated him for the presidency of the railroad in 1858. After a hard-fought battle, Garrett was elected president by a narrow margin. The private stockholders had won.

The New President of the Railroad

From that moment on and for the next 20 years, Garrett exercised autocratic control over the railroad. Moreover, from his position as president, he exerted a commanding economic and political influence in Baltimore, in Maryland, and throughout the country.

During the Civil War, his railroad transported federal troops to battle. In the postwar expansion, it was the lifeline of an expanding American market. Beginning with a comparatively weak system, Garrett built up the Baltimore and Ohio to become one of the most powerful railroads in the country, with lines stretching from Baltimore to Pittsburgh, Chicago, Cincinnati, West Virginia, and Kentucky.

In addition, Garrett's presidency was hugely successful with his stockholders. In its first year he managed to slash operating costs (including wages) from 65 percent of revenues to 46 percent. In the second year, he cut costs to 41 percent, announced a net profit of well over $2 million, and began distributing the proceeds to stockholders. The railroad paid dividends of 6 percent throughout the war years, and these climbed to 10 percent by 1872. From 1872, Garrett continued to pay 10 percent dividends through periods of depression as well as prosperity. Meanwhile, he paid his workers the lowest wages of any railroad.

Garrett's Political Power

With his financial success ensured, Garrett became a political force to be reckoned with. Through his control over the railroad, Garrett helped put down John Brown's rebellion, then helped the Union win the Civil War.

The first time Garrett intervened in the struggle between the states was on the night of October 17, 1859, when he heard that the Harper's Ferry express train had been stopped by a band of abolitionists led by John Brown. (Brown had planned to seize the federal arsenal at Harper's Ferry, arm his followers, and march south at the head of an army of liberation, rousing the slaves to rebellion.)

Garrett telegraphed the secretary of war, who sent Robert E. Lee with a contingent of troops on the Baltimore and Ohio Railroad. They quickly put down the slave rebellion and captured John Brown. Garrett intervened again at Brown's trial by controlling railroad ticket sales to prevent Northern sympathizers from attending. After Brown was hung in the presence of thousands of federal troops, Garrett received a personal commendation from the governor of Virginia for his fast, effective action against the Northern troublemakers.

But as the conflict over slavery grew, John Work

John Work Garrett (1820–
1884), president of the
Baltimore and Ohio Railroad.

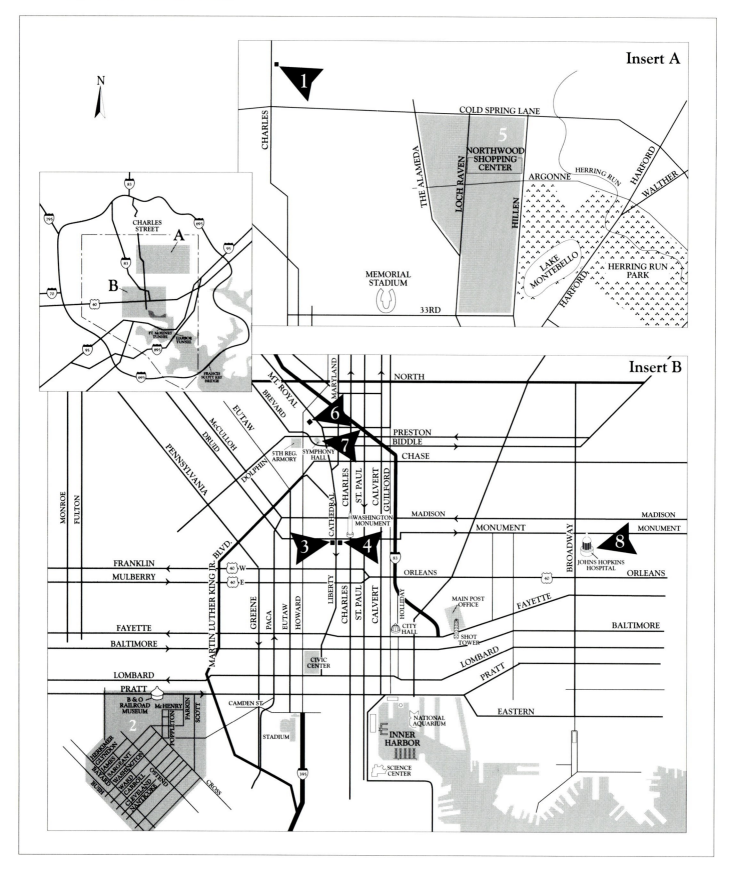

Garrett faced an agony of choice. Members of the Garrett family were Southern sympathizers, yet the loyalties of Baltimore and Maryland were divided in the developing struggle. More important, his railroad lay along the troubled borderline between North and South.

Forced to decide, Garrett went with his business interests over personal and family values. Since his railroad faced west and north through Union territory, its future clearly lay with Northern capitalism rather than Southern slaveholding. After some hesitation, Garrett gave his full support to the Union.

His railroad played an important role throughout the Civil War. A vital source of troops and supplies, it was a frequent target of Southern raids. Costly lines, bridges, and track were blown up again and again by Confederate soldiers. But Garrett continued to make repairs and expand services for the Union army.

He was richly rewarded. The volume of civilian and military shipments kept the railroad operating at peak capacity, with high rates, record profits, and no competition. In 1865, when the railroad carried 233,000 happy Union soldiers home from Washington, a profitable war was over and an even more profitable postwar boom lay ahead.

The Most Powerful Man in Maryland

After the war, unbelievable riches flowed down on those who were skillful enough or fortunate enough or ruthless enough to seize the main chance at the right moment. The scramble for wealth was fueled by speculation and easy credit.

Baltimore became known as the Liverpool of America because so much trade was conducted through its port, much of it transported by Garrett's railroad. In fact, four major, fiercely competing private railroads were at the center of the postwar expansion, including, of course, the Baltimore and Ohio.

To cash in on the boom and stay ahead of the competition—the Pennsylvania, the Erie, and the New York Central—Garrett worked to establish a Southern rail network linking Baltimore to the Southern states. He also continued to believe in what he called "conservative management." Despite huge profits, he kept shareholders' dividends to 10 percent per year, reinvesting the remainder.

During Garrett's management, operating costs (including wages) were usually kept below 50 percent of income, sometimes below 35 percent. The rest was used to expand lines, add railroad cars, and build wharves, warehouses, and even steamships. His reach got ever longer, as profits were used to link the B & O to world markets.

Garrett started a steamship service to England, bringing floods of European immigrants to Baltimore to work in the expanding postwar economy. He bought war-surplus ships from the government, and even built special piers to transfer immigrants directly from the steamships into B & O passenger trains headed straight for the prairies. The steamships returning to England were filled with grain brought east by the B & O and with coal from Garrett's own coalfields in Cumberland, Maryland, and West Virginia.

Many immigrants who stayed in Baltimore found work building and extending the railroad tracks. Still others built railroad cars at the Mt. Clare Shops on Pratt Street, the largest railroad shops in the world and one of the largest employers in Maryland. Immigrant railroad workers lived in densely packed rowhouses clustered around the shops, and around Camden Station (*site 2*).

John Work Garrett became perhaps the most powerful man in Maryland. It was said that no governor, state senator, congressman, or judge could be elected without his approval. His early years as director of the B & O had doubtless taught him the economic importance of political control. In any case, he became a close ally of the political bosses of the Maryland Democratic machine. As far as the courts were concerned, the B & O never lost a legal suit. According to one history:

At the time when Mr. Garrett was made President of the great Maryland Railway, and for many years thereafter, the State of Maryland really owned the road, and the city and state Directors were in a majority on the board. In order therefore to maintain his influence in the management, Mr. Garrett realized that he must have a dominant influence in the State Government, and that, most important of all, he must have a Governor who would be guided by him in all matters pertaining to the affairs of this great property, which was then,

When immigrants arrived at Locust Point, B & O trains were waiting to carry them to all points west.

The B & O Railroad's grand Victorian office building stood at the northwest corner of Baltimore and Calvert Streets. Designed by E. Francis Baldwin, it was completed in 1882 and all but destroyed in the great fire of 1904.

as it is now, the greatest asset Maryland possessed. To that end, his agents were busily engaged in politics from one end of the state to the other, and to the day of his death, the word of the President of the Baltimore and Ohio was law to Governors, all state officials, including senators and members of the National House of Representatives.

Financial Wizard and Strikebreaker

In 1873, stock speculation and the overextension of credit led to a financial crisis and touched off a major depression throughout the nation. The postwar boom was over. But Garrett's management helped the railroad survive the financial upheavals of the 1870s.

When the panic hit, Garrett was in Europe with his wife, Rachel Ann Garrison ("Rit"), and daughter, Mary Elizabeth ("Lissie"), enjoying a relaxed tour through Italy, Switzerland, Germany, France, and England. Unperturbed by frantic messages from Baltimore, Garrett extended his tour for 18 months. His calm was justified. B & O stock climbed from 50 to 170 and was still issuing dividends of 10 percent, despite panic, depression, and unemployment at home.

By 1876, the Baltimore and Ohio Railroad had an annual income of almost $10 million and profits of over $4 million. Its surplus fund stood at over $36 million. Despite the continuing depression, the railroad was in splendid financial health.

Mount Vernon Square

In the mid-nineteenth century, Baltimore's social elite lived in elegant townhouses, many of them built around Mount Vernon Square, near the cathedral. These houses were double the width of workers' houses built at the time, and six times as large inside. They were of handsome design, with such details as Italian marble fireplaces, ornamental brickwork, Ionic columns, hot-water heating, gas lighting, and patent water closets. The design of the Mount Vernon houses was so successful that by 1860 a half-dozen new

squares were attracting residents: Franklin Square, Union Square, and Madison Square, among others.

In 1893, a London reporter described Mount Vernon: "Elegant ladies slip out of great spacious doorways into roomy family carriages driven by old colored servants in livery. Colored men are also sweeping the stone steps of the houses and washing the large fine windows . . . you feel that it is always afternoon here." In the long, hot Baltimore summers, the owners of the Mount Vernon townhouses escaped to their country houses, often built on hilltops 10 or 12 miles from town.

But Garrett was not satisfied. He thought competition with other railroad lines had cut railroad rates too low. If only he could have charged an extra 10 cents per 100 miles, he could have made an additional $2 million in profits for the year's work. And things got worse: In 1877, the railroad's earnings fell to $8 million and profits to less than $4 million. Always the expert cost cutter, Garrett decided to cut workers' wages.

The depression had created so much unemployment that labor was cheap, and desperate workers were readily available. Garrett cut their wages by 10 percent, then cut them again, and then again. With the abolition of overtime, many workers found their wages cut by more than half.

The lowest-paid railway workers could barely survive. Driven to desperation, they declared a strike. Even the *Baltimore Sun* was sympathetic: "There is no disguising the fact that the strikers in all their lawful acts have the fullest sympathy of the community. The 10 percent reduction after two previous reductions was ill-advised. The company for years has boasted of its great earnings and paid enormous dividends."

The full story of the 1877 strike is told in the preceding chapter. Suffice it to say that Garrett broke the strike the same way he stopped John Brown and the abolitionists: with the help of state and federal troops.

The Master of Evergreen House

A year after the strike, John Work Garrett bought Evergreen House, one of Garrett's many homes. Garrett's style of life was typical of Baltimore's

wealthiest families, who copied the manners and pleasures of the European aristocracy, with fashionable townhouses on Mount Vernon Square and country manors and estates on the outskirts of town. They enjoyed a constant round of balls, parties, concerts, and weddings; they also traveled frequently to Newport, to Cape May, and to Europe. The women managed extensive and busy social calendars. The men concentrated on business.

When in town, Garrett stayed at his mansion on Mount Vernon Place, at the southwest corner of Cathedral and Monument Streets (*site 3*), where the Peabody Court Hotel now stands. Garrett then bought the townhouse at 11 Mount Vernon Place as a wedding present for his son Robert and his daughter-in-law Mary Frick. They acquired the two houses next door at 9 and 7 Mount Vernon Place and combined them into one; the resulting 40-room mansion now belongs to the Engineering Society (*site 4*). This Garrett townhouse was as large as several ordinary Baltimore dwellings and included spacious drawing rooms, a central courtyard, an extensive art gallery, and a ballroom.

The scale of Garrett's Evergreen House also contrasts vividly with the cramped two-story rowhouses clustered around the Mt. Clare Shops, about a mile west of Camden Station along Pratt Street, where immigrant Irish railroad workers lived with their families. Railroad workers' houses were small, narrow, and dark. They had few amenities and no indoor plumbing. There were no gardens, no trees, no safe places for children to play. Indeed, there were few prospects for the children growing up in these families. The boys, if they were lucky, would work on the

Evergreen House, view from the rear gardens. The house was situated on 26 acres of wooded grounds with a formal garden, complete with classical sculptures, in the back.

Mount Royal Station's expansive train shed welcomed passengers beginning on September 1, 1896. The *Book of the Royal Blue* said that "this magnificent railway station was erected by the Baltimore and Ohio for the convenience of North Baltimore residents, being a mile and a half from Camden Station, the original railway station of the B & O in the southern part of town. The two stations are connected by the famous double-track tunnel, under the city, which is lighted by electricity and through which the trains are propelled by the same wonderful force." The station is now part of the Maryland Institute, College of Art.

railroads. The girls, if they were lucky, would find husbands with steady work.

Garrett also owned Lansdowne, a country estate in southwest Baltimore, and a huge estate at Montebello in northeast Baltimore (*site 5*). At that time, the Montebello estate was a Baltimore showplace, featuring a large mansion, greenhouse and stables, racetracks, blooded stallions, and prize cattle. The stables, along 33rd Street, provided stalls for 198 horses. Here Garrett could enjoy occasional respites from business and play the role of gentleman farmer. For variety, he also owned Deer Park, a home in Garrett County, Maryland.

A Declining Man, a Declining Railroad

By the 1880s, the bleak days of the depression were over, and competition increased between the main railroad lines. John Work Garrett was growing old. When the Pennsylvania Railroad outbid the B & O to buy the railroad line from Philadelphia to Baltimore, a furious John Work Garrett decided to build a parallel competing railroad between the two cities. He was in such a hurry that he failed to connect his two lines of track—his southern and western railroad lines met at Camden Station, but the northern line started some miles distant at Mount Royal Station (*site 6*). Baltimore lay in the middle.

In the midst of heavy competition for the expansion of railroad track, and therefore eventual control of the whole rail transport system, Garrett's health started to fail. He now spent his time in his elegant Mount Vernon townhouse or his summer estate at Montebello, summoning railroad officials when he wanted to discuss business.

In 1883 his wife Rit died. Garrett was inconsolable. He lost all interest in his main passions—money and his railroad—and he died the following year. His railroad never recovered from the loss.

Garrett had personally overseen virtually every aspect of the railroad business, examined every expenditure, made every decision. When in good health, he had spent much of his time riding the lines in his private railroad car, personally supervising the foremen and crews. The B & O was truly a one-man railroad.

But Garrett had not named anyone to take his place; he did not think his sons were qualified. His first son, Robert, he said, cared only for amusement. His second, Thomas Harrison ("Harry"), went into the family banking business, and his youngest son, Henry, was an invalid, cared for on the Montebello estate by Garrett's daughter, Mary Elizabeth. Garrett thought highly of her: "If the boys were only like Mary, what a satisfaction it would be to me. I have often wished in these last few years that Mary was a boy. I know she could carry on my work after I am gone."

But since it was inconceivable to put a woman in charge of a railroad, the presidency of the B & O passed to Robert Garrett after John Work's death. He stayed less than two years and was succeeded by two other presidents in quick succession. The fortunes of the railroad, once so strong, sank ever lower. Lines failed to expand, and tracks fell into disrepair. Then came the financial panic and depression of 1893. For the first time, the Baltimore and Ohio reduced, then abandoned, the payment of dividends. Quarrels broke out among the stockholders and members of the board. President Charles Mayer was forced to resign in January 1896, and the railroad entered into receivership.

The B & O was recapitalized by the financier J. P. Morgan, shifting control to wealthy men in New York and Chicago. In 1901, the Pennsylvania Railroad gained control by buying out the holdings of the Chicago group. The B & O finally lost out to its old competitor, and Baltimore—once the center of the nation's most extensive and powerful railroad line—became just a provincial stop on the way from New York to Washington.

Mary Elizabeth: A Different Garrett

When John Work Garrett died, he left $5.6 million—the largest estate of his generation of extremely wealthy Baltimore men. His daughter, Mary Elizabeth, inherited one-third of this fortune. She could not run a railroad, but she would leave her mark on Baltimore and the nation.

An intelligent, restless, and talented woman, she was impatient with the expectation that she would devote her life to dinner parties, husband, and children. She agreed with the sentiments of her closest

Mary Garrett with her friends: *left to right*, M. Carey Thomas, Julia Rogers (*seated, back*), Mamie Gwinn (*seated, center*), Bessie King (*standing*), and Mary Garrett (*seated, floor*).

The Bryn Mawr School basketball team in 1922. The school placed great emphasis on physical as well as intellectual training for girls.

friend, M. Carey Thomas, who had written in her diary at the age of fourteen: "If I ever live and grow up, my one aim and concentrated purpose shall be and is to show that women can learn, can reason, can compete with men in the great fields of literature and science and conjecture . . . that a woman can be a woman, and a true one, without having all her time engrossed in dress and society."

As young women, M. Carey Thomas, Mary Garrett, Mamie Gwinn, Julia Rogers, and Elizabeth King formed a small group of feminists who met once a fortnight to discuss literature, love, marriage, and education. Members of Baltimore high society, they longed for education and a chance to participate in a wider, male world of learning. Thomas managed

to persuade her reluctant father to send her to college at Cornell University, which had just opened its doors to women. She then applied to Johns Hopkins graduate school. She was admitted, but forbidden to attend classes.

In frustration, Thomas set out for Europe. She attended universities at Leipzig and Göttingen, but both refused to grant doctoral degrees to women. Finally she was admitted to the University of Zurich in Switzerland and earned the Ph.D. degree *summa cum laude,* an unprecedented accomplishment for a woman. The great suffrage leader Susan B. Anthony met her in Paris to tell her that her victory was a triumph for all women.

Thomas returned to Baltimore and enlisted her friends in a project to open up educational opportunities for women in the United States. First, the five feminist friends founded the Bryn Mawr School for Girls (*site 7*). The unconventional school was equipped with a swimming pool, a running track, and a gym with rowing machines—unheard of in a girls' school. As treasurer and president of the school's board of managers, Mary Garrett displayed the same passion for administrative and financial detail that had characterized her father's control of the railroad. She insisted that every bill and request be sent to her and that she make all decisions, from the pencils to be bought to the choice of books for the library.

Precise about small financial matters, Garrett was generous with large sums of money. She devoted her considerable fortune toward helping other women gain access to higher education. Her gifts went to Bryn Mawr School and to Bryn Mawr College, where her friend M. Carey Thomas became president. But Garrett's most important bequest to the cause of women's higher education involved the Johns Hopkins Medical School.

The Making of a Medical School
In 1889, after opening the Johns Hopkins Hospital on North Broadway, the trustees of Johns Hopkins University found they still needed $500,000 in endowment funds to begin the medical school they had planned. Mary Elizabeth Garrett and M. Carey Thomas saw the university's financial predicament as an opportunity. They announced they would raise

Women's Suffrage Meeting in Baltimore

The support of Mary Elizabeth Garrett and M. Carey Thomas helped make women's suffrage respectable, even fashionable, in Baltimore. In 1906, the two women responded enthusiastically to an appeal from Susan B. Anthony, the national suffrage leader, to help organize a meeting of the National American Woman Suffrage Association in Baltimore. The ladies drew on their Johns Hopkins connections for the event. They persuaded Ira Remson, president of Johns Hopkins University, to preside over a "College Women's Evening"; Goucher College undergraduates, dressed in academic caps and gowns, acted as usherettes. William Henry Welch, dean of the Johns Hopkins School of Medicine, chaired a session on "Women's In-

fluence in Municipal Government," at which Jane Addams, the famous social reformer and founder of Hull House in Chicago, was the main speaker. Welch, who had previously refused to commit himself on the suffrage question, declared that "the administration of a city was largely housekeeping on a large scale, and that the more women's influence was felt in such matters, the better for the people." Welch was favorably impressed by the meeting and privately concluded that "the suffragists are not such a queer lot of people as many suppose." Despite the success of the meeting in publicizing the cause of women's suffrage in Baltimore, and in gaining at least the qualified support of some prominent citizens, it would be 14 more years until women nationally were permitted to vote.

the money for the medical school on the condition that it admit women on the same terms as men.

Elizabeth King, Mamie Gwinn, M. Carey Thomas, and Mary Elizabeth Garrett were all daughters of Hopkins trustees and therefore in a good position to influence the university. To publicize their cause and raise the money, they organized a national fundraising effort. In 1890, they formed the Women's Medical Fund Committee in Baltimore, with committees in Boston, Washington, D.C., New York, Philadelphia, Chicago, Madison, the Pacific Coast, Maine, St. Louis, Buffalo, and Annapolis. They involved the First Lady, Mrs. (Caroline Scott) Benjamin Harrison, and other politically influential wives: Mrs. (Frances) Grover Cleveland, Mrs. (Jane Elizabeth) Leland Stanford, and Mrs. (Frances) John Quincy Adams II.

Mary Elizabeth Garrett's talent for organizing brilliant social affairs was now fully displayed. Elegant society ladies, patrons of the arts, literary figures, prominent women physicians, leading feminists, social reformers, and the wives of newspaper editors all received invitations to Women's Medical Fund events. These gathered glowing newspaper reports and growing support across the country. When Mary Elizabeth held an "At Home" at Garrett House in Mount Vernon, jointly hosted by the First Lady, almost every socially prominent citizen of Baltimore responded to the invitation. It was the society event

of the season. The press declared that only old fogies could be opposed to higher education for women.

The founders of the Medical Fund wanted Johns Hopkins to be much more than an ordinary medical school; they wanted it to match the leading schools in Paris and Vienna, a considerably higher standard than that met by any other American medical college. Garrett insisted that it be a graduate medical school, that its students have a reading knowledge of French and German, and that physics, chemistry, and biology be required for admission.

The Women's Medical Fund Committee finally raised the $500,000 needed to open the medical school (*site 8*), with more than $300,000 personally contributed by Garrett herself. After prolonged negotiations, the university trustees agreed to accept the women's terms: to require the highest admission standards of any medical school in the country, and to admit women on the same basis as men. Only one member of the faculty, William Councilman, resigned when he heard the news.

Evergreen House Today

Evergreen House was inherited by Mary Elizabeth's brother, T. Harrison Garrett. When he married Alice Whitridge and had three sons, they added a wing containing a billiard room, a bowling alley, and a gymnasium. One of the boys was called John Work after his grandfather. The younger John Work Garrett became

The library of Evergreen House contained 8,000 volumes. It now serves as the Rare Book Library of Johns Hopkins University.

an ambassador, serving terms as U.S. ambassador to the Hague, Paris, Rome, Argentina, and Venezuela.

On his return to Baltimore, he and his wife, also called Alice, turned Evergreen House into an artistic and cultural center. They made the bowling alley into a gallery for the display of Japanese and Chinese art, and converted the gymnasium into a theater, decorated by Leon Bakst, which became the setting for concerts and dance programs given by Alice and professional artists. Alice collected modern art, filling the house with paintings by such artists as Bonnard, Dufy, Modigliani, and Picasso. Since they had no children, John Work bequeathed the house to Johns Hopkins University in 1942.

The Garrett Family and Johns Hopkins
Evergreen House stands as a fitting memorial to the intertwined fortunes of the Garrett family and Johns Hopkins, the man and the university. The first John Work Garrett and Johns Hopkins, the Baltimore merchant and financier, were directors of the Baltimore and Ohio Railroad, together struggling for control by the private stockholders. Hopkins nominated Garrett in his successful run for the presidency of the railroad. And as president, Garrett's management of the railroad greatly increased Johns Hopkins's fortune.

When Hopkins left much of that fortune to found a university and a medical school, he named Garrett to the board of trustees. Garrett, in turn, left much of his money to his daughter, Mary Elizabeth, who used it to fund the Johns Hopkins Medical School.

When the second John Work Garrett left Evergreen House to Johns Hopkins University in 1942, he closed the circle of historical connections between Hopkins and the Garretts. The house is now a standing reminder of fortunes made on the railroad, and fortunes spent; of class divisions that made such wealth possible for one generation, and of the efforts of a second to use that wealth to overcome some of the inequalities of gender.

Acknowledgment: The author would like to express her appreciation to the Johns Hopkins Women's Medical Alumnae Association.

Elisabeth Gilman: Socialist Candidate for Mayor of Baltimore

Baltimore's upper class has produced many radical women. Besides Mary Elizabeth Garrett and M. Carey Thomas, one of the best known was Elisabeth Gilman, daughter of Daniel Coit Gilman, the first president of Johns Hopkins University. Like many ladies of her time, Elisabeth began social work as a volunteer and board member of charitable organizations; she started a boys' club and an emergency workshop for the unemployed in 1915. During World War I, she volunteered to serve as a lay nurse and canteen worker for the soldiers in France. But Elisabeth's experiences in Europe pushed her beyond her class and family background; they introduced her to socialist ideas.

When she returned to Baltimore, Gilman organized a weekly open forum for political discussions, and she invited a distinguished list of liberal and labor speakers to address large audiences. In the 1920s she visited a tent colony of striking West Virginia miners and organized carloads of provisions for their relief; she defended members of the International Workers of the World (iww), under attack in the courts. She was Maryland chair for the women's division supporting the national candidacy of Robert La Follette on the Progressive ticket in 1924.

In 1929, Elisabeth Gilman decided to run for political office herself. She joined the Socialist party, visited the USSR and socialist centers in Europe, and took lessons in public speaking. In 1930 she was Socialist party candidate for governor of Maryland; in 1934 and 1935, she was the Socialist candidate for the U.S. Senate; and in 1935, she ran for mayor of Baltimore. In 1945, at the age of seventy-eight, she ran again for governor of Maryland on the Socialist party ticket. Her platform emphasized international peace and cooperation within the framework of the United Nations, full-employment policies at home, and guarantees of civil liberties and "civil rights for Negroes." "I'll frankly admit I don't think I have a chance in the world of being elected," she said, "I'm running for office to spread the Socialist point of view. . . . Mine will be an educational campaign, educational, that is, for the voters of Maryland."

Elisabeth Gilman's home at 513 Park Avenue was a gathering place for all those working for peace, civil rights, enlightened race relations, improved housing and education, and protective labor legislation. Those harassed for their views became her guests for long periods. Gilman held office in many progressive organizations; she was board member of the League for Industrial Democracy, secretary of the Maryland Civil Liberties Union, and founder of the Christian Social Justice Fund. On her seventy-fifth birthday, Elisabeth Gilman was honored at a public dinner as the leading social reformer of Maryland.

Roland Park and Guilford

Roland Park, one of Baltimore's first suburban developments, represented an ideal model of gracious living for the urban elite, bent on escaping the heat, noise, and social pressures of the inner city. The Roland Park Company, incorporated in 1891, assembled hundreds of acres for development by buying up large country estates. Its local manager, Edward H. Bouton, brought in the renowned landscape architect Frederick Law Olmsted, Jr., as planning consultant. He provided a new style of elegant living, with large and well-designed houses, curving and landscaped streets, and a golf and country club, all built with painstaking attention to the details of style, comfort, and privacy.

Roland Park lots were large, irregular, and curved, giving a pleasantly informal appearance. Great care was taken to preserve existing trees and to plant new ones, to give the impression that the houses were scattered throughout parkland—offering visions of a return to nature away from the artificialities of city living. The elder Frederick Law Olmsted, designer of New York's Central Park and Brooklyn's Prospect Park, had spoken of suburban neighborhoods of "detached dwellings with sylvan surroundings yet supplied with a considerable share of urban convenience." Roland Park thus offered residents a safe haven from the dangers of city life and provided a community where relatively wealthy families could create a social life unsullied by contact with the working-class European immigrants and black migrants who were moving to Baltimore in such numbers in the late nineteenth century.

The restrictions on the initial sale of lots in Roland Park

established the *minimum* cost for houses as from $2,000 to $5,000 in pre-1900 values (worth at least 40 times that today), required setbacks of 30 to 40 feet, and prohibited the raising of hogs and the construction of privies or vaults or "other nuisances noxious or dangerous to health." All building plans had to be approved by the company, which ensured high property values by maintaining a consistent architectural style; the company also assessed rates for the maintenance of roads and common grounds and for street lighting, garbage removal, and sewers. Bouton organized the Roland Park Civic League to collect these monies and maintain the property. The Roland Park sewer system was a matter of particular pride.

Transportation between Roland Park and Baltimore initially was difficult, but by 1903, the Lake Roland Elevated Electric Railroad was carrying people back and forth to the city center within 30 minutes. For local shopping, the company built a business block, set back from the street, with grocery store, drugstore, and post office; all other businesses, bars, and stores were banned from the area by deed restrictions.

Deed restrictions are commonly associated with racial restrictions, but these were not included in the first Roland Park deeds in the 1890s; that any black person might have the money to buy such property was unimaginable. But after the turn of the century, as more rights were being claimed for blacks and immigrants, informal rejection was replaced by formal, written restrictions.

The possibility of a black family purchasing a home in Roland Park remained remote throughout the 1920s. Of more immediate concern to the "high class" developers was the real possibility that they might be faced with potential sales to Jews. Bouton made his position about selling to minorities abundantly clear during the meetings of the High Class Developers Conference in 1917 and 1919. In these sessions he was adamantly opposed to selling to Jews and Catholics, let alone blacks. Bouton considered some developers' willingness to sell to Jews a "perfectly ghastly mistake," as he believed that his property owners would not willingly accept Jewish neighbors. Such attitudes relaxed only slowly; in the 1930s, Julius Levy was the only Jew with a house in Guilford, and the newspaperman, the breadman, and the milkman wouldn't deliver to him.

Roland Park developed rapidly; it had 250 houses in 1904 and 500 in 1910. Baltimore's Social Register, first published in 1892, provides a measure of Roland Park's success in attracting socially prominent families. Before World War I, 60 percent of Social Register families still lived on Mount Vernon Square and in Bolton Hill, 8 percent in Roland Park, and most of the others somewhere in between. By 1932, only a third lived in Mount Vernon and Bolton Hill; nearly half lived in the Roland Park suburbs of Roland Park, Guilford, and Homeland, or along University Parkway. As one commentator complained: "It is no idle jest that Baltimore society is moving further and further out; from all signs soon there will be no Baltimore society, literally speaking, as everyone will live in the country."

Guilford was an extension of Roland Park, begun in 1908. Guilford had probably the most extensive set of restrictions applied to any development in the United States at that time. The "nuisances prohibited" included businesses, manufacturing, and public buildings (except in approved locations); livestock, poultry, swine, and cattle; dark-coal smoke; and occupancy by blacks (except as servants).

The lush new green suburban areas were thus reserved for whites, with a selection system that continued to operate through the collusion of realtors, developers, banks, and the suburban residents themselves. The selection process was rigorous with regard to race, and precise with regard to religion, national origin, and income. Deed restrictions, enforced by homeowner associations, proved an effective method of protecting property values and at the same time reinforcing the segregated nature of residential areas. Although challenged in courts, racially restrictive covenants were continually upheld as constitutional until a Supreme Court case in 1948. At that time, the Court held that such restrictions were unenforceable in a court of law, but it took two more decades until the civil rights movement effectively challenged them in practice. By this time, Roland Park and Guilford were long established as socially exclusive areas where Baltimore's elite families could enjoy the pleasures of elegant homes, landscaped gardens, country clubs, women's clubs, and garden clubs, and with good private schools for the children—an aura of country living. Families in these new enclaves could establish a clear social distance between themselves and the urban working-class and immigrant populations, while still being within comfortable geographical reach of the amenities of city life.

Caroline Hammond: A Runaway Slave Tells Her Story

"I was born in Anne Arundel County near Davidsonville about 3 miles from South River in the year 1844," Caroline Hammond told an interviewer in her home at 4710 Falls Road in 1938. She was "the daughter of a free man and a slave woman, who was owned by Thomas Davidson, a slave owner and farmer of Anne Arundel."

Davidson "had a large farm and about 25 slaves on his farm, all of whom lived in small huts, with the exception of several of the household help who ate and slept in the manor house. My mother being one of the household slaves enjoyed certain privileges that the farm slaves did not. She was the head cook of Mr. Davidson's household.

"Mr. Davidson and his family were considered of high social standing in Annapolis and [by] the people in that county. Mr. Davidson entertained on a large scale, especially many of the officers of the Naval Academy at Annapolis and his friends from Baltimore. Mr. Davidson's dishes were considered the finest, and to receive an invitation from the Davidsons meant that you would enjoy Maryland's finest terrapin and chicken besides the best wine and champagne on the market.

"All of the cooking was supervised by mother, and the table was waited on by Uncle Billie dressed in a uniform decorated with brass buttons, braid, and a fancy vest, his hands encased in white gloves. I can see him now, standing at the door, after he had rung the bell. When the family and guests came in, he took his position behind Mr. Davidson ready to serve or to pass the plates after they had been decorated with meats, fowl, or whatever was to be eaten by the family or guests.

"Mr. Davidson was very good to his slaves, treating them with every consideration that he could, with the exception of freeing them. But Mrs. Davidson was hard on all the slaves whenever she had the opportunity, driving

Like Caroline Hammond, African-American women, free and slave, were frequently employed as domestic workers for white families. Here a Mrs. Chapman poses with her white charges.

them at full speed when working, giving different food of a coarser grade and not much of it. She was the daughter of the Revells of the county, a family whose reputation was known all over Maryland for their brutality with their slaves.

"Mother with the consent of Mr. Davidson married George Berry, a free colored man of Annapolis, with the proviso that he was to purchase mother within three years after marriage for $750 and, if any children were born, they were to go with her.

"My father was a carpenter by trade [and] his services were much in demand. This gave him an opportunity to save money. Father often told me that he could save more than half of his income. He had plenty of work, doing repair and building both for the white people and free colored people.

"Father paid Mr. Davidson for mother on the partial payment plan. He had paid up all but forty dollars on mother's account when, by accident, Mr. Davidson was shot by one of the duck hunters while ducking on the South River, dying instantly. Mrs. Davidson assumed full control of the farm and the slaves. When father wanted to pay off the balance due—forty dollars—Mrs. Davidson refused to accept it. Thus mother and I were to remain in slavery.

"Being a free man, father had the privilege to go where he wanted to, provided he was endorsed by a white man who was known to the people and sheriffs, constables, and officials of public conveyances. By bribery of the sheriff of Anne Arundel County, father was given a passage to Baltimore for mother and me.

"On arriving in Baltimore, mother, father, and I went to a white family on Ross Street—now Druid Hill Avenue— where we were sheltered by the occupants, who were ardent supporters of the Underground Railroad. A reward of fifty dollars each was offered for my father, mother, and me—one by Mrs. Davidson and the other by the Sheriff of Anne Arundel County.

"At this time the Hookstown Road was one of the main turnpikes into Baltimore. A Mr. Coleman, whose brother-in-law lived in Pennsylvania, used a large covered wagon to transport merchandise from Baltimore to different villages along the turnpike to Hanover, Pennsylvania, where he lived. Mother and father and I were concealed in a large wagon drawn by six horses. On our way to Pennsylvania, we never alighted on the ground in any community or close to any settlement, fearful of being apprehended by people who were always looking for rewards.

"After arriving at Hanover . . . it was easy for us to get transportation farther north. They made their way to Scranton . . . in which place they both secured positions in the same family. Father and mother's salary combined was $27.50 per month. They stayed there until 1869.

"In the meantime I was being taught at a Quaker mission in Scranton. When we came to Baltimore, I entered the 7th grade grammar school in South Baltimore. After finishing the grammar school, I followed cooking all my life before and after marriage.

"My husband, James Berry, who waited at the Howard House, died in 1927 aged 84. On my next birthday, which will occur on the 22nd of November, I will be 95. I can see well, have an excellent appetite, but my grandchildren will let me eat only certain things that they say the doctor ordered I should eat.

"On Christmas Day, forty-nine children and grandchildren and some great-grandchildren gave me a Christmas dinner and one hundred dollars for Christmas. I am happy with all of the comforts of a poor person not dependent on anyone else for tomorrow."

(This account was excerpted from *Slave Narratives, Vol. 15: Kansas, Kentucky, and Maryland Interviews*. These interviews were originally conducted in the 1930s by WPA researchers and historians in the Federal Writers' Project and were republished in 1976 by Scholarly Press, Michigan. The interview has been edited by Elizabeth Fee.)

Richard Macks: A Former Slave Tells His Story

"I was born in Charles County in Southern Maryland in the year of 1844." So begins a 1937 interview with Richard Macks, a former slave, in his home at 541 Biddle Street in Baltimore.

"I lived with my mother, father, and sister in a log cabin built of log and mud, having two rooms; one with a dirt floor and the other above, having two windows, but no glass." Macks lived "on a large farm or plantation owned by an old maid by the name of Sally McPherson on McPherson Farm.

"I slept on a home-made bed or bunk, while my mother and sister slept in a bed made by father on which they had a mattress made by themselves and filled with straw, while dad slept on a bench beside the bed and that he used in the day as a workbench, mending shoes for the slaves and others.

"I have seen mother going to the fields each day like other slaves to do her part of the farming. . . . My father was the colored overseer. He had charge of the entire plantation and continued until he was too old to work.

"As a small boy and later on, until I was emancipated, I worked on the farm doing farm work, principally in the tobacco fields and in the woods cutting timber and firewood. I being considered as one of the household employees, my work was both in the field and around the stable, giving me an opportunity to meet people, some of whom gave me a few pennies. By this method I earned some money which I gave to my mother. I once found a gold dollar. That was the first dollar I ever had in my life.

"We had nothing to eat but corn bread baked in ashes, fat back and vegetables raised on the farm—no ham or any other choice meats—and fish we caught out of the creeks and streams.

"We had a section of the farm that the slaves were allowed to farm for themselves. My mistress would let them raise extra food for their own use at nights.

"During hot weather we wore thin woolen clothes, the material being made on the farm from the wool of our

sheep. In the winter we wore thicker clothes made on the farm by slaves, and for shoes our measures were taken of each slave with a stick. They were brought to Baltimore by the old mistress at the beginning of each season. If she or the one who did the measuring got the shoe too short or too small you had to wear it or go barefooted.

"We were never taught to read or write by white people. . . . We had to go to the white church, sit in the rear, many times on the floor, or stand up. We had a colored preacher. He would walk 10 miles, then walk back. I was not a member of church. We had no baptising. We were christened by the white preacher.

"We had a graveyard on the place. Whites were buried inside of the railing and slaves on the outside. The members of the white family had tombstones, [while] the col-

Richard Macks achieved success as a caterer, one of the few business opportunities open to African Americans in the late-nineteenth and early-twentieth centuries. Here a group of waiters stand ready to serve a dinner party in the 1940s.

ored had headstones and cedar posts to show where they were buried.

"When the slaves took sick or some woman gave birth to a child, herbs, salves, home linaments were used or a midwife or old mama was the attendant, unless [there was] severe sickness. [When that happened], Miss McPherson would send for the white doctor, [but] that was very seldom.

"When I was a small boy I used to run races with other boys, play marbles, and have jumping contests. At nights the slaves would go from one cabin to the other, talk, dance or play the fiddle or sing. Christmas everybody had holiday, [but] our mistress never gave presents. Saturdays were half-day holidays, unless [it was] planting and harvest times. Then we worked all day.

"In Charles County and, in fact, all of Southern Maryland, tobacco was raised on a large scale. Men, women, and children had to work hard to produce the required crops. The slaves did the work, and they were driven at full speed, sometimes by the owners and others by both owner and overseers.

"The slaves would run away from the farms whenever they had a chance. Some were returned and others getting away. This made it very profitable to white men and constables to capture runaways. This caused trouble between the colored people and whites, especially the free people, as some of them would be taken for slaves. I had heard of several killings resulting from fights at night.

"I had one sister named Jenny and no brothers. Let me say right here it was God's blessing I did not. Near Bryantown, a county center prior to the Civil War, was a market for tobacco, grain, and a market for slaves.

"When I was a boy, I saw slaves going through and to Bryantown. Some would be chained, some handcuffed, and others not. These slaves were brought up from time to time to be auctioned off or sold at Bryantown, to go to other farms in Maryland, or shipped south.

"The slave traders would buy young and able farm men and well developed girls with fine physiques to barter and sell. They would bring them to the taverns where there would be the buyers and traders, display them and offer them for sale.

"In Bryantown there were several stores, two or three taverns or inns, which were well known in their days for their hospitality to their guests and arrangements to house slaves. There were two inns both of which had long sheds, strongly built, with cells downstairs for men and a large room above for women. At night the slave traders would bring their charges to the inns, [and] pay for their meals, which were served on a long table in the shed. Then afterwards they were locked up for the night.

"Let me explain to you very plain without prejudice one way or the other, I have had many opportunities . . . to watch white men and women in my long career. Colored women have [had] many hard battles to fight to protect themselves from assault by employers, white male servants, or by white men, many times not being able to protect [themselves] in fear of losing their positions. Then on the other hand they were subjected to many impositions by the women of the household through woman's jealousy. . . . There are several cases I could mention, but they are distasteful to me.

"I remember well when President Buchanan was elected, I was a large boy. I came to Baltimore when General Grant was elected, worked in a livery stable for three years, [worked] three years with Dr. Owens as a waiter and coachman, three years with Mr. Thomas Winans on Baltimore Street as a butler, three years with Mr. Oscar Stillman of Boston, then eleven years with Mr. Robert Garrett [president of the B & O Railroad] on Mount Vernon Place as a head butler, after which I entered the catering business and continued until about twelve years ago.

"In my career I have had the opportunity to come in contact with the best white people and the most cultured class in Maryland and those visiting Baltimore. This class is about gone. Now we have a new group, lacking the refinement and culture and taste of those that have gone by."

(This account was excerpted from *Slave Narratives, Vol. 15: Kansas, Kentucky, and Maryland Interviews*. These interviews were originally conducted in the 1930s by WPA researchers and historians in the Federal Writers' Project and were republished in 1976 by Scholarly Press, Michigan. The interview has been edited by Elizabeth Fee.)

Chapter 3 Hampden–Woodberry: Baltimore's Mill Villages

BILL HARVEY

The few Baltimoreans who know where Hampden–Woodberry is probably think first of Hampden's main shopping district on West 36th Street—"The Avenue," as Hampden residents call it (*site 1*). Still fewer are aware of the ways in which the textile mills of "The Bottom" or "The Hollow," as the old-timers called the mill district in the deep valley along the Jones Falls, shaped the neighborhood (*sites 2–8*). Only after the mills became firmly established did a community grow eastward up and out of the valley to take in the "downtown" district of contemporary Hampden. Today it retains a small-town flavor rarely found in big cities—without, however, the sustaining powers of the mills that originally nourished its growth.

Pop was talking to Uncle Lee about farmwork being so hard and he says, "Why don't you take these kids you got and bring them to Baltimore and put them all to work in the mill."—Mary (Hall) Proctor, 1979

Mary (Hall) Proctor was born in 1902 or 1903 "down in around Culpepper, Virginia." Her father was a day laborer and, like millions of rural workers in the 1910s, usually had trouble finding enough work to keep the family going. After several moves in the Culpepper area, Mr. Hall took the family to Cherrydale, a small Virginia town near Washington, D.C. Mary, by then a young woman in her late teens, fared pretty well in Cherrydale. She worked as a messenger and had a budding romance. She was happy in the new town, but the family continued to have trouble making ends meet. Mary's Uncle Lee, who had recently migrated from Culpepper County to Hampden–Woodberry in Baltimore, came to Cherrydale for a visit. He suggested that Mary's father "take these kids you got and bring them to Baltimore and put them all to work in the mill." In search of better financial prospects, and over Mary's protests, Mr. Hall brought the family to Hampden–Woodberry. And that's how Mary Hall came to be a spooler at the Mount Vernon–Woodberry Cotton Duck Company. She lasted only a few months in the mill; a bad case of "the cough" prompted a doctor to advise her to get out of the dusty working conditions. But she stayed on in Hampden–Woodberry for 60 years until her death in 1979.

Mary Proctor's story, in broad outline, was the story of tens of millions of Americans. Between the Civil War and the Great Depression, immigrants from the American countryside and Europe poured into industrial cities and towns. More often than

A view of Hampden–Woodberry facing east from Druid Hill Park, showing the growth of the area up from the Jones Falls valley, *ca.* 1920. In the foreground is one of the area's "brick hills," originally built as workers' housing. The Meadow Mill is at left center; beyond it are more workers' houses.

Meadow Mill, which opened in 1877, was the largest Hampden–Woodberry mill and was regarded by mill owners as a symbol of the industry's progress. Recently, the building was occupied by Londontowne, a manufacturer of rainwear that shut down operations in the 1980s. The fate of the building is now uncertain.

This boardinghouse, which formerly stood close to Clipper Mill Road and Ash Street, was opened in the 1870s to accommodate young single women from the countryside. It was closed in 1911, just a few years after a strike spearheaded by "boardinghouse girls."

not, they were in flight from a depressed farming economy. Tens of thousands came to Hampden–Woodberry.

The first mill in Hampden–Woodberry was a flour mill, established on the banks of the Jones Falls in 1802. Baltimore had been founded in 1729 in the hope that it would become a center for the tobacco trade. The town floundered, however, until the 1750s when the settlement of western Maryland (then Frederick County) created the need for a port for the export of grain. Baltimore became the hub of a network of grain-milling operations along the many falls in the vicinity. Hampden–Woodberry's first mill was part of that network.

Starting in the 1830s, most of Hampden–Woodberry's flour mills were converted to cotton mills. By the time of the outbreak of the Civil War, there were four cotton mills along the Jones Falls, primarily under the ownership of the Gambrill family.

These remained rather small operations; by 1870, there were still only 631 workers in all the mills. Hampden–Woodberry as such had not yet been consolidated into a distinct mill town; it remained little more than a grouping of seven villages—Mount Vernon, Clipper, Druidville, Woodberry, Hampden in Woodberry, Sweetaire, and Hampden Village—most of them clustered around one of the mills (sites 9–15).

The 1870s were a turning point in the development of Hampden–Woodberry. In a single decade the workforce grew nearly fivefold, to 2,931 workers. This increase was propelled by the expansion of Woodberry Mill and the building of Meadow Mill under the ownership of William E. Hooper and Sons. Meadow Mill was the largest and most imposing mill building; its long lawn and flower garden spread out to a new train station, a symbol to all travelers of Hampden–Woodberry's growth and prosperity. Word spread quickly along the rail line into Baltimore and Carroll Counties and into southern Penn-

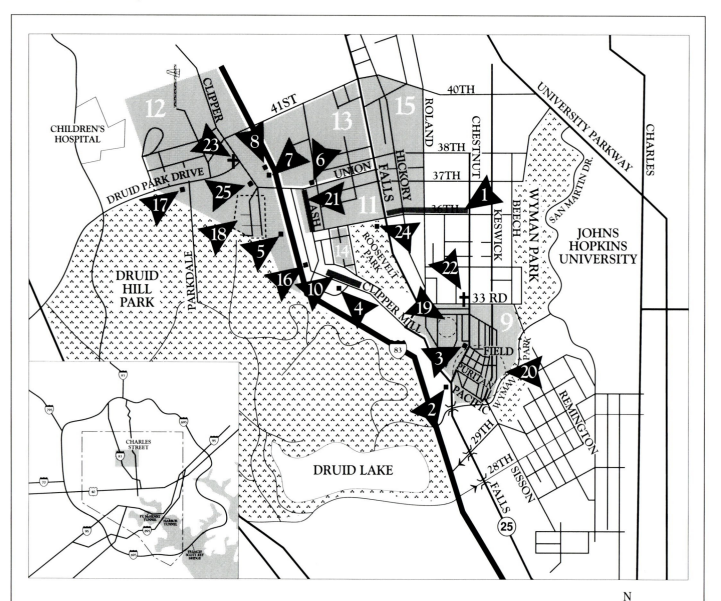

Italic type indicates original building site or function.

* indicates original building is not extant.

1. "The Avenue"

Hampden–Woodberry mills, sites 2–8

2. *Mount Vernon Mill #1*, now Lifelike Products

3. *Mount Vernon Mill #2*, now The Mill Centre

4. *Clipper Mill*, now Sekine Brush Company

5. *Meadow Mill*

6. *Druid Mill*, now Lifelike Products

7. *Park Mill*, now Clipper Mill Printers and other small companies

8. *Woodberry Mill*, now Jazz Cabinets and other small companies

Mill villages, sites 9–15

9. Mount Vernon

10. Clipper

11. Druidville

12. Woodberry

13. Hampden in Woodberry

14. Sweetaire

15. Hampden Village

*16. *Hooper Hotel*, now Jones Falls Wastewater Pumping Station

17. *William E. Hooper and Sons*, now WBFF-TV (Channel 45), Hooper Textiles, and other small businesses

Company housing, sites 18–21

18. Brick Hill #1

19. Brick Hill #2

20. Stone Hill

21. Ash Street

22. Mt. Vernon Methodist Church

23. Woodberry Methodist Church

24. Roosevelt Recreation Center

25. *Poole and Hunt Foundry*, now Clipper Industrial Park

Probably the Clipper Mill. The rural setting of the Hampden–Woodberry mills eased the transition to industrial labor for many mill workers, most of whom were from the surrounding countryside.

sylvania. Hooper Hotel, a boardinghouse formerly on the corner of Ash Street and Clipper Mill Road, was built to lodge young women who left their families in the countryside to come work in the mills (*site 16*). Several churches were established in the 1870s and 1880s.

This enormous project, begun in the throes of the depression of the 1870s, was evidence of a good bit of optimism and business acumen on the part of a small circle of men who undertook the effort to capitalize the mills. The Hooper family and their allies were the only people on the scene with the vision and the wherewithal—the capital—to take on the project.

By the 1890s, the mills were operating at their

peak. With nearly 4,000 people at work, they constituted one of the largest workplaces in the entire country. Again, in the face of a severe nationwide depression, Hampden–Woodberry was a relatively prosperous place for a working-class family to live. As part of a national wave of mergers, the owners of the various mills consolidated their holdings and incorporated as the Mount Vernon–Woodberry Cotton Duck Company. Although the Hooper family pulled out of the new arrangement in 1903 and reestablished the name of William E. Hooper and Sons just adjacent to Druid Hill Park (*site 17*), the mills of Hampden–Woodberry held a dominant position on the national market for cotton duck (heavy canvas used for tents,

Workers' housing along Clipper Mill Road. The stone for the houses was quarried a few miles north, in the Jones Falls valley.

Scott's general store, *ca.* 1900. Shopping at neighborhood stores, in Hampden–Woodberry and throughout Baltimore, encouraged informal networks and kept money in the community.

family knew hard work. And the family economy of the farm was well adapted to the textile industry's demands for a workforce. Men, women, and children could find jobs in the mills. Often a family would keep a child working in the mills so that it could take advantage of cheap company rental housing (*sites 18–21*), while other family members, especially the men, sought higher-paying work elsewhere. Of course, children did not always take to mill work, as witnessed by countless stories of such unworkmanlike activities as sleigh riding during working hours and swimming on lunch break.

Hampden–Woodberry's geographic isolation from the rest of the city led local working people to believe that the community belonged to them; it was their own. With Druid Hill Park to the west (after 1860) and Wyman Park and Johns Hopkins University to the east (after 1916), Hampden–Woodberry did not share a thoroughfare, shopping district, or school with any other neighborhood for most of its history. To the north, there was only the Jones Falls Valley and farmland, which did not become Medfield, a "suburb" of Hampden–Woodberry, until after World War II. To the northeast, Roland Park, an exclusive upper-class enclave founded in the 1890s, formed a social wall as real and as formidable as any natural barrier. To the south, the Northern Central Railroad Yards blocked the way of an imagined onslaught from "the city" and the immigrants and blacks who lived there. Formal annexation of Hampden–Woodberry into the city in 1888 aside, many Hampden residents to this day think of themselves as living in a distinct community with closer ties to "up the country" than to city neighborhoods like ethnic Highlandtown or black Johnston Square. The links with the countryside are still a vital part of life. Some of my own schoolmates migrated to Hampden–Woodberry as late as the 1950s. My mother, who came down in 1940 to work for the Commercial Envelope Company in the old Park Mill building, returned to the countryside, repeating a journey made by most of her ten brothers and sisters before her.

Once they reached Hampden–Woodberry, workers scraped to build a life for themselves. Although unions were successful in a number of scattered organizing drives, they never achieved real stability

tarpaulin, mailbags, etc.). Their preeminent position undoubtedly helps explain the relative prosperity of the working people of Hampden–Woodberry in this period.

With jobs beckoning, thousands of native-born Americans left their rural homes for the opportunity of steady work. From the Maryland, Virginia, and Pennsylvania countrysides, they poured into Hampden–Woodberry. Their most precious possession was their ability to work. But they also brought with them a determination, rooted in their rural background, to make a better life for themselves. Hard work was not new to them; every member of a farm

Teeny Thompson, a well-known boxer of the 1930s and a product of Roosevelt Recreation Center in Hampden–Woodberry.

and Woodberry Methodist at Druid Park Drive and Clipper Road—were funded and partly overseen by mill owners (*sites 22 and 23*). Mill owners were instrumental in the founding and operation of savings and loan associations and the Roosevelt Recreation Center on the corner of Falls Road and West 36th Street (*site 24*). Company-sponsored baseball teams and holiday outings helped round out the total environment the owners hoped to achieve. Not least important was the fact that the mills hired very few "outsiders"; virtually the entire workforce consisted of native-born rural white Americans. This arrangement—one is tempted to call it a deal—lasted until the World War I period.

The war created a spectacular boom time in the mills. War demand for cotton duck brought more jobs, longer hours, and higher wages. One family reported an astonishing total earnings of $75 a week. With the new situation came bolder expectations among the workers; owners' profits were high, so they were more likely to concede to workers' demands. Sensing this, mill workers and machinists at Poole and Hunt Foundry on Clipper Road (*site 25*), an important local company, struck and secured union recognition and wage gains in 1915, 1916, 1917, and 1918. Working-class opposition was not new to Hampden–Woodberry; many instances of it can be cited for the 50-year period prior to World War I. Hampden–Woodberry railroad workers struck the Northern Central in the Great Strike of 1877, which is described in Chapter 1; the Workingmen's party had a strong following in the election of 1877; the Knights of Labor, whose activities are detailed in Chapter 6, established several local assemblies during the Great Upheaval of 1885–1887; workers resisted the annexation of Hampden–Woodberry by Baltimore City in 1888; and a mill workers' strike occurred in 1906. The mill owners, however, were able to turn back these challenges to their power, and it is accurate to portray the period from the 1870s until the strike of 1923 as the heyday of Hampden–Woodberry as a cotton mill town. It was not so after the strike.

here, as we shall see. Churches and fraternal organizations were the most powerful institutions in the neighborhood. But even these were strongly influenced by the mill owners, who undoubtedly felt the need to stamp their imprint on every aspect of life. Sociologists and historians call this management approach "paternalism," by which they mean a company's fatherly interest in the well-being of its workers. The cornerstone of this paternalism was the provision of cheap housing. The boardinghouse for young single women and hundreds of company-owned family homes provided a strong incentive to come to Hampden–Woodberry and "to keep your nose clean." In addition to providing housing, the company ran a store for a time. There were periodic experiments with company unions. Company owners went still further in an attempt to influence the religious and social lives of the people. Many of the churches—including Mount Vernon Methodist on the corner of Chestnut Avenue and 33rd Street

Before we turn to that strike, though, we need only to listen to the words of two Hampden residents to realize how it was that many people came

The Poole and Hunt Machine Shops, established in Woodberry in 1853.

Interior of Poole and Hunt Machine Shops, *ca.* 1910.

The Problem of Social Memory

We usually think of "memory" as a personal matter. A good memory is thought to be a gift we are born with or a skill we master. Forgetting, then, is just a slip, a mistake, a personal shortcoming.

This issue of remembering and forgetting presents a serious problem for historians, especially those who deal with oral testimony. Historians puzzle over ways to blend oral testimony with more traditional historical sources. There are, of course, the more immediate problems of forgetfulness and intentional and unintentional distortion. And in a few cases there is the possibility of outright lying.

But what can we make of it when a *whole community* "slips" or "makes a mistake"? From such traditional sources as newspapers and the reports of the Maryland Bureau of Industrial Statistics (BIS) we learn of the 1923 strike. The strike drew a good bit of attention from the Sun papers, trade unions, Mayor Jackson, many clergymen and businessmen of Hampden–Woodberry, and the U.S. Department of Labor. The Maryland BIS judged it to be the biggest strike in the state that year. Taking a longer historical perspective, we see that the company soon began to leave Hampden–Woodberry. No historian working from these sources could avoid concluding that the 1923 strike was pivotal to the community's history. Any historian, moreover, would quickly connect these events to a nationwide pattern in a period when many New England mill owners deserted their towns for cheaper labor in the South.

But here's the rub: Suzy Hawes and I worked for a year and a half on the Baltimore Neighborhood Heritage Project in 1979 and 1980 doing oral history interviews with older people in Hampden–Woodberry. We talked to roughly 250 people about the strike specifically, mostly by reading Sun papers' accounts to members of Golden Age clubs at the Roosevelt Recreation Center. We taped interviews with nearly 50 Hampdenites. Still, we have no information on tape about the 1923 strike. Some people remembered bits and pieces; others were unwilling to talk about it. No one would discuss it on tape. One obvious explanation is that since the strike had occurred more than 50 years before our interviews, many strike participants would have died or moved out of the area. But many of the people we talked to had lived in Hampden–Woodberry in 1923—a few were even working in the mills at the time! And doesn't it seem reasonable to expect that the story of such an event would be passed down from generation to generation?

Other historians around the country—in Manchester, New Hampshire, Lawrence, Massachusetts, and Birmingham, Alabama—have come up against a similar problem, especially in the period from 1910 to 1930. How can we begin to explain it when a whole community loses track of an important part of its past? I admit to being puzzled by this situation, but let me try to stumble toward an answer.

A question of this kind does not yield readily to the usual "rules of evidence" that are said to govern the study of history. The answer to a question about the consciousness of large numbers of people over time will not be so tidy as the would-be "scientific" historian would require.

First, let's admit the bias of the question. "History" has a very different meaning for historians and for working people. Whereas historians look for patterns of behavior and development over a long period of time, most people get to live only a brief and cheated life. Given the press of family and work, few people have the luxury and the time, much less the inclination and tools, to reflect on broad historical patterns. Given this structure of everyday life, it takes a special effort to keep our history alive for many people.

The second point follows from the first. Few people in Hampden–Woodberry have been in a position to make this effort. The ministers were probably not inclined to do so; perhaps they saw no reason for it. Unions have never been able to achieve the kind of stability in Hampden–Woodberry that would be necessary to establish an institutional structure that could "naturally" carry along the memory of past struggles.

Besides these problems, the strike would only make a bad memory. Workers lost. Who needs to be reminded of a loss? Not only did they lose, but the memory only serves to remind us of everyday realities that we believe we cannot afford to confront: here, the basic inequity of capitalism and the pride we must sacrifice just to scratch by in the workaday world.

However we decide to answer the question, one thing is certain: We can no longer regard memory as a simple personal matter. And this, I think, is one of the most important reasons to study history. In doing so, we begin to see that *nothing* is a simple personal or individual matter. Instead, we are shaped by our circumstances as much as we shape our own lives. Our successes and failures are part of the successes and failures of the human race. That realization may help us to see our lives more clearly and to see the road to democratic change.

to regard Hampden–Woodberry as a place of blessed opportunity. I think of Mary Proctor's comments about slapping mud into the sides of her family's Virginia farmhouse to keep the winter wind out. Or, in a more positive vein, another old resident said: "I thought, 'This place looks so prosperous and all compared to what we had there.' People dressed nice and coming home from work and, my God, here you got a job. We thought we were in paradise here when we seen everybody working and everything. It was really nice. Oh God, we thought we were good."

On Wednesday, November 28, 1923, the *Baltimore Evening Sun* ran a front-page article entitled "Woodberry Area Hardly Touched by City Advance." The subtitles read: "District, Including Hampden, Much as It Was 50 Years Ago. Cotton Mills Afford Chief Means of Work. Nearly All People There Americans for Generations." These headings are instructive. To characterize the area as "hardly touched by city advance" reflects important realities that persist to the present day. And the mills *were* the chief employers, and the majority of the people *were* descendants of native-born Americans. Even the notion of a timeless 50 years, curious and outlandish as it seems on the face of it, hints at Hampden–Woodberry's uniqueness. But what the headlines do not say is even more striking. We read further into the article and find this passage: "There was a strike in the Woodberry district this year, when the mills decided to go back to a nine hour day, after working for some time 48 hours a week. The strike lasted for several months, and was finally lost by the mill workers." This short passage is the lone mention of a strike that signaled the beginning of the end of a way of life so heartily celebrated in the article.

After World War I, textile manufacturers in the United States found themselves hard pressed. Wartime demand had slackened, and owners faced an expanded and restive workforce. Several textile mill towns, especially in New England, experienced bitter strikes in the postwar years. Many New England towns were gutted by capital's flight to the South. In the middle of April 1923, the management of Mount Vernon–Woodberry Mills announced a new 54-hour workweek at a 7.5 percent increase in pay. The work-

ers responded with a demand for the continuation of the 48-hour week at a 25 percent increase in pay. The company refused; the workers struck.

Almost 1,000 workers stood solid in their demands. With the help of the United Textile Workers Union, they developed a routine of activities that kept spirits high and sights clear. Regular meetings at the Recreation Center drew as many as 800 strikers and sympathizers. "Eight hours" became the preferred greeting on 36th Street. Support came from the many businessmen and clergy who knew well the hardships of mill work. But company stonewalling proved to be the strikers' undoing: Eight weeks was just too long for many families to go without a paycheck.

The strike, the biggest in the state in 1923, was thoroughly reported by the Sun papers throughout its duration. Although a minority of workers did not honor the strike, production was crippled, and the company had to make a decision. This time, however, their response was very different from that of the previous decade, when they had granted wage increases and other demands. First, they refused to recognize the United Textile Workers as the bargaining agent for the strikers. Second, they refused categorically even to meet with a committee of strikers and Hampden–Woodberry businessmen and clergymen that had been constituted by Baltimore's Mayor Howard Jackson. Third, they evicted several strike leaders, including the local union president, William Eckert, from company-owned housing. The company's strategy amounted to an absolute rejection of any negotiation. Eventually, the strikers were forced to accept the end of the strike, and most returned to work.

Within 18 months of the conclusion of the strike, Mount Vernon–Woodberry's management moved to break a long-lasting connection with the people of Hampden–Woodberry. In early 1925, the company began to sell off much of the workers' housing. Three mill buildings were sold, and the mills' operations were moved south to Tallasee, Alabama, and Greenville, South Carolina. So ended the era of paternalism, an idea that makes little sense anyhow, since it takes no account of the unequal power wielded by workers and capitalists.

Working in the Mills

Fenton Hoshall was born in Hampden in 1909 and lived there all his life. Between 1935 and 1940, he worked at Hooper Mill, first in the opening room, then in the finishing room. In an interview conducted by Bill Harvey in 1979 for the Baltimore Neighborhood Heritage Project, Hoshall described the work process at Hooper's. The precision of his description suggests the complex knowledge many "ordinary" working people routinely possess.

"In making cotton duck, twine, thread, and many other products, the cotton was shipped into the warehouse of the mills for storage under government control. As the mills needed cotton, the number of bales, which was compressed and usually weighed about 500 pounds, was drawn from the warehouse and paid for at the bank before it could be used. [Then] it was moved into the opening room, and the metal straps were cut and laid on the floor.

"Some bales of cotton run different from others. Now you used to get a cotton from down around Biloxi, Mississippi. The opening room was painted green up about 4 foot or 5 foot and the rest of it was all painted white. When you got done running that cotton, the whole inside of that building was red because of the red clay from where it was [brought] in."

After the bales had been opened, "the operator would take a layer of cotton, usually about 3 inches thick, and put it into a hopper that kept turning it over and over, [pulling] little pieces of cotton off of the layer and dropping it onto a belt, which carried it to a series of beaters and cleaners. These cleaners would take and clean the cotton—all the dirt and dust out of it. It was then passed through big pipes across to the finishing room."

There, "the cotton was dropped into hoppers and fed into machines, which made a lap of cotton about 3 foot wide and weighing about 40 or 50 pounds. The laps was put on a wagon and carried out to the carding room.

"I guess the picking house—the opening room and the finishing room—was two of the cleanest places in the mill. Still . . . if you didn't keep your filters clean, your cotton didn't run right. Your machines had to breathe. If those filters wasn't brushed down . . . before you started up and running them for three, three-and-a-half hours . . . then your machines would run bad. . . . If you started cotton bad in the picking house, then you had it all through the mill. If you started it right, most of the time the cotton run good through the mill."

In the carding room, "the laps was fed into the carding machine from which a soft ropelike thread was fed into a can, which passed on to the slubbers [and] from which a smaller and more workable thread was put onto spools and passed to the spinning frames. The spinning frames were used to make a single thread of cotton and then spooled.

"Then it went to the twisting room, where it was made into a cord, which was usually from 3 to 7 ply. From the twisting room it was taken to the beaming room, the rope room, and to the Brownell twisters. The beaming room was where it was put onto pipelike beams with gears on the ends for the heavy duck looms. The Brownell twisters was to make heavier thread for heavy duck.

"Hooper Mill made a duck that on one side was asbestos and the other side it was cotton for pulp mills. The looms was called 'Big Liz' and 'Little Mary.' Some of the duck must have been as much as 30 foot wide. The asbestos was put next to the rollers to keep it from burning. Hooper waterproofed its own duck and dyed its own duck. During World War II, millions of yards of duck was shipped in for waterproofing and dyeing. Hooper built a brand new dye house to take care of all this increased amount of duck. Hooper also made a fireproof paint. They made lamp wicks, sash cord, oil filters for the oil companies, and many other things for commercial use."

Mr. Hoshall went on to describe the sexual division of labor within the mill: "Sixty percent if not more of the people in the mill were women. . . . In the cloth office, where they did most of their packing, that was mostly all women. They dressed nice. . . . It was a good clean job.

"Then in your lamp-wick weaving you had mostly women and in your automatic weaving. . . . Mostly all the big looms were men, but the small automatics—they made a duck maybe 4 foot wide . . . most of the operators on that were women. On your heavy duck machines you had men because they had to take and set the tensions and all like that.

"On your twisting frames, your spinning frames, most of them were women. On the cards, most of the men run the card because they had to put them heavy laps of cotton in there. But your slubbers were run mostly by women, your braiders were run mostly by men making sash cord."

A Hampden family, posing
by their wood frame house,
ca. 1900.

to seek employment outside the neighborhood when such prospects were available.

The Great Depression of the 1930s was a time of bleak prospects. Mill workers were placed on a short workweek, sometimes working only three days. Many had no employment whatsoever. Children scavenged coal along the railroad tracks and firewood wherever they could get it. The hills of Woodberry were picked bare in those days. Along with the rest of America, Hampden residents despaired of their economic prospects.

And, like the rest of America, many Hampden residents turned with hope to the Democratic party of Franklin Delano Roosevelt and the New Deal. The election of Herbert R. O'Conor, a New Dealer, as governor of Maryland in 1938 was a watershed in state politics. Hampden–Woodberry also underwent a transformation in this election. Older neighborhood political analysts mark this election—and O'Conor's excellent showing here—as the major turning point in Hampden–Woodberry politics in the twentieth century.

Hampden–Woodberry had been a Republican stronghold since the Civil War. It was little affected by Baltimore Democratic party machine politics in the late nineteenth century and indeed played an important role in the decisive defeat of the Democrats in the 1890s by providing two Republican mayors, Alcaeus Hooper and Clay Timanus, both from mill-owner families. Both men were key figures in the Republican "reform" effort at the turn of the century. These reformers, who were largely upper- and middle-class, native-born Americans, campaigned successfully to gain control of the city government from the Democratic party and its largely immigrant working-class followers. The native-born Americans of Hampden–Woodberry supported the Republicans in this contest.

Thus, O'Conor's victory in Hampden–Woodberry was important for many reasons. First, it reflected a shift away from the attitudes and perceptions that had characterized the old pact with the mill owners. In the face of the Great Depression, Hampden residents showed that they would vote in coalition with other working people, despite their ethnic differences. Second, support for an Irish Catholic like

The period from the 1920s to the 1960s represents another distinct phase in the history of Hampden–Woodberry. Although they were no longer as dominant as in the earlier period, the mills continued to be the community's largest employer. But Hampden–Woodberry, unlike most other textile mill towns, is located very near the center of a major city, and so Hampden residents had the advantage of being able

O'Conor indicated a new willingness to look beyond narrow neighborhood interests and to seek alliances with "outsiders," who had always been greatly mistrusted. Hampden–Woodberry seemed to be coming into the larger world of city and state politics. But the transition was not to be a smooth one.

World War II brought a breather to Hampden–Woodberry's textile industry. Wartime demand helped revive the depressed mills. Soon after the war, though, the drop in demand caused the mill owners to cut back operations. The mills would never again reach the heights of their early years. Hooper Mills closed down completely in 1961, and Mount Vernon Mills closed the last of its Hampden operations in 1972. The 1960s, then, mark the time that Hampden–Woodberry turned away from textile production for good. But the mills had been only a shadow of their old selves ever since the postwar contraction. From then on, the culture of a cotton mill town became more a legacy than a reality.

Yet, even today, Hampden–Woodberry is a remarkably close-knit and durable community—a marvel to other Baltimoreans and to sociologists. The community rests squarely on the legacy of the mills and the culture of the rural white Americans who came to work in them.

Perhaps the most important factor in Hampden–Woodberry's ability to survive the departure of the mills was its close proximity to the rest of Baltimore. In many important respects Hampden–Woodberry resembled the mill towns of the South, but people who lived in Southern mill towns simply had to leave when mill owners decided to close down operations. Hampden residents were able to look elsewhere for work while continuing to live in the community.

A combination of factors helped create an unusual community that is often forthrightly scorned for what outsiders call its "boosterism." The term implies a lot of style and little substance, but Hamp-

Looking east along 36th Street in the late 1950s. Shopping and socializing along "the Avenue" has been an important part of Hampden's distinctive small-town flavor.

den residents know that what some call boosterism is actually what constitutes the bone and sinew of Hampden–Woodberry, what makes it different from other neighborhoods. Frequent holiday parades enable people to get together in their own public space. A first-rate Recreation Center with one of the best boys' athletic programs in the city is another favorite gathering place. And a strong network of churches, old folks' clubs, and fraternal and women's organizations help sustain these activities. For example, when drug use became increasingly evident among Hampden's young people, community leaders were able to mobilize quickly to form Neighbors Against Drug Abuse (NADA). Hampdenites seem to know that they have only their own resources to fall back on, although outsiders often fail to recognize this strength.

Nevertheless, criticism of Hampden–Woodberry's boosterism does underscore residents' ambivalence about the neighborhood's unique place in the history of Baltimore. That is, Hampden residents often seem defensive about their relationship to the rest of the city. They appear to feel a mixture, on the one hand, of guilt and fear, and, on the other, of pride and strength. In this ambivalence Hampdenites reflect two of the most important realities in American society: class and race, issues that challenge Hampden–Woodberry's century–old sense of community.

First, the national recession–recovery cycles of the 1970s and 1980s have had their impact on Hampden–Woodberry, as they have on so many working-class neighborhoods and towns around the country. The large numbers of older people in the neighborhood are more vulnerable to swings in the economy than they were during their working years. And young people find secure and good-paying blue-collar jobs harder to find than did their parents' generation in the boom period of the 1950s and 1960s. Many middle-class whites have also begun to regard Hampden–Woodberry as an attractive and safe haven in a city that is now 60 percent black. The "gentry" have started to move in and fix up, thereby driving property values beyond the reach of the old-timers and changing the character of the neighborhood. Although this process is not yet so great a problem as it has been for other working-class neighborhoods, many Hampdenites are beginning to view it with sus-

picion. Hampden–Woodberry, then, finds itself still caught in the grip of outside economic forces, as it has been for more than a century.

The second and more important challenge to Hampden–Woodberry's hard-earned sense of community is the changing demographics of Baltimore City. As the city's black population grows, Hampden–Woodberry becomes even more isolated, both socially and politically. As we have seen, Hampden residents have a poor record of getting along with "outsiders." Historically, this has meant a good bit of antagonism toward immigrants, especially Jews and, to some extent, Catholics. And more than any other group, blacks have been the object of Hampdenites' prejudice.

Unwillingness to get along with other ethnic groups has left its stamp on Hampden–Woodberry politics. As far back as the 1940s, one could hear suspicion and even hatred in the code phrase "the people on the other side of the park." The term referred first to Jews and later to blacks, who moved out along the northwest corridor just west of Druid Hill Park. Hampdenites saw these groups as competitors for city and state resources, and there is some truth in that view. But the political toll for Hampden–Woodberry's unwillingness to make alliances has been enormous. Today, Hampden–Woodberry finds itself gerrymandered into three different City Council districts and three different state legislative districts, left without proportional representation in city or state government.

Ironically, then, Hampden–Woodberry's chief source of strength—its close-knit community—may yet contribute to the neighborhood's downfall. Today Hampden–Woodberry stands at a crossroads in its history. The most important issue facing Hampden–Woodberry is whether it will be able to make creative alliances with the city's black majority. Only such a coalition will be strong enough to defend against the "outside" economic forces that have always dictated the neighborhood's fortunes. Let's hope that Hampden residents will turn the strength of their community to this good and constructive purpose.

Acknowledgments: The author expresses his thanks to the Baltimore Neighborhood Heritage Project, especially D. Randall Beirne, W. T. Dürr, and Suzy Hawes, and to the people of Hampden–Woodberry, especially Joan Kirkendall.

St. Luke's Lutheran Church
at Chestnut Avenue and West
36th Street, 1988. One of
the numerous churches in
Hampden–Woodberry.

Civil rights activists in the
1960s waged a campaign in
Old West Baltimore to get out
the vote.

Chapter 4   Old West Baltimore: Segregation, African-American Culture, and the Struggle for Equality

KAREN OLSON

On the day we moved into a new school building—it was my sophomore year—they had a big inauguration ceremony. Everybody was there. City officials, school department officials, parents, leaders in the community, ministers, everybody. The auditorium was packed. Negroes were proud as hell of having this new school. —Cab Calloway

Much of the history of Baltimore is dominated by the social dynamics of race. The contemporary consequences of those dynamics are nowhere more evident than in Old West Baltimore.

Drive northwest of downtown Baltimore, through the city's oldest African-American neighborhood, and you'll see a study in contrasts. On the one hand, there are imposing churches, faithfully maintained by attentive congregations; clean streets; modest brick rowhouses, looking sturdy and comfortable. On the other hand, there are telltale signs that the community has seen better days. Driving down Pennsylvania Avenue, you get a glimmer of its past glory as a thriving entertainment and commercial district. But today the clubs and shops look shabby. There are too many vacant lots and too few shoppers.

Before 1960, housing segregation forced African Americans at all economic levels to live together in this community. Today, residential segregation in Old West Baltimore is based as much on class as on race; the community has been virtually abandoned to older and poorer blacks.

This community was created in the late nineteenth century by racial segregation and deliberate, often mean-spirited exclusion. But, paradoxically, its citizens used their excluded status to build a center of African-American culture that made Old West Baltimore a highly desirable place to live. This chapter tells the story of Old West Baltimore's struggles for racial equality by touring three of its most significant landmarks—a church, a school, and a theater—and portraying some of its most active leaders.

Turn-of-the-Century Beginnings

A predominately African-American residential area did not exist in Baltimore before 1890. In 1880, blacks were widely distributed throughout Baltimore City. Although African Americans constituted 10 percent or more of the total population in three-fourths of the city's 20 wards, no single ward was more than one-third black.

By the end of the nineteenth century, however, there was a sharp rise in the size of Baltimore's African-American population, the result of migration

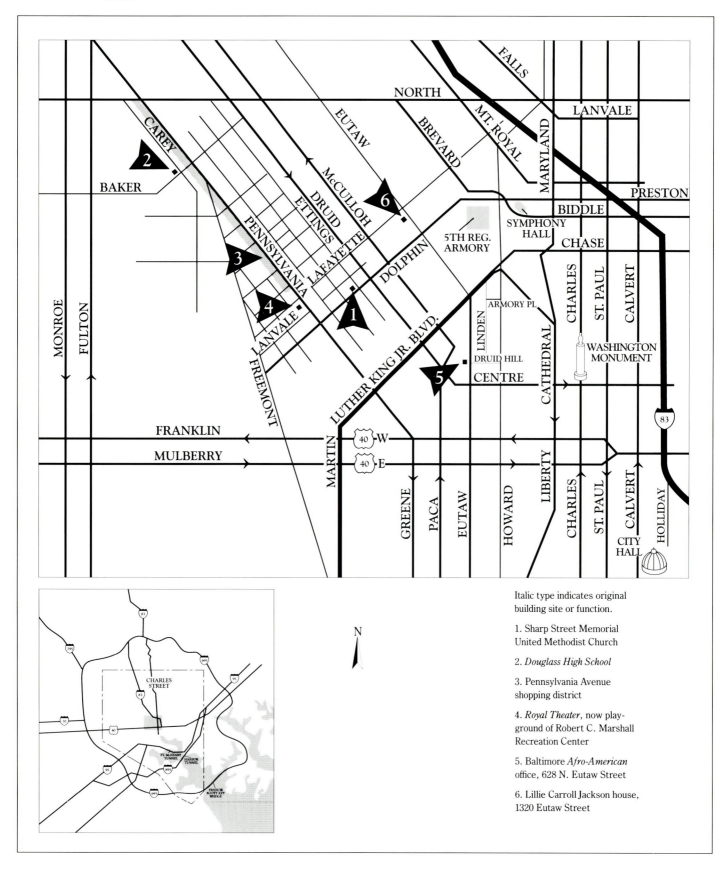

Italic type indicates original building site or function.

1. Sharp Street Memorial United Methodist Church

2. *Douglass High School*

3. Pennsylvania Avenue shopping district

4. *Royal Theater*, now playground of Robert C. Marshall Recreation Center

5. Baltimore *Afro-American* office, 628 N. Eutaw Street

6. Lillie Carroll Jackson house, 1320 Eutaw Street

This view of the 900 block of Druid Hill Avenue in the mid 1920s shows a bustling urban neighborhood.

from the South and from rural areas of Maryland. It was during this time that a segregated African-American community first emerged.

Old West Baltimore, as this neighborhood was originally called, is bounded by North Avenue on the north, Franklin Street on the south, and Madison and Fulton Streets on the east and west. The movement of African Americans to Old West Baltimore began in about 1885 in response to overcrowding and poor sanitation in the alley districts of South Baltimore. The shallow wells in South Baltimore were frequently polluted. Consequently, the rate of epidemic disease in that area was significantly higher than in neighborhoods farther north of the harbor.

African Americans who could afford to move relocated to Old West Baltimore, following a radial line directly northwest from their original neighborhood and displacing German families who moved even farther to the northwest. After the turn of the century, more than 200 black dwellings were demolished in South Baltimore to accommodate the expansion of Camden Station. This forced even more migration to the north.

By 1904, one-half of the African-American population of the city was living in Old West Baltimore. It was a socially and economically diverse neighbor-

African-American family in a Baltimore alley house, 1916.

Until World War II, most African-American men were low-paid, irregularly employed laborers like these sugar baggers.

hood that included within its geographic boundaries the most prominent of Baltimore's black citizens, a substantial group of modest renters, and the poorest of the city's working class.

Even today, as you drive through the neighborhood, you'll notice a sharp difference between the substantial three-story rowhouses on Druid Hill Avenue and the much smaller homes on the surrounding side streets. Black professionals—doctors, lawyers, teachers, undertakers, and business people—bought houses on Druid Hill Avenue; black working-class families rented more affordable dwellings.

The least desirable dwellings in Old West Baltimore were alley houses—small structures built along narrow back alleys and lacking the basic amenities of urban life. These alley houses no longer exist, but one observer in the 1920s remembered the Biddle Alley neighborhood as an area in northwest Baltimore "known as Lung Block. It was bounded by Pennsylvania Avenue, Druid Hill Avenue . . . Biddle and Preston Streets. The area was called Lung Block because so many Negroes down there had tuberculosis. The death rate for TB in the area was 958 per 100,000 people, compared with a rate of 131.9 for the city as a whole."

According to a housing survey done in 1907 by the Association for the Condition of the Poor, the houses in this area were generally dilapidated, with leaking roofs and broken plaster on cracked walls that let in the cold and rain. There was no indoor plumbing— only one outdoor toilet for every two houses. One-third of the houses had indoor sinks, one-third had water available from outdoor hydrants, and one-third had no attached running water.

The houses themselves, as well as the yards, were exceedingly damp. Water mixed with waste from overflowing privies. It collected in yards, oozed into cellars and walls.

African Americans were not the only slum dwellers in turn-of-the-century Baltimore. Between 1870 and 1900, the population of the city doubled from 250,000 to 500,000. The result was a drastic shortage of affordable housing for the European immigrants and rural migrants who flooded the city looking for jobs. City services—police and fire

protection, schools, water, and sewers—were inadequate or nonexistent.

The depression of the 1890s exacerbated the problems of unemployment and low wages that plagued residents of African-American ghettos on the west side as well as the immigrant ghettos on the east side where Russians, Jews, and Poles lived in much the same conditions.

Though poor blacks and recent immigrants shared a similar plight of job scarcity, low wages, and squalid housing, African Americans bore the added burden of discrimination. Three times before World War I, the Baltimore City Council passed ordinances forbidding blacks from moving into white neighborhoods. Although the courts overturned these ordinances, they nonetheless reflected the social practice of housing discrimination that became entrenched after the turn of the century. In a system that one historian has compared to apartheid, African Americans were imprisoned in overcrowded and isolated slums from which there was no escape.

Discrimination in employment has also hampered African-American aspirations for a comfortable standard of living. With the exception of a few middle-class professionals, most African Americans experienced emancipation principally as a move from slave labor to cheap labor. At the beginning of the twentieth century, most black men were low-paid, irregularly employed laborers and personal service workers. Black women, about half of whom worked, were overwhelemingly laundresses and domestics.

Not until World War II did black men and women find employment as clerks, bus drivers, fire fighters, police officers, or in any but the most undesirable industrial jobs. As late as 1943, when Bethlehem Steel attempted to train 15 black riveters, 7,000 white employees went on strike, insisting on their traditional monopoly of skilled work.

Even the Enoch Pratt Free Library closed its training school to African Americans because "the trustees considered the other members of the staff in making appointments and felt most other staff members do not want to work with Negro librarians. . . . Such are the customs of Baltimore." In a job market where all but the most menial and lowest-paying work was closed to black citizens, poverty was a life-

African-American workers were customarily hired for janitorial jobs even by industries and businesses that refused to employ them in any other job catagories.

threatening problem for a large number of Old West Baltimore families.

The Sharp Street Church

Our tour of Old West Baltimore most appropriately begins with the Sharp Street Memorial United Methodist Church at Dolphin and Ettings Streets (*site 1*). The enormous structure towers above the unpretentious rowhouses that surround it. On Sunday mornings, the narrow streets are clogged with cars and pedestrians drawn to this church that has for so long been a physical and spiritual center for the neighborhood. The history of the Sharp Street Church reveals much of the early story of racial segregation in Baltimore City.

Baltimore always had a large population of free black citizens. In fact, by 1820, the majority of African Americans in Baltimore were not slaves but "free people of color." In the late eighteenth century, free blacks attended services at the predominantly white Lovely Lane Methodist Chapel on German Street (now Redwood Street), but were required to sit in the back of the church and were forbidden to commune with whites at the altar.

Unwilling to tolerate this strikingly un-Christian form of worship, African-American members left Lovely Lane Methodist to form the Colored Methodist Society. In 1802, they built a church at 112–116 Sharp Street in South Baltimore.

Before long, people gathered at the Sharp Street Church not only to worship but also to discuss the abolitionist and African colonization movements, to raise money to buy freedom for slaves, to hear itinerant speakers, and to receive schooling. In 1864 the Sharp Street Church hosted the first regional conference for African-American Methodists, and from 1867 until 1872 the Centenary Biblical Institute, precursor of Morgan State University, met at the Sharp Street Church.

In 1898 the Sharp Street Church joined the stream of black migration out of South Baltimore and erected a new building at its present site. Dozens of other churches were established in Old West Baltimore, including Union Baptist, Bethel A.M.E., and Douglass Memorial. Through the decades, these churches provided places of worship and solace for their congregations; they also served as social, cultural, and political centers for a community excluded from many of the city's white institutions.

Douglass High School

The second stop on our tour is Douglass High School, located at Baker and Carey Streets (*site 2*). The building was erected by the city in 1925, but vacated in 1954 when the high school moved to a new facility on Gwynns Falls Parkway. The building at Baker and Carey Streets has been redeveloped and now houses low- and moderate-income rental units, an innovative family support program called the Baltimore Program, and a museum of Douglass High School memorabilia.

Douglass High School was named after Frederick Douglass, the Maryland slave who became an internationally renowned statesman and reformer. Douglass learned about the liberating possibilities of education when he overheard his master forbid reading lessons: "If you teach that nigger to read, there will be no keeping him." At that moment, the path to freedom became clear to Douglass. He pursued his reading lessons on the streets of Fells Point before escaping to the North and a career as an abolitionist (see Chapter 7).

Well into the twentieth century, Baltimore school officials were echoing the slavemaster's fear of, and resistance to, education for African Americans. In 1913, school commissioner Richard Biggs issued a familiar warning: "Stop at once the so-called higher education that unfits [Negroes] for the lives that they are to lead and which makes them desire things they will never be able to reach."

Schools for African-American children became a state responsibility following the Civil War, but facilities were entirely separate and vastly inferior to the schools provided for white children. The original funding formula stipulated that school taxes paid by whites would go to white schools, while taxes paid by blacks would go to black schools, thus guaranteeing that black schools would remain inferior.

Black schools were run by white teachers and principals until the turn of the century, when African-American professionals were hired at lower wages. Between 1900 and the 1930s, overcrowding was so

severe in black schools that most held half-day sessions. In 1934, a Baltimore reformer reported that public schools were careful not to teach African-American children any of the skills that would enable them to encroach on the white monopoly of trades and professions.

Despite official discouragement, Baltimore's African-American citizens clamored, petitioned, sued, and demonstrated for good education for their children. Beginning in 1865, a group of 40 African-American citizens pooled their resources to buy a building at Lexington and Davis Streets for the Douglass Institute, organized for the "intellectual advancement of the colored portion of the community." Agitation from African-American leaders gradually won improvements in all the facilities provided by the public school system, but jazz musician Cab Calloway remembered the opening of the new Douglass High School in 1925 as a particularly important event: "On the day we moved into a new school building—it was my sophomore year—they had a big inauguration ceremony. Everybody was there. City officials, school department officials, parents, leaders in the community, ministers, everybody. The auditorium

was packed. Negroes were proud as hell of having this new school."

Although Douglass High School was a segregated school, it was also the focus of enormous pride and enthusiasm for Baltimore's African-American community. The school was another example of how segregation served as a double-edged sword, excluding African Americans from white institutions, yet unifying them in institutions they could claim as their own and within which they flourished.

During the first decades after the school's founding, one-third of Douglass graduates went on to college or normal school. Thousands of Baltimore's teachers, salespeople, business owners, clerical workers, industrial employees, and governmental officials received their education at Douglass.

The list of illustrious alumni includes Justice Thurgood Marshall of the U.S. Supreme Court; former U.S. Representative Parren J. Mitchell of the seventh congressional district; Verda Welcome, the first African-American woman to serve as a state senator in the Maryland legislature; Calvin Lightfoot, first African-American warden of the Baltimore City Jail; Lillie Mae Carroll Jackson, longtime leader of the

Frederick Douglass High School, housed in this building at the corner of Baker and Carey Streets from 1925 to 1954, has been the focus of enormous pride for Baltimore's African-American community.

In the 1930s and 1940s, white as well as black patrons packed the Royal Theater, formerly on the 1300 block of Pennsylvania Avenue, to hear jazz greats.

Maryland NAACP; Carl Murphy, editor of the *Afro-American*; jazz singer Ethel Ennis; Avon Long, who played "Sportin' Life" in the original cast of *Porgy and Bess*; band leader Cab Calloway; and pro-football star Raymond Chester.

The Royal Theater

At our third stop, imagine that the playground adjoining the Robert C. Marshall Recreation Center in the 1300 block of Pennsylvania Avenue is a theater with blazing neon signs advertising the jazz greats of the 1930s and 1940s and drawing hundreds of excited patrons. In its heyday, Pennsylvania Avenue was a bustling shopping center for Old West Baltimore residents by day (*site 3*). At night, the street came alive as an entertainment mecca, featuring clubs, music, dancing, and—most important—the Royal (*site 4*).

Built in 1921, the Royal Theater sat nearly 1,400 people. But it was in the late 1930s and just after World War II that the Royal enjoyed its best years. A name band was billed every week, along with the country's top African-American singers and comedians.

The Royal owed much of its success to segrega-

tion because African-American spectators and entertainers were barred from white theaters. African-American performers traveled the "chitlins circuit," a national network of white-owned but black-patronized vaudeville and movie houses that included the Apollo in Harlem, the Howard in Washington, D.C., and the Royal in Baltimore. All the black jazz greats—Fats Waller, Count Basie, Cab Calloway, Dizzy Gillespie, Duke Ellington, and Louis Armstrong—played exclusively at the Royal when they were in Baltimore. Singers Ella Fitzgerald and Billie Holiday were regulars at the Royal, and Pearl Bailey got her start there as a chorus girl.

A show at the Royal typically included a movie, a chorus line, acrobats, tumblers, an exotic dancer, and a team of comedians to augment the big-band performance. Comedians Moms Mabley and Pigmeat Marcum played the Royal to capacity crowds. One spectator remembers "an audience of 2,000 folks in the old Royal literally out of their seats and in convulsions in the aisles. . . . To generate that kind of laughter is true power."

For over 30 years, the Royal was a source of cultural pride among Old West Baltimore residents. In

During the 1950s, the Sphinx Club was one of several Pennsylvania Avenue nightspots where West Baltimore residents enjoyed the sociability and cohesiveness of their neighborhood.

In the 1940s, standards of black beauty reflected the biases of a white-dominated world. Apex Barber College, Pennsylvania Avenue.

its heyday, it was remembered as "the most beautiful place you ever want to find," the place where "everything was jumpin'." A job at the Royal was "a prestige thing," whether you were an usherette or a musician. "You knew you were something if your date took you to the Royal; you wore your best outfit," an Old West Baltimore resident remembers.

The Royal Theater was just the first of several "good time" spots visited on "The Avenue." After the show, the audience stopped at Mannheimer's on Eutaw Street for a bite to eat, then drifted back to the Strand Ballroom or the Albert Hall on Pennsylvania Avenue to dance or listen to "cutting contests between visiting musicians who tried to outdo each other with improvisations."

In the 1930s and 1940s, whites flocked to Pennsylvania Avenue to hear the pioneers of jazz—men and women who were making musical history, who were in great demand, but who could not perform anywhere in Baltimore except the Royal because of the restrictions of racial segregation.

The eradication of Jim Crow laws in the 1950s and 1960s, along with the advent of television, the construction of the Civic Center, and the decline of big bands, made the Royal Theater obsolete. The opening show in 1921 had been appropriately called *Rarin' to Go*. By 1965, the Royal had stopped its live performances and was strictly a movie house. On July 21, 1970, the theater was formally closed with the double feature *Alley Cats* and *I Spit on Your Grave*. The building was demolished in 1971 and replaced by a public school.

Throughout the twentieth century, the movies, bars, pool halls, and theaters along Pennsylvania Avenue were an important source of income for Old West Baltimore residents. The white establishment frowned on pool halls and numbers games, but those enterprises provided capital by making loans to African Americans attempting to buy houses or establish businesses at a time when Baltimore's banks refused to lend to them.

Leaders of the Struggle for Equality

Although the fight against racial discrimination dates back to the creation of the Sharp Street Church in 1781, it was in the 1930s that an organized, sustained campaign against segregation began that would transform social relations in Baltimore.

By that time, the lives of Baltimore's African-American citizens had become totally circumscribed by racial restrictions. Blacks were segregated by law into separate schools, hospitals, jobs, parks, restaurants, and railroad cars. Separate toilets and water fountains were provided for "colored" and "whites only." In 1920, the Maryland public schools spent $36.03 per year for each white child; only $13.20 was allotted for each black child.

Two unusually skilled leaders, Carl Murphy of the *Afro-American* and Lillie Carroll Jackson, head of the Baltimore NAACP, mobilized the opposition to segregation in the early 1930s. Together these two Old West Baltimore residents and former schoolmates championed a series of successful legal, political, and economic challenges to racial discrimination.

For nearly 50 years, Carl Murphy published the *Afro-American* newspaper out of the small brick office you can still visit at 628 North Eutaw Street (*site 5*). The Reverend William Alexander founded the *Afro-American* in 1892 to encourage political militance in the African-American community. In 1896, a former slave, John H. Murphy, Sr., and his wife, Martha Murphy, replaced Alexander as the editors.

In this 1930s photograph, Lillie Mae Carroll Jackson (*front row, third from left*) sits at the center of the leadership of the Baltimore chapter of the NAACP, a group that included Carl Murphy (*back row, third from left*) from the *Afro-American*, several West Baltimore ministers and community leaders, and Jackson's two daughters, Virginia (*front row, second from left*) and Juanita (*back row, extreme right*).

To this day, the newspaper continues to be published by members of the Murphy family.

When John Murphy died in 1922, control of the *Afro-American* passed to his son Carl, a graduate of Frederick Douglass High School, who had degrees in German from both Howard University and Harvard University. Under Carl Murphy's direction, the *Afro-American* grew from a Baltimore weekly to a national chain.

The paper's headlines and editorials fought a continual battle against segregated education and recreation, as well as discrimination in employment, housing, and justice. The *Afro-American* also reported civil rights activities, bolstering the efforts of African-American churches that served as meeting places and area ministers who encouraged members of their congregations to join the NAACP and participate in its campaigns.

Murphy's colleague, Lillie Carroll Jackson, headed the Baltimore NAACP from the mid 1930s until the mid 1970s. During this time, she increased the organization's membership from a handful of people to more than 20,000 and recruited a governing board of militant activists.

Mrs. Jackson's home at 1320 Eutaw Street (*site 6*) stands as a reminder of her role as pioneer in dismantling the barriers of segregation in Baltimore. The graceful, three-story rowhouse is located on a tree-lined boulevard from which black residents were barred for most of Lillie Carroll Jackson's life. It was not until 1953, when Baltimore's Jim Crow laws were crumbling in the face of NAACP challenges, that Mrs. Jackson was able to purchase a house on once-exclusively white Eutaw Street. During her lifetime, the house was undoubtedly a nerve center for NAACP activism. In the late 1980s it functioned as a museum,

Civil rights activists in Baltimore City in the 1940s: "Your vote is your ticket to freedom."

housing a collection of memorabilia from the local civil rights movement.

Jackson's devotion to the civil rights struggle was prompted by a burning desire for social justice and personal outrage at incidents of racial violence and discrimination that had affected her family. Her husband, Keiffer Jackson, witnessed the lynching of three African Americans in his home town of Carrolltown, Mississippi, when he was only nine years old. In the late 1920s, her daughters, Virginia and Juanita, were denied admission to the Maryland Institute and the University of Maryland because of their race. And when Virginia Jackson married, a downtown department store refused to sell her a wedding gown because the store would not serve African Americans.

In 1933, Lillie Carroll Jackson's daughter Juanita Jackson organized the Citywide Young People's

Forum, which met each Friday night to hear W. E. B. Du Bois, Walter White, James Weldon Johnson, and other powerful civil rights speakers. The Forum met initially at the Sharp Street Church, but growing attendance forced them to move to the larger auditorium at Bethel A.M.E.

In November 1933, the Forum launched the "Don't Buy Where You Can't Work" campaign, directed at merchants on Pennsylvania Avenue who "wouldn't employ colored young people . . . although their patronage was a hundred percent black. . . . These white merchants were getting their sustenance from the black community and wouldn't let us work." Backed by the *Afro-American* and the African-American churches, the Citywide Young People's Forum persuaded A & P stores in West Baltimore to hire 42 black clerks after just three days of picketing.

This victory was followed by a decades-long series

The Fight against Lynching

The lynching of African Americans on the Eastern Shore of Maryland was symptomatic of the deterioration of race relations throughout the rural South between 1890 and the mid 1930s. Eastern Shore counties were poor, isolated from the amenities and economic opportunities of urban life, and, according to H. L. Mencken, lacked political leadership with the courage to "speak out boldly for sense and decorum." The 1933 lynching of George Armwood in Somerset County mobilized civil rights activists in Baltimore City. Outraged by the brutality of the lynchings and aware that African-American citizens on the Eastern Shore were prevented from effectively protesting the terrorism aimed against their community, black residents of the city organized a campaign that helped end lynching in Maryland and then mushroomed into a challenge to segregation and discrimination on all fronts. The following article was written by Clarence Mitchell, Jr., then a young reporter for the Afro-American, *who covered the racial unrest in Princess Anne in Somerset County in September 1934. Mitchell went on to become the chief lobbyist for the national* NAACP.

Flames of race antagonism that have been smouldering in Princess Anne since the lynching of George Armwood, last October, burst into fever heat on Saturday night when a gang of white hoodlums attacked several colored citizens.

Reports circulating to the effect that the entire colored population was being driven from town on Saturday night were denied by colored residents who would talk to *Afro* reporters on Monday. Many of the terror-stricken townsfolk refused to talk for fear of reprisals.

Residents were prone to dismiss the disorder as trivial, despite the report that men, women and children had been set scurrying in all directions by the enraged whites. Varying reports give the number of whites in the mob from 200 to 500.

The small force of three policemen, headed by Chief Marion Austin, was ignored as if it did not exist.

The town was in a turmoil for more than an hour on Saturday night, and outside help was summoned by Sheriff Luther Daugherty as officials recalled the burning of George Armwood in the courthouse square during an outbreak last October.

Eye-witnesses charge that a mob, led by a white man named Stacey, attacked Roy Shields, a native of the town, and severely beat him with clubs and other weapons.

Shields was rescued from the crowd by officers, according to a witness, but his attackers were not dispersed until one of them had made a speech.

The speech is thought to have centered around recent arrests of colored men on the shore for alleged crimes against white women.

In one of these cases, which was that of Sam Jones, several blood-stained garments that were offered as evidence in attempting to prove that he (Jones) was the murderer of a Mrs. Brumbley, were found to have been dipped in turkey blood.

Jones was released, and is now living at his home in Crisfield, Maryland.

Another of these cases is that of James Boland, a former Sunday school teacher, who is accused of having attempted to rape Mrs. Anna Waddy, 65-year-old white woman, last week.

According to some current rumors in the community, Boland is not guilty but he was trying to collect $118 in salary that he said was owed to him by Mrs. Waddy.

Certain white elements, however, have taken these cases as indications of danger signals in the colored community and are said to have been planning such an affair as took place Saturday.

A variety of reasons why a gang of whites attacked colored citizens in Princess Anne, Saturday, have been given, but some residents are firmly convinced that the trouble was a political move by which whites hoped to make wholesale arrests of colored voters.

With primary elections coming off today (Wednesday), it is said that the gang of trouble makers had counted on the aid of the authorities in keeping the colored people in cells on charges of disorderly conduct.

A decided opposition is growing, among colored people, for Sheriff Luther Daugherty and John B. Robins, state's attorney. Both of these men were in office during the lynching of George Armwood, and Sheriff Daugherty has since figured in the arrest of another man, who was declared not guilty in an Eastern Shore court.

Regardless of what the motive for Saturday night's outbreak was, however, it has left the people of Princess Anne in a state of fear and anger.

The lynching of George Armwood in 1933 on the rural Eastern Shore of Maryland inspired three decades of intense activism among Baltimore City's African-American community.

Ethnic Tensions

Conflict among ethnic groups characterizes all urban areas where people must compete for scarce resources like jobs and housing. In February 1936, The Crisis, *the official journal of the* NAACP, *published an article by Baltimore Rabbi Edward L. Israel entitled "Jew Hatred among Negroes." The article reveals in a particularly poignant way the strained relations between Jews and African Americans, two of Baltimore's most significant ethnic groups. Rabbi Israel's remarks confirm the evidence provided by historians that real differences in their relations with African Americans separated Jewish merchants from other members of the Jewish community. Lillie Mae Jackson's comments exemplify the position of her son-in-law, Clarence Mitchell, Jr., who argued that what appeared on the surface to be an ethnic conflict was, in reality, the predictable antipathy between merchant and consumer.*

As one of the by-products of Hitlerism, there seems to be a great increase in anti-Semitism among Negroes. . . . There have been outbreaks such as the Harlem riotings, when the chief target of Negro wrath seemed to be the Jew. Again, only a few days ago, a prominent Negro social worker told me of the growing disinclination of the colored members of his interracial board to have Jews as white representatives. That this anti-Jewish feeling is not confined to the Negro intelligentsia is demonstrated by the "Situations Wanted" columns of a paper like the *Baltimore Sun*, where more and more applications for domestic service by Negroes stipulate that they want to work for "Gentiles only."

My personal experience brought me a keen insight into this feeling several nights ago when I addressed a Negro forum. The subject was a symposium on the question, "Germany's Treatment of the Jews: Is It Justified?" . . . In the course of the question period I was asked why Jewish department store owners in Baltimore refused to sell to Negroes. This condition is true in one or two instances. It is also true that several Jewish department stores have no such attitude and that, moreover, the department stores controlled by non-Jews almost universally exclude Negroes. I explained my own complete lack of sympathy with this situation, told of my efforts at changing it, and announced that some of these merchants had told me that they would welcome a general agreement of all stores to eliminate all racial discrimination. I pointed out that it was the 90 percent non-Jewish trade which was primarily responsible for this anti-Negro stand, and while I did not consider this a moral justification of the merchant's action, the real solution of the Negro problem lay not with the Jewish minority but with the anti-Negro Gentile majority, even to the extent of challenging the segregation of Negroes in Christian churches. . . .

After the meeting, a young colored woman . . . asked me why it was that since the Jews controlled most of the money in the United States of America, they didn't use that financial power to better the condition of the Negro. . . . She saw the successful Jewish merchant, so she considered all Jews wealthy. She did not come into contact with the great masses of poor Jews, nor did she see the much wealthier holders of big securities who were not Jews.

Herein lies the source of a great deal of anti-Jewish feeling among the Negroes. For reasons of persecution, too intricate to explain in detail, the Jews have been pushed disproportionately into the tradesman group just as the Negro has been pushed by persecution primarily into domestic service and unskilled labor. The Negro frequently buys his wares from a Jew. Often he rents his house from a Jew. Some of these Jews are petty exploiters who not only act in a cold-blooded manner, but who further often enrage the Negro by discriminating against Negro help. But mark you well, they do not do these things because they are Jews. This type of person exploits his fellow Jews just as much as he exploits the Negro. I can vouch for that from wide experience. It is no more fair to take him as typical of the Jew than it is to take the drunken, razor-toting Negro roust-about as typical of the colored man. . . .

I write this article not as a defense of the Jew, nor as an attack upon any Negro or group of Negroes. I write it in the hope that two minority groups who have so many problems in common, particularly in these trying times, . . . will come to understand each other a little better. If any individuals of either group are guilty of actions against the other, let the rest set an example of justice by judging this unworthy person as an individual, and not by hating the whole group because of him. We minorities are always preaching that idea to the world. Why not practice it in our relations with each other?

In the April 1936 issue of The Crisis, *Lillie Mae Jackson responded to Rabbi Israel's article as follows:*

The discrimination in the majority of the large downtown stores owned and controlled by Jews against Negroes has aroused our ire. Rabbi Israel errs when he says the Gentiles own most of the stores that discriminate. When the Gentiles controlled the large stores downtown (having been born and reared in Baltimore), there was no such thing as Negroes not being able to buy in any of the stores. One of the largest stores owned by Jews has always had an attitude of "we don't want colored people here," but quite a number of the better class Negroes who were able to buy expensive garments bought there—now, even that store as well as others, have actually told these refined colored people, "we don't want your patronage." The Negroes understand that Jewish merchants downtown, in order to help the poorer Jewish merchants, have agreed to restrict the Negroes from the larger stores thus forcing them to buy from the smaller stores which the Negroes find selling mostly all "seconds" and their goods sell higher. All Negroes resent this. . . .

May I add, Negroes do not hate Jews; they resent those Jews who practice injustices upon them, believing firmly that minority groups should be most sympathetic rather than join in the persecution with the majority.

of struggles for equality. In 1934, Baltimore lawyer Thurgood Marshall and the NAACP pressed a successful lawsuit to get Donald Gains Murray admitted to the University of Maryland.

University officials at first insisted that Murray have a vacant seat on either side of him so he wouldn't offend white students. Eventually, they designated a $20,000 fund to send African-American students out of state for an education. Unwilling to accept this compromise, the NAACP pursued a legal battle that lasted from 1935 to 1950 and eventually opened the University of Maryland Schools of Law, Engineering, Pharmacy, Dentistry, and Nursing to black students.

During the 1940s, African Americans used voter registration and bloc voting to gain a measure of black power in Baltimore City. Between 1940 and 1952, the number of black voters nearly doubled. The Colored Democratic Women, organized in 1946 by Victorine Adams, mobilized black support for Mayor Theodore McKeldin and other white officials who supported racial change.

Using the power of the ballot and the lawsuit, African Americans won one victory after another in the post–World War II period. In 1952, Ford's Theater agreed to admit African Americans after seven years of NAACP picketing. During that same year, downtown department stores agreed to sell to black customers, although they were not permitted to try on clothing. The Lyric booked Marian Anderson, its first African-American performer, in 1953, although no hotel would give her a room. Also in 1953, municipal parks were desegregated, and the fire department began hiring black employees.

In 1954, Baltimore sent its first African-American delegate, Harry Cole, to the Maryland General Assembly, and Baltimore City schools became the first system in the nation to comply with the Supreme Court's integration order. In 1956, the city passed an equal employment ordinance, and the state ended the practice of listing separate job openings for "white" and "colored." By 1958, most movie theaters and first-class hotels in Baltimore City accommodated African-American patrons.

By the 1960s—the era of civil rights activism in the Deep South—most Jim Crow laws had been

Even in the depths of the Great Depression, blacks beautified their modest row-houses with potted plants, like these along the 600 block of Archer Street.

struck down in Baltimore City. The vestiges of segregation were challenged by a younger, more militant generation of blacks and whites, who expanded their activities across the city and denounced economic inequality as well as racism.

Organizations like the Congress of Racial Equality (CORE) and the Union for Jobs or Income Now (UJOIN) went beyond issues of legal equality. They demanded changes in the distribution of wealth and resources: decent housing, more jobs and better wages, reform of the welfare system.

The demands of the 1960s articulated the needs of Baltimore's poor blacks. Nevertheless, the work of Lillie Carroll Jackson and the NAACP initiated the campaign that made employment and upward mobility a reality for what would become a vastly expanded African-American middle class. Ironically, that mobility has further impoverished the Old West Baltimore neighborhood by enabling the most successful African Americans to move to suburban areas, a process described in Chapter 10.

Old West Baltimore Today

Despite the exodus of many of its more prosperous residents, Old West Baltimore has continued its tradition of social activism. Community associations organized since the 1960s work closely with area churches to improve housing, sanitation, education, and employment and to fight crime. Low-income residents take part in food cooperatives and a program that employs neighborhood men and women to renovate vacant homes.

Agitation for political change at local, state, and national levels is organized through the Black Ministerial Alliance and a network of political clubs that has sent a series of outspoken activists to the Baltimore City Council, the Maryland General Assembly, and the U.S. House of Representatives.

The political sophistication of Old West Baltimore citizens today is the result of a long history of confronting racial discrimination and economic adversity. The tenacity with which this community campaigned for social justice has repeatedly challenged the city as a whole to be a more democratic and more humane place to live.

Acknowledgment: The author wishes to thank Mrs. Juanita Jackson Mitchell for generously sharing her time and her vast knowledge of the campaign for civil rights in Baltimore, Maryland, and the nation.

Dr. John E. T. Camper: Civil Rights Activist

"Patrolman Glass used to shoot colored people, just like you'd shoot ducks," Dr. John E. T. Camper recalled, thinking back to the 1940s when a soldier was killed on Pennsylvania Avenue and Pitcher Street. A general practitioner in Baltimore for more than 57 years and a founding member of the NAACP, Camper was chairman of the Citizens Committee for Justice, a coalition of groups that campaigned during the 1940s against police brutality and for jobs and representation for African Americans. He was also a member of the Me-De-So Club, which was made up of black professional men who helped finance civil rights activities in the city.

A soldier in World War I, Camper remembered African-American veterans as being "particularly bitter. We felt we put our lives on the line to fight for America and didn't get any consideration or protection. In fact, we received less of the benefits of democracy."

When he returned from the war on a train from Washington to Baltimore, Camper was sitting up front, the only African-American passenger in the car. The conductor told him repeatedly to move to the back, but "I refused. I wouldn't move back." Finally, the conductor called a policeman. "He came and looked at me and said, 'Well, he isn't drunk.' Then he asked, 'Buddy, you got your ticket?'

"When I assured him I did, he said, 'Well, he's in the uniform of the United States Army. He'll ride where he damn pleases!' You could see everybody in that car was hoping the conductor would jump me, but he was afraid. I told him if he touched me I was going to kill him."

Camper was born in Baltimore in 1894, the son of two educators. "My father was a teacher in the county, then a principal of the elementary school at Sparrows Point. My mother, before her marriage, was one of the first colored teachers who ever taught in Baltimore back in the 1890s."

A respected physician and civil rights leader, Camper graduated from what is now Douglass High School and Howard University Medical School. He remembered his struggles against job discrimination and other injustices "heaped upon the Negro population." During World War II, he led a picket line up and down Pennsylvania Avenue until "we won out and all the stores hired colored clerks. And then we set out to get the telephone company. I threw a picket line downtown, and we walked that picket line for weeks.

"In the end, the telephone company hired colored coin collectors. Later they put up a division of the company across from the old Provident Hospital and staffed it with colored people. They were dead set against having colored operators in the beginning, but eventually they hired the hello girls, the operators, too."

His campaign to get department stores to allow African-American customers to try on clothing was not so successful. The plan was to bring a case against the stores and take it to the Supreme Court, with the help of Charlie Houston, a well-known and well-feared constitutional lawyer.

Accordingly, Houston, Camper, NAACP president Lillie Carroll Jackson, and her daughter Juanita went to the menswear and womenswear departments of Stewart's, Hutzler's, and other Baltimore stores where they asked to try on various garments. "Juanita bought a coat. Houston bought some underwear. We bought stuff we didn't even want—we just wanted a case so we could carry it to the Supreme Court."

For the first time, all the stores let them try on the clothes; they didn't want to tangle with Charlie Houston. Unfortunately, "we didn't get the case, because all the stores cooperated. Then, when they found out Houston was gone, they reverted to the same discriminatory procedures."

In the 1940s, Camper was active in the campaign to encourage blacks to register and vote. Of the campaign, he says, "There never has been one like it since. We went from neighborhood to neighborhood, from church to church.

"I remember we had a line of colored people standing ready to register, and people tried all kinds of discouragement." It was a hot day, and when people asked for water, a policeman told them there was none available. "I remember I had my children bring buckets of water and go down the line to give people a drink."

The defiance that the young soldier had shown the bus driver in the 1920s was still present in the middle-aged civil rights activist of the 1940s and 1950s. In 1942, as president of the Citizens Committee for Justice, Camper coordinated the march on Annapolis that was to confront Governor Herbert O'Conor with the injustices black people were suffering. At a meeting of the Governor's Commission on Problems Affecting Negroes, set up to deal with the Citizens Committee's complaints, a commission member offered Camper a deal: "If you go along with me, I'll make you black governor of Maryland as far as appointments are concerned. No Negro will have a job in the state if he doesn't come by you." A feisty Camper replied, "I would rather shoot craps up and down Pennsylvania Avenue than accept any such thing as that."

Camper was not easily cowed by bullies like Jack Pollack, a machine politician. "I remember we found one of his men coming in the place where you vote with a bottle of whiskey. He went to each colored person, offered them a drink of whiskey, and put a slip in his hand.

"I objected to that, and told them I was going to make some calls and have it stopped. Five minutes later, here

Dr. John E. T. Camper

comes a truck full of hoodlums and they all surrounded me, trying to scare me away. Well, I come from the country where you fight. They didn't intimidate me in the least," said Camper, a college letter man in track, basketball, and football.

In contrast, Camper was willing to make allowances for people like "Little Willie" Adams ("he was practically in the underworld, you know") if they were active in the struggle for justice. "The truth of it is," said Camper about the man known as the "numbers king" of Baltimore, "Little Willie had done a lot for the black people in Baltimore. A lot of people would never have been in business if it hadn't been for Little Willie.

"Little Willie didn't make himself prominent in the NAACP, but when I gave a talk I saw him sitting in the back of the audience. He supported the NAACP and he supported me in my efforts to get Negroes jobs. When I needed money for these things, I went to Little Willie."

A founder of the Progressive party, Camper supported Henry Wallace for president and ran for Congress from the Fourth District on the party's ticket. "When I was in the Progressive party, a lot of my acquaintances called me a communist. But in actual fact I never even thought of becoming a communist. If I believed in it, I would have said openly, 'I'm a Communist,' and I would have stood up for it. I believe," said Camper with characteristic tenacity, "if I wanted to be a communist, I would have had the right to be one."

Camper died in 1977 at the age of 83 in Provident Hospital, where he had been a visiting staff member for 57 years.

(This account was excerpted from an interview with Dr. J. E. T. Camper by Leroy Graham, in the McKeldin-Jackson oral history collection of the Maryland Historical Society. The interview was edited by Elizabeth Fee.)

J. Broadus Mitchell: An Activist Scholar

Broadus Mitchell, economic historian and socialist, learned practical economics while he was a graduate student in political economy at Johns Hopkins University in the early 1900s. As a volunteer for the Family Welfare Association, a local social agency that organized poor relief, he worked with "a boy who . . . was roller skating and was hit by a streetcar and terribly hurt. [T]his little boy was illiterate but he was fourteen years old. His legs were injured, but he could get a job driving a delivery wagon, delivering packages if he could read . . . the street signs . . . and the addresses on the packages. I tried to teach him to read.

"He lived in a small house in a poor district in southwest Baltimore. I remember how cold it was. They had no heat or almost none. . . . The family was on relief, and I used to take the basket of groceries and soap at the same time that I went to try to help this boy."

Mitchell felt this work deepened his university education: "Without this actual experience in how people lived in poverty and under discrimination, including the Negroes,

I think my economic education would have been lacking."

A native Kentuckian, Mitchell received his Ph.D. from Johns Hopkins in 1918 and began teaching there in the Economics Department. In the 1920s, he served as president of the Baltimore Urban League, an interracial organization designed to improve living and working conditions for local blacks. During the 1930s, the league produced a study of social conditions in West Baltimore's Lung Block, an area where deplorable housing and sanitary conditions had produced an extraordinarily high rate of tuberculosis.

The league tried to convince the city that the block was unfit for housing: "We took our finished study to the Park Board and said, 'Can't you tear down some of this and make a playground?' The man, a white politician, didn't want to shake hands with R. [Maurice] Moss [secretary of the local Urban League]. Moss was a Negro. He didn't want to call him Mr. Moss. He said, 'Oh, we're putting our money into the Baltimore Stadium.' They were trying to attract the Army–Navy game, out on 33rd Street. 'We don't have any funds for this.'"

According to Mitchell, school authorities proved more

J. Broadus Mitchell

responsive. They had a number of the houses torn down and built the Henry Coleridge Taylor elementary school and an adjacent playground. Encouraged by this, the remaining residents began a neighborhood improvement campaign, repairing and beautifying their homes and demanding more city services.

In 1934, Mitchell ran for governor of Maryland on the Socialist party ticket against the Democratic incumbent, Albert Ritchie, and his Republican challenger, Harry Nice. Describing the campaign, Mitchell recalls, "We went around in my car to many parts of Maryland, mining districts in the West, and we went to the eastern part of the state. . . . A staple of our appeal to voters was anti-Eastern Shore lynchers, see, so we didn't go over there.

"My most vivid recollection of that campaign is with Frank [Trager, a fellow socialist], who'd go out on a street corner in Baltimore and stand on a soapbox. . . . We'd get under an arc light and try to collect a little crowd around us. I remember vividly the thing that always got a response from the crowd. . . . We said to them, 'Very few of you who are 50 years of age or over and unemployed will ever work again.' And maybe it was an exaggeration, but by golly you could see it struck home."

Nice won the election, but the Socialist party amassed about 5,000 votes, double its total in past elections. Mitchell attributed the Socialist gains to the severity of the depression in Maryland, as well as to a protest against the Eastern Shore lynchings. He also conceded that he didn't run to win, but as "an opportunity to say some things about the economy."

During his years in Baltimore, many of Mitchell's social commitments were clearly aimed at protesting racial injustice. He investigated a second lynching on the Eastern Shore in the 1930s at the request of the World Council of Churches and published a report to arouse public condemnation. Through this work he met Baltimore's H. L. Mencken, then a writer for the *Sun*. "When I was a student, Mencken was writing articles for the *Baltimore Sun*, making fun of all the do-gooders. . . . [He was] very gifted and very irritating to people who didn't agree with him," Mitchell recalls.

"I had known of him only as, I thought, a rather cynical and destructive person. [But] when we had the second one of those lynchings on the Eastern Shore . . . all of his indignation was turned on the lynchers and those who supported them.

"When my report was published, Mr. Mencken wrote me a nice little note and said, 'Please come to see me. I'm interested in what you experienced over there.' He explained to me that he worked until 10 o'clock at night, but then he was free and I should come to his apartment . . . on Mount Vernon Place. He was most cordial, and he offered me the biggest cigar I've ever seen. And beer.

"Anyway, he sympathized strongly with what I had said

. . . and then when I began to get criticisms in the paper from the Eastern Shore, Mencken wrote a piece in my defense. The university had received some protests, and the president of the university, a man I liked very much, President [Joseph] Ames, he hadn't assented to those protests, but he didn't come very strongly to my support, so Mencken said they ought to cut off the ears of that corpse and send them to the president of the university. I liked it, you know."

During the late 1930s, Mitchell's civil rights activities increasingly aroused the ire of Johns Hopkins administrators and its board of trustees. Along with other Urban League members, Mitchell urged Edward Lewis, then secretary of the Baltimore League, to apply to the Johns Hopkins graduate program in political economy. Lewis was an African American, and Johns Hopkins, as Mitchell explained, "hadn't had any Negroes.

"Now here was a splendidly equipped man, mature . . . married, several children, appointed on commissions by the governor, by the mayor. He was the number one black social worker in Maryland." Lewis applied, but "his application was met with a conspiracy of silence, first. . . . Then opposition became vocal."

Mitchell worked to persuade the university to admit Lewis. "It had been said to me, 'The charter forbids it.' So

I went back to the charter. It didn't. Not a word. Hopkins was an old Quaker, you know." Mitchell also uncovered the fact that in the nineteenth century Hopkins had admitted an African-American, Kelly Miller, who went on to become a dean of Howard University.

But "it didn't do any good. . . . Well, I pressed this thing. Some of the trustees of the university were adamant against it, and they were large contributors to the university, and it came to me unmistakably that it was their opposition which was holding the university up."

During this same period, Mitchell had been proposed for promotion to full professor. But an injudicious remark in the classroom—he referred to the conservative Supreme Court as "nine old bastards"—led to his censure by the academic governing body of the university. Isaiah Bowman, the president of the university, raged at him. As Mitchell put it, "Instead of being promoted, I got bawled out and left. I can't recall exactly what was done with Mr. Lewis's application, but I suppose it was turned down, because he came instead to a new job here in New York."

After resigning from Johns Hopkins in 1939, Mitchell taught in universities around the country, ending his career at Hofstra University in New York in 1967. He published prolifically and remained active in political causes, serving as chairman of the New Jersey Civil Liberties Committee. While on the faculty of Rutgers University in New Jersey, he led a protest against the discharge of two faculty members for their political views during the McCarthy era.

Mitchell died in 1988 at the age of 95.

(This account was excerpted from an interview with J. Broadus Mitchell by Daniel Joseph Singal for the Oral History Research Office, Columbia University, in 1972. The interview was edited by Linda Shopes.)

In 1940, striking Amalgamated workers blocked the entrance to Kaylon plants at 5 North Haven and 1500 Eagle Streets to force the manufacturer to comply with federal standards for wages and hours.

Chapter 5 — # The City That Tries to Suit Everybody: Baltimore's Clothing Industry

JO ANN E. ARGERSINGER

We made frequent complaints and he [the foreman] told me if I wanted my job very badly I would keep my mouth shut. —Marion Vigneri, a garment worker

Baltimore—"the city that tries to suit everybody," as local officials proclaimed with pride—consistently ranked among the nation's top five centers for the production of clothing. During World War I, the clothing industry employed more workers than Bethlehem Steel. Clothing manufacturers methodically turned out men's garments, from cheap-grade summer suits to higher-quality woolen overcoats and business suits. Manufacturers also produced off-the-rack clothes for working- and middle-class women, although the production of women's clothes never matched that of men's.

Baltimore early took advantage of its status as a major port in the Atlantic trade to boost its clothing industry. In 1838, Robert Walker established the city's first manufacturing plant for boys' and men's clothing. Other entrepreneurs followed in quick succession, many of them German Jews who knew well the evils of anti-Semitism and were eager to become economically independent. Henry Sonneborn, for example, whose firm was to become the city's

largest employer of clothing workers by 1919, got his start in 1855.

Baltimore's geographical location also made it ideally suited for trade with the Southern states. Spurred by demands for clothing during the Civil War and assisted by technological advances in cutting and sewing, the manufacture of garments grew rapidly after 1870. A series of good crops in the postwar South enabled that region to purchase over one-third of the clothes produced in Baltimore. By that time, the city's major clothiers—L. Greif & Bros., Strouse & Bros., J. Schoeneman, and the Schloss Bros.—were well under way, employing thousands of workers.

Baltimore's garment district took shape at the turn of the century when large plants were built to satisfy the demand for ready-made clothing among an increasingly urban population. Today there are only a few reminders of it and its once thriving clothing industry, located in the area west of Lexington Market, bound by Baltimore Street to the north and Pratt to the south and heavily concentrated on West Redwood and Paca Streets. The Henry Sonneborn building (*site 1*) at Paca and Pratt Streets, recently renovated to reveal its architectural splendor, still stands, and to the north, at Paca and Lombard Streets, the Strouse & Bros. clothing plant can still

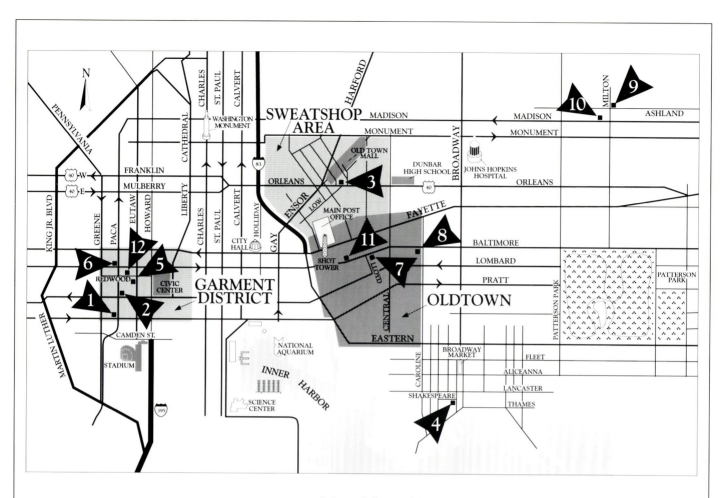

Italic type indicates original building site or function.

1. *Henry Sonneborn*, now Paca–Pratt building

2. *Strouse & Bros.*, now Marlboro Square Apartments

3. *Sweatshop*, 1122 Low Street, now public housing

4. *Sweatshop*, 1631 Shakespeare Street

5. *L. Greif & Bros.*, now Classic Apartments

6. *Schloss Bros.*, now University of Maryland Law School

7. *United Garment Workers union hall*, 1119 E. Baltimore Street, now a parking lot

8. *Amalgamated Clothing Workers' labor hall*, Lewis Building, 1441 E. Baltimore Street

9. *L. Greif & Bros.*, now MarLenn Company

10. *Strikers' "safe house,"* 2410 E. Madison Street, now boarded up

11. *B'rith Sholom Hall*, 1012 E. Baltimore Street

12. *J. Schoeneman*, now Redwood Square Apartments

Hundreds of these sweatshops were located in East Baltimore rowhouses in the late-nineteenth and early-twentieth centuries.

be seen (*site 2*). But the sewing machines are silent in these firms, as well as the other major clothing producers.

Also gone are the sweatshops of East Baltimore, where sewing rooms in rowhouses provided cramped quarters for workers and their bosses. In the 1890s, more than 300 sweatshops filled with Italian, Lithuanian, Bohemian, and Russian-Jewish workers lined Baltimore's streets. Strewn with clippings and, according to one contemporary observer, "swarming with half-clothed children," the sweatshops were concentrated in the area bounded by Lexington Street, Eastern Avenue, Caroline Street, and the Jones Falls, where different ethnic groups lived and worked, learning how to cope with the challenges that an industrializing city presented.

They're Only Girls

More than half of Baltimore's 10,000 clothing workers were women, many young girls barely in their teens. On any day in the 1890s, shortly after sunrise, you could see them leaving small houses and apartments located primarily in Oldtown and East Baltimore to go to work in Baltimore's clothing shops. Many of these women were Russian Jews who had traded the repression and limited opportunities of their homeland for the sewing machines and squalor of city sweatshops.

The shop owners were often fellow Jews, who attempted to win a measure of independence and prosperity as petty entrepreneurs. They sweated their workers, crowding them into rooms in rowhouses and establishing production quotas so high that they could not be met in a 12-hour day. Workers were often forced to labor two days in order to receive what the shop owner claimed was a day's wage.

Although men were always paid higher wages than women garment workers—even for the same jobs—they still earned a meager $450 a year. Only cutters and trimmers could earn more. Their skills were

The employees of Moses Isaac Berman's vest-making shop in East Baltimore, 1893.

highly valued, for they had to be precise in driving the gas-powered (and later electrically powered) cutting knives through as many as 40 layers of cloth.

Women were usually confined to lower-paying jobs —stitching collars, running sewing machines, or sewing hems or buttonholes. They earned barely enough to live, just over $200 a year. Even small children, who fetched bundles of cloth or pulled loose threads, labored from dawn to dusk, receiving about $110 a year for their efforts.

Children also brought bundles of clothes to their mothers at home, where stitching collars or cuffs kept these women up past midnight after they had finished their domestic duties. Employers considered

them unskilled and, like most women in the factories and sweatshops, paid them "by the piece." They received no weekly wage based on the number of hours worked; payment depended on the number of collars stitched or coats hemmed. Even skilled buttonhole makers were paid by the piece. After all, as one employer explained, "They're only girls, and girls can't expect to make a lot of money."

The system failed to benefit even the most efficient and rapid workers, for piece rates were usually set so low that a constant and exhausting work pace was required to earn $1 a day. And employers often changed the piece rates, usually without notifying workers in advance. Stretched to the limit, working-

Inside the Henry Sonne-
born and Company garment
factory, 1902.

class families depended on the collective wages of their members, including the small change earned by children. Unexpected hardship often meant disaster, whereas saving money usually required some deprivation.

The Darker Side of Progress

Teeming with social and economic evils, the sweatshop became the symbol of the darker side of industrial progress. The Maryland Bureau of Industrial Statistics (BIS) reported that, at 1122 Low Street (*site 3*), "a terrible odor pervades the whole house and the only entrance is through a filthy alley." At another shop, located at 1631 Shakespeare Street

(*site 4*), where portions of letter-carrier uniforms were produced, the bureau found it "difficult to conceive a more filthy and unwholesome place in which to manufacture clothing."

The bureau's reports aroused the community. From the press to the pulpit, demands were heard to end the unhealthy conditions surrounding the sweatshops. Socially minded reformers sympathized with the immigrants caught in a web of poverty and deprivation and called for a halt to the sweating system. Other citizens fretted more about the prospect of contagious disease spreading beyond the confines of the sweatshops and endangering their own lives.

Laws passed in 1894 and 1895 established guidelines for proper sanitary conditions at the workplace. But not until a 1902 amendment did the BIS receive the authority to enforce the statutes. Even then, the bureau was allowed to hire only two inspectors to investigate the entire city.

Skyscraping Factories

From the turn of the century through World War I, the rapid expansion of large manufactories, known as inside shops, led contemporary observers to believe that the modern factory would eliminate the toil and inefficiency of the sweatshop system. More efficient and less resistant to technological change, the inside shops practiced the science of production, performing all the steps of clothing manufacture under one roof. Unlike the sweatshops, which might employ five to nine workers, a single inside factory could have as many as 3,000 workers laboring in specialized departments. Garments could be made with greater efficiency and precision, and workers, it was argued, could be relieved of the filth and drudgery of sweatshop conditions.

Modern and imposing, the inside shops—also called Baltimore's "skyscraping factories"—appeared to herald a new era of industrial progress and prosperity. In an inside shop that employed 650 workers, for example, as many as 7,000 men's woolen suits could be produced in a week. Each day, about 6,000 yards of material would arrive to be sponged and shrunk, laid out on 100-foot-long cutting tables, chalked, cut, and delivered to a sewing room of at least 400 operators. Most of them sewed only one seam, as the garments passed through the departments in a steady, monotonous stream. It was, by the accounts of local business leaders, an industrial marvel.

By the early twentieth century, Baltimore's major inside companies included Sonneborn's, Strouse & Bros., Greif's (*site 5*), and Schloss Bros. (*site 6*). They were all firms of German-Jewish ownership, and by 1915 they accounted for nearly three-quarters of the city's production of men's garments and employed more than half the city's clothing workers.

Coexisting with sweatshops—and exempted from the public outcries the sweatshops produced—the multistory inside shops followed certain principles of scientific management to maximize efficiency and profits. By diluting skills through the subdivision of labor, disciplining workers more completely on the shopfloor, and standardizing work rules and processes, employers sought to eliminate what they regarded as inefficiencies in the production process. For example, Sonneborn's speeded up the pace of work by eliminating less fit workers and carefully monitoring workers' motions during production.

Although the owners of these factories often joined the chorus of opposition to sweatshops, inside shops benefited from the labors of sweated workers by contracting work out to small shops. Large clothiers pitted these contractors against one another until the successful bidder promised to complete the task for an absurdly low price. The contractor then sweated his workers or, even worse, cheated them by claiming their work had been performed improperly and refusing to pay them at all. Finally, inside shops whose workers were unionized occasionally set up their own sweatshops to avoid paying union wages for the less-skilled tasks.

During World War I, many of the city's major clothiers expanded their operations to satisfy government orders for war-related apparel. Workers labored extra shifts to turn out uniforms, and women were allowed to perform the skilled jobs traditionally reserved for men.

One garment worker and labor organizer, Sarah Barron, fondly recalled her war days at Sonneborn's: She received higher wages and learned new skills. And, without the knowledge of the foreman, she and her union sisters routinely stitched their names and addresses in soldiers' overcoats in hopes of receiving letters from the boys at the front.

After the war, the withdrawal of government contracts hit the clothing industry especially hard. Wages declined, and workers were laid off. The once vigorous Strouse & Bros. closed permanently in 1922 and, by mid decade, such firms as Philip Kahn (the "Overcoat King") had also shut down. Even Sonneborn's was forced to close in 1931.

Other major companies survived by cooperating through the Baltimore Association of Clothing Manufacturers, formed in the 1920s, and by using the sweatshop system they had once deplored. But the

The Henry Sonneborn and Company factory is the most prominent building in this 1928 view of the city's former garment district. Renamed the Paca-Pratt Building, Sonneborn's has been renovated and is now used as offices.

clothing industry never regained its earlier vitality.

The clothing industry continued to decline throughout the Great Depression. Sweatshops increased in number, but total production dropped, as did Baltimore's national standing among clothing manufacturing centers. The revitalization of the union movement, which brought hope and higher wages to garment workers, challenged nonunion clothiers. A few left the city rather than recognize the rights of workers.

World War II, unlike the first world war, did not significantly revitalize the industry. Government clothing contracts were diverted to other cities so

that Baltimore workers could take jobs in industries deemed more essential to the war effort: shipbuilding, steelmaking, and jobs in airplane and munitions factories.

After the war, local manufacturers predicted another golden era, hoping to duplicate the heyday of clothing production between 1914 and 1919. By the early 1950s, almost 17,000 workers—nearly three-quarters of them women—labored in 340 clothing shops. About a third of the shops were contract shops similar to the old sweatshops. Once again, the large manufacturers pitted contractors against each other, wages were fairly low (under $50 a week), immigrants predominated in the shops, and in spite of better sanitation and less overcrowding, working conditions were still harsh.

But skyscraping factories were, for the most part, gone. By the end of the 1950s, the industry began a new decline as corporations shifted production to nonunion areas all over the world.

Strength in Numbers

The Italian, Jewish, Lithuanian, and Bohemian women and men who worked in Baltimore's sweatshops often found that even talking about forming a union threatened employment. Unionization was no easy task. And long hours of hard work often left garment workers "too damn tired to organize," as one union leader put it. Language barriers among workers also discouraged organizing, as did employers who circulated blacklists of union "troublemakers" to deter unionization. So, to register their protest against working conditions, clothing workers engaged in slowdowns at work, or they changed employers with some frequency.

Nevertheless, the strike was the workers' primary weapon, and the intransigent boss was their foe. In the 1890s, laborers organized under the United Garment Workers of America (UGW)—an affiliate of the American Federation of Labor—and used the strike to win a 10-hour workday and the weekly payment of wages from 20 shops in the city.

As a craft-based union, the UGW, whose hall was located at 1119 East Baltimore Street (*site 7*), attempted to win concessions from employers through the organized power of those most skilled in the garment trades: the cutters and trimmers. Critical to the production process and possessing skills not readily acquired, these aristocrats of labor were usually able to halt production when they struck.

In 1895 and 1896, just as the industry had begun to change with the construction of larger, more modern inside shops, UGW workers, especially the trimmers and cutters, turned to the strike again to protest the rapid pace of work required in the inside shops and to demand higher wages in both contracting and inside shops.

Although not fully successful, the strikes focused public attention on the miserable working conditions of clothing workers and encouraged reform-minded middle-class citizens to lobby for legislation against sweatshops. Laws were passed to ensure at least a modicum of space, light, and ventilation for workers. But the laws were enforced only sporadically, and sweatshops continued to operate.

The strikes also demonstrated the value of organization to clothing workers. As one garment worker recalled, "There really was strength in numbers." Worker dissent became more vocal and more visible, attracting press attention as well as producing employer concern. Indeed, the unionization of the trimmers and cutters led employers to band together to minimize the UGW's power at the workplace.

The formation in 1914 of the Amalgamated Clothing Workers of America (ACW), with headquarters in the Lewis Building at 1441 East Baltimore Street (*site 8*), added to the turbulence of the period. As a union open to all clothing workers, regardless of skill, the ACW appealed especially to the city's newest immigrants, offering them a voice in union matters— a voice they believed had been too often muffled under the traditional and native-born leadership of the United Garment Workers.

Spearheaded by Jewish immigrants and influenced by socialist teachings, leaders of the ACW hoped to rid the country of clothing sweatshops, to bring economic order and justice to the industry. In Baltimore, Sonneborn's most nearly approximated what the ACW regarded as an enlightened employer. But that assessment came only after a bitter struggle with Sonneborn's and a divisive battle with the United Garment Workers.

Degrading Physical Examinations

A highly efficient skyscraping factory, Sonneborn's boasted the most modern equipment on the eve of World War I. But workers resisted the streamlined production process: They occasionally became ill and missed work, they socialized when they were supposed to be working, they took too much or too little time for their tasks.

The managerial changes Sonneborn's introduced to regiment the workforce and eliminate inefficiency were unpopular. Workers denounced them, especially the degrading physical examinations designed

This group of tailors was among those who walked off the job at Sonneborn's in 1914 to protest company efforts to "streamline" the production process. The 16-week strike that followed resulted in the Amalgamated Clothing Workers' first contract with a Baltimore firm.

to weed out the unfit. With the assistance of the ACW, workers launched a strike against Sonneborn's.

But workers were also fighting against each other in the strike of 1914, which marked the beginning of a two-year struggle between the ACW and the UGW. Workers hurled both rocks and epithets at one another, forcing Sonneborn officials, especially Sieg-mund Sonneborn, an ardent opponent of sweatshops

and an advocate of scientific management practices, to resolve the difficulties. Impressed by the plans of the ACW, Sonneborn's supported negotiations that ended the strike, brought recognition of the ACW, and eliminated the dreaded physical tests.

Within a short time, the ACW and Sonneborn's mu-tually established an arbitration system that prom-ised a more disciplined workforce as well as employer

L. Greif & Bros., at Milton and Ashland Avenues. In 1916 a militant strike here and at other factories of the company sparked Amalgamated Clothing Workers' efforts to organize the labor force. Greif successfully resisted unionization until the 1940s.

commitment to signed agreements. The company also introduced a pension plan, improved safety features (including fire drills), and a medical department staffed with a trained nurse. Workers benefited from many of these changes, and Sonneborn's system of collective bargaining, as it was called, meant that fewer strikes would occur.

But workers also had to forfeit the custom of immediate redress at the workplace, for grievances now wended their way through the arbitration system. Union officials joined with employers to condemn spontaneous or unauthorized strikes. Worker stability did not always ensure industrial democracy. Further, the armistice between the UGW's 200 cutters and the ACW's thousands of clothing workers at Sonneborn's was an uneasy one—in fact, on the verge of collapse.

If Anyone Kicks, Run Her In

In 1916, as war in Europe increased demand for mass-produced uniforms, city clothiers expanded their operations. But visions of profits often faded

before the realities of what employers derisively termed "labor troubles," as the ACW and UGW struggled for supremacy in the men's clothing industry in Baltimore.

The ACW turned first to the Greif factories—an essential part of the city's clothing industry. Many of Greif's women workers were ready to join the union; they attended meetings and signed union cards, pledging their loyalty to the ACW. Greif responded swiftly, dismissing 20 of the most outspoken women. The ACW called a strike, even bringing workers from Sonneborn's to picket the Greif plant on Milton and Ashland Avenues (*site 9*). About 3,500 garment workers—two-thirds of them women—crowded the streets surrounding the Greif factory.

Newspapers reported that riot police met the picketers with clubs. Ordered not to "stand any guff" from the strikers, the police warned them against becoming "obstreperous." "If anyone kicks, run her in," the city police commissioner said. Swearing and swinging at the picketers, the police were greeted by strikers who "hooted in derision" and by 10,000

spectators shouting their disapproval. At 2410 East Madison (*site 10*), an elderly woman, enraged by the behavior of the police, threw open her doors to the strikers, and 60 garment workers crowded into her rowhouse, mocking police and vowing never to "give up." The jeering further angered the riot squads. They stormed the house, arresting everybody inside, including the elderly woman, who was hustled off to jail.

The strike continued for two days, and arrests grew more frequent. "I must have been arrested 10 or 11 times," recalled ACW member Sarah Barron. But news that a general strike might occur, paralyzing the city, prompted the chief of the Bureau of Statistics and Information to hold a conference between workers and the Greif firm. The ACW, now 9,000 members strong, bargained hard. "The result was a victory for the clothing workers on every point involved," the *Sun* reported.

Few employers resisted unionization so completely as the firm of L. Greif & Bros. The shared Jewish faith that had helped bring Sonneborn's and the ACW's leadership together in 1914 proved unable to generate similar sentiments among the Greif leadership. The apparent victory by the workers disturbed both the Greif firm and the competing union, the UGW. Both looked for ways to undo the results of the peace conference.

In late February, Greif fired the ACW's most vocal members, then abruptly announced a signed agreement with the UGW. More than 800 ACW workers walked off their jobs: 200 quit work at Greif's factory at Milton and Ashland Avenues, and all of Greif's employees at its other plants stopped work. The Baltimore Federation of Labor, with which the UGW was affiliated, condemned the strike and organized groups of Federation members to patrol Greif's factories to insure against another ACW demonstration.

But they failed to halt the strike. Instead, the actions of city police against the strikers served to generate public sympathy, even encouraging civic reformers to organize an open forum at the city's Academy of Music to protest "police brutality," especially toward "girl strikers." Middle-class women listened with shock as Greif's female employees detailed both the force and the language used by the

police. Admonishing the police chief, a few prominent attorneys even accompanied women workers to the police department to prefer charges against officers for "unnecessary brutality" and for "using language which cannot be repeated in dealing with girl strikers."

Yet little came of these protests. The police commissioner concluded that his officers had behaved responsibly, and strikers returned to Greif's or looked elsewhere for jobs. The ACW strike fund had been too small. "The class of people that we have out [on strike]," explained one organizer, "must be paid from the very first minute," for these workers had no resources to fall back on. Even the UGW felt betrayed when Greif's hired nonunion trimmers and later began hiring women to cut cloth—a job traditionally reserved for men. Having successfully repelled efforts at labor organization in 1916, L. Greif & Bros. remained a bastion of nonunionism in the city's clothing market until the 1940s.

The Battle of the Scissors

But the year 1916 was not over, and industrial strife in other clothing factories led the *Sun* to conclude in late summer that "strike fever is spreading." Wartime orders continued to increase, placing a premium on reliable labor and giving unions a slight edge in their struggle against manufacturers. In need of workers in wartime shops hastily established throughout the city, employers circulated brochures in immigrant neighborhoods promising "good wages while learning piecework" and boasting of the "coolest workrooms in the city."

For the ACW, the economic conditions offered a ready invitation to unionize the men's garment industry. In particular, the ACW sought to break the grip of the UGW on cutters and trimmers by encouraging these workers to switch affiliation and by training the newer male immigrants for jobs as cutters. For the UGW, the time had come to regain lost membership and flex its muscles, showing the strength of its union among the most skilled of the garment trades.

The struggle between the ACW and the UGW reached a violent climax at Sonneborn's in August 1916. In what the press labeled the "battle of the scissors," UGW cutters physically resisted the introduc-

Her name is misspelled, but union organizer Sarah (Borinsky) Barron is arrested during the 1932 strike against Greif's and Schoeneman's.

Hurt in Strike

Sara Bornsky

Miss Bornsky, of the 1200 block N. Caroline St., reported she was knocked down by a policeman and her glasses broken as she was arrested with a large group of striking garment workers today at Oliver St. and Central Ave.

Portrait of Sarah Barron

"I remember it was a big boat" and "we were on the bottom," recalled Sarah Barron. The year was 1914, and Sarah, her two sisters, and her brother stayed near their mother on the passage to their new home: Baltimore. Their father, a tailor from a small Russian village, had come to Baltimore in 1912 to find work. He found a small house in the predominantly Jewish neighborhood of Oldtown and a job in a clothing factory, and he saved his money until he could send for his family.

A 12-year-old child, Sarah had little time for schooling or play in her new community. Her mother fell ill—a "weakened heart," Sarah explained—and her father lost his job because he refused to work on the Sabbath (a demand of even Jewish manufacturers during the boom years of World War I). As a consequence, Sarah left school in the fourth grade to accompany her sisters to the garment factories. She worked in a basement at Wohlmuth's factory, pulling loose threads for 10 hours a day and hiding in a large bin of scraps when the occasional child-labor inspector came in. "It was hot," Sarah remembered, "and there wasn't even no payroll. They used to give my sister the money for me too."

Within the year, Sarah and her sisters left Wohlmuth's for Sonneborn's. By 1916, she had advanced from thread puller to sewing machine operator and had joined the union. Her oldest sister had already joined the UGW, following in the footsteps of their father, who became a UGW member shortly after his arrival in Baltimore. But Sarah's first union affiliation was with the newly formed ACW. She was recruited to the union by Dorothy Jacobs Bellanca, an outspoken woman who in 1909 had organized a UGW Local of Buttonhole-Makers when she was barely 16. Like most of the unionized Jewish immigrant community, Dorothy Jacobs Bellanca left the UGW for the ACW—a union with a Jewish leadership that took in all workers, regardless of skill or gender, and was influenced by the socialist principles many Russian Jews believed necessary for the new industrial order.

Once Sarah had signed her union card, labor organizing took precedence over other interests, for building a union required time, persistence, and, as Sarah recalled, a willingness to go to jail. Arrested a number of times along with other "Sonneborn girls" who picketed the Greif firm in 1916, Sarah remembered the event vividly: We were "just a bunch of young kids, but we had a lot of spunk in us." We were told that "the girls" were to march in the front of the picket line to protect the men from the police clubs. Then there was "a lot of shouting . . . and a lot of us landed in the police station. Some of them had to nurse their babies. They let them out but they didn't let us out until the following day. . . . We didn't get the union so easy," Sarah added.

Throughout the 1920s and 1930s, Sarah Barron rose through the union ranks. Her organizational skills, enthusiasm, and unwavering commitment to increasing the ranks of union women all made her union sisters, and many of her union brothers, look to her for guidance and support. She took a prominent role in the 1932 strike, which revitalized the ACW in the midst of the economic depression and landed her in jail 13 times. Later in the decade, she worked hard to assist the CIO in its organizational campaigns: "Take Sarah [with you]," an ACW leader instructed a United Automobile Workers organizer, setting out to unionize the auto workers, "she's got a lot of nerve."

After World War II, as a paid union organizer, Sarah had the difficult task of chasing "runaway shops" into the far reaches of the Eastern Shore or rural Pennsylvania. She encountered not only the usual array of hostile local officials but also the fear of outsiders among workers, racial tensions in integrated shops, and antiunion sentiment springing from hysteria about communism. Indeed, just after the war started, Sarah officially changed her name from Borinsky to Barron, on the advice of fellow ACW member, Jacob Edelman. Jake warned her to "drop the 'sky,' lest you be called a communist."

But Sarah Barron was no communist, for by the end of the 1930s she was already firmly committed to the party of the New Deal and a loyal follower of Franklin Roose-velt. Although previously a socialist, her commitment to the Democratic party remained firm after 1936.

Her primary loyalty, however, was always the union. But the ACW was not always as kind in return. Union brothers resisted efforts among women members to gain a greater voice in the union, and Sarah Barron had been among those women in the 1920s who attempted to form a women's local. Denied the necessary support, shouted down at meetings, ridiculed at the workplace, and even deprived of grievance representation, these women unionists—with Barron in the forefront—were ultimately forced to abandon their hopes for a women's local. Paid less for the same job and denied access to better-paying jobs, women workers also found barriers in the union organization. Becoming a paid organizer was often the highest position a woman could achieve in the ACW.

There were, however, victories along the way. Barron remembered how she and other women led the fight in 1919 to keep one ACW woman's job as a cutter, despite serious opposition by the all-male local. She spoke with pride of the achievements of ACW women. "We helped to make the union stronger. . . . Our women were really wonderful." She added, "We picketed plenty. . . . They could always count on us."

Sarah Barron grew up with the union, and after the death of her family members, she regarded the union as her family. "I didn't have too much social life outside the union. But I loved it. We accomplished a lot of exciting things." Officially retired in 1972, Barron has been active in helping senior citizens, and when she visits her senior center she provides leadership and support. "It makes me feel like I'm still in the union," she explained.

Scene Of Garment Makers' Riot This Morning

FACTORY OF HENRY SONNEBORN & CO., INC., PRATT AND PACA STREETS

The photograph was taken immediately after the riot this morning in which 400 men fought like madmen with shears, knives and clubs. The building has been under strong police guard since the fight.

Policemen stood guard at Sonneborn's in 1916 after an intraunion struggle spilled out into the streets in what the press called "The Battle of the Scissors."

tion of four ACW cutters into the ninth-floor cutting room of Sonneborn's. (The other 2,800 Sonneborn workers were ACW members.) The fight began on the ninth floor, but as both unions sent in reinforcements, the struggle spilled into Pratt and Paca Streets. Blackjacks, clothing shears, and iron knuckles left bloodied and bruised victims, some seriously injured and requiring hospitalization. Riot police arrived, according to the *Sun*, "all wielding clubs and some with drawn revolvers . . . charging the mob, striking right and left." An hour later, 12 men had been arrested, and the streets had been cleared of "rioters."

With Sonneborn's support, the ACW cutters remained on the job, and additional ACW cutters were soon hired. UGW cutters and trimmers became disillusioned with their union, as the entire leadership of the Baltimore Federation of Labor came under fire for "losing" the garment industry to the ACW. Although the UGW continued to serve as an irritant,

the ACW reigned supreme in the men's garment industry, celebrating its victory by establishing a new local for cutters and trimmers.

The success of the ACW continued throughout the war years. The union organized every major firm in Baltimore, with the exception of L. Greif & Bros. Smaller clothiers also warmed to the ACW, for it introduced an element of stability into the industry. For their part, the large clothing manufacturers found the ACW arbitration system effective and efficient. Strikes became less frequent, although neither workers nor employers were entirely satisfied with the new grievance procedures. Still, wages rose, profits soared, and workers won a number of major concessions.

The End of an Era
During the postwar slump of 1920–1922, the loss of government contracts hit the major clothiers hard,

and workers, fearful of losing their jobs, challenged their bosses reluctantly. The postwar "Red Scare," the xenophobic drive for 100 percent Americanism, and the open-shop campaign of the 1920s all meant that organized labor had once again become suspect, and unions, castigated by local businesses as dangerous instruments of revolution and radicalism, rarely called strikes or expanded their influence in the 1920s.

ACW membership peaked in 1919 at about 10,000, falling in the 1920s to under 3,000. Only Sonneborn's maintained its union contracts in the depressed 1920s, and this resulted primarily from its unusually cooperative relationship with the ACW.

Workers had much to complain about, for the depression in Baltimore's clothing industry signaled a return to sweatshops. Large manufacturers increasingly relied on contract shops, and small entrepreneurs sweated their workers to enhance their profits. Meanwhile, outcries against sweatshop conditions had dwindled to being barely audible. It was a time for middle-class consumption, not reform—a time of radios, autos, and Sunday excursions into the countryside, far away from the dimly lit workrooms of garment workers. As a consequence, conditions in the industry declined, while the ACW tried to preserve a few of its earlier gains.

"Feminist Conspirators"

As immigrants became Americanized and new immigration declined, ethnic ties became less important within the union, but inequality between men and women workers persisted. Empowered by the right to vote in 1920, women workers sought to widen their role in the ACW. Inspired by the existence of an Italian local, a Jewish local, and a Lithuanian local, among others, and by the existence of women's locals in Rochester, Chicago, and New York, women workers attempted to form their own local of the ACW in Baltimore.

Their efforts were supported by the ACW's only woman official at the national level, Dorothy Jacobs Bellanca, who had migrated to Baltimore from Latvia in 1900 and had entered a sweatshop near her home in Oldtown at the age of 13. She organized the predominantly female local of buttonhole makers before

she was 16 and, in 1914, led her local to abandon the UGW in favor of the ACW.

She rose rapidly in the union, ultimately becoming a member of its national executive board. Although acknowledging what she termed the "ever-present tension between men and women," Dorothy Jacobs Bellanca worked to overcome the division and promote working-class unity. But she agreed with her union sisters in Baltimore that a separate women's local was needed until women held a more active role in the union and men treated them as equals.

In 1925, about 100 union women set out to form their own local. They sponsored weekly lectures on the role of women in the labor movement and organized a union party attended by some 500 people. "I don't think there was ever a group of women with so much hope, determination, and strong willpower to succeed in this undertaking as we are," one woman worker exclaimed.

But their determination and enthusiasm failed to change the minds of local union officials, men who ignored economic realities and objected to women working for wages or who tolerated women at the workplace only as long as they were submissive. Labeling the women "feminist conspirators," union officials refused to grant the proposed women's local a charter.

A United Army of Workers

The union did make some attempts to soothe tensions between men and women and among ethnic groups. Education, union leaders believed, was the best way to reach out to members, erase old prejudices, and build new alliances based on a common class identity. Along with other forces, union leaders urged members to become more Americanized. In 1928, for example, the ACW halted publication of the Yiddish and Italian versions of its paper, declaring that the English version was sufficient. The union also featured stories in its paper celebrating the role of women in the labor movement and often encouraged union brothers to extend the principle of equality to their union sisters.

In Baltimore, the ACW's educational activities were among the most popular events sponsored by the union. A number of professors from Johns Hopkins University and Goucher College consistently attracted large gatherings at the B'rith Sholom Hall on East Baltimore Street (*site 11*). Broadus Mitchell, a socialist professor at Hopkins (see Chapter 4 interview), was a particular favorite, frequently speaking to packed houses or conducting weekly seminars for eager unionists. As Sarah Barron recalled, "We paid Dr. Mitchell a quarter a week to learn what the union was about." She said it was one of the best investments she ever made.

Because family obligations or parental restrictions sometimes left women workers unable to attend evening lectures, the Women's Educational League of the ACW also held talks on weekend afternoons or at picnics in local parks. But the educational work went on, telling workers to stand united behind their union. By the 1930s, what one local ACW leader called a "tightly knit, united army of workers" had been established.

Throw the Girls in the Wagon

The unity among clothing workers was particularly evident in the 1932 strike during the Great Depression. Called by the ACW, the strike was intended to unionize Greif's and Schoeneman's (*site 12*), the city's major nonunion clothiers, and the hundreds of contract shops they used.

According to the ACW, cut-throat competition by Baltimore's garment industry had become a menace to clothing markets in Rochester and Philadelphia. No longer dominated by large, modern factories systematically turning out men's clothes, Baltimore's clothing industry was also made up of small entrepreneurs who sweated their workers in primitive workrooms.

In September 1932, some 5,000 garment workers responded to the ACW's call to action. Two-thirds of them were women, who turned out to protest working conditions and wages and to demand recognition of their union. Over 200 clothing shops were affected by the strike, but most attention focused on Greif's and Schoeneman's. Both firms operated their own contract shops where wages rarely exceeded $8 a week for 60 hours of work.

At Schoeneman's industrial building, pickets and police clashed when the police commissioner ordered

his force to reduce the number of pickets to four. Under instruction to "throw [the girls] in the wagon," the police arrested hundreds of strikers at Schoeneman's, while others moved in with clocklike precision to take their places.

Sarah Barron later recalled with pride, "We [women] were really the ones who had something to do with mass picketing" in Baltimore in the 1930s. She added cheerfully, "I was locked up thirteen times" in the 1932 strike. But, Barron noted, there was little enthusiasm for going to jail, and some of the women workers who spent the night in jail were reluctant to join a picket line again. Even those, like Barron, who became regular visitors to the city jail during the strike never forgot the attitudes of the arresting officers. They treated us like streetwalkers, complained one woman striker.

Calling the strike a civic nuisance, concerned citizens demanded that the city's mayor investigate it. Schoeneman refused to attend the public hearings, but his workers patiently waited hours to have their stories recorded, shocking the public with their accounts of pitiful wages and conditions.

Marion Vigneri of Little Italy, who worked in the cellar of Schoeneman's, told this story to the investigators:

We had a cooler in the cellar which was filled only twice a day for 150 girls. If we wanted any more water we were told to go and get it in the toilet. Our lunches we placed on work benches where rat poison was thrown around and roaches crawled up and down continuously all day. We made frequent complaints and he [the foreman] told me if I wanted my job very badly I would keep my mouth shut.

Producing her pay envelopes, Vigneri testified that she earned $6.50 for a 60-hour week.

Esther Buzi and Agnes Stankowski of East Baltimore corroborated her testimony, as did Margaret Baker of East Oliver Street. Others complained of inadequate light and ventilation, of severe rodent infestation, of low wages, and of intimidation by male foremen, who forced them to work overtime or lose their jobs, refused to allow them leave for personal or family illness, arbitrarily changed the piece rates, and regularly harassed women they found attractive.

Striking female garment workers attempting to organize Greif's and Schoeneman's in 1932 were "girls" to the press, as the headline indicates. A woman identified as Miss Mataiozza points to a bruise she received from a policeman.

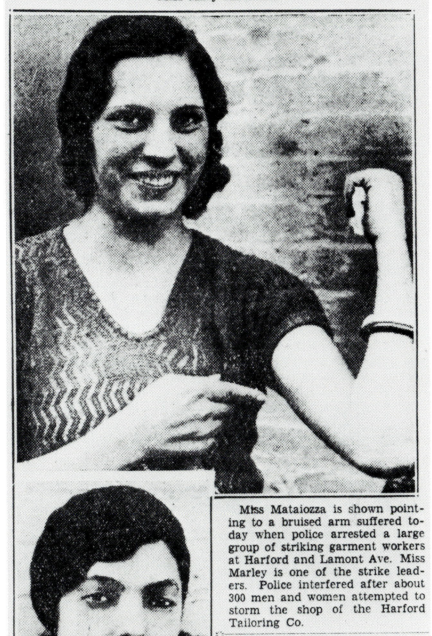

Girls Arrested in Strike Riot
Miss Mary Mataiozza

Miss Mataiozza is shown pointing to a bruised arm suffered today when police arrested a large group of striking garment workers at Harford and Lamont Ave. Miss Marley is one of the strike leaders. Police interfered after about 300 men and women attempted to storm the shop of the Harford Tailoring Co.

Miss Emma Marley

Portrait of Jacob J. Edelman

"You have to be quite articulate in debating labor issues," the late Jacob Edelman once explained, noting the formidable resources business can use against unions. And Jack, as he was called, early developed a reputation for his oratorical skills, despite having arrived alone at Locust Point from Russia in 1912, speaking no English whatsoever.

The son of an attorney in Rovno, Russia, Jack had already completed his secondary education when he set out for Baltimore at age 16, and his enthusiasm for learning remained with him until his death in 1984. Though he labored long hours by day in the city's clothing factories, he also attended evening classes at the University of Maryland Law School. Graduating in 1925, he became one of the city's most important labor lawyers and an advocate for all workers.

Offended by the degrading conditions in the sweatshops, numbed by his own long hours and low wages, committed to socialist principles, and fiercely attracted to the promise of unionism, Jacob Edelman joined his first strike only months after his arrival in Baltimore. By 1914, he had earned a place on the employers' blacklist as a "revolutionary" and was unable to find work in any clothing factory in the city.

He went to New York for a few months in search of a job. While there, he became especially attracted to the new brand of unionism heralded by the ACW. In late 1914 he returned to Baltimore and found work at Sonneborn's where the ACW had just been accepted by management. He fought the cutters of the UGW in the "battle of the scissors" in 1916, and with the ACW victory was able to work his way up to the position of cutter at Sonneborn's. Subsequently, he became a shop chairman for his union, and in 1918 was elected a business representative for the ACW.

By that time, Jack Edelman cut a striking presence. He spoke eloquently and dressed stylishly. In union negotiations, he impressed company officials, who were also unnerved by his obvious academic achievements.

With his law degree, Edelman defended workers thrown in jail for picketing and represented unions in fighting injunctions. Edelman was known to bail out strikers as well as defend them. Sarah Barron remembered him fondly, for, as she explained, she would have spent "more nights in jail" had it not been for Jack.

His legal efforts were instrumental in advancing organized labor's cause in Baltimore in the 1930s, and despite the rift between the AFL and the CIO, and despite Edelman's preference for the latter, he defended craft as well as industrial unionists. After the passage of the Wagner Act in 1935, U.S. Secretary of Labor Frances Perkins selected Edelman to serve as a federal labor referee, which he did with distinction until 1939. In that year, Edelman successfully accomplished another goal: election to the City Council of Baltimore, where he served for 32 years.

Never enamored of politics—a plaque in his law office stated that *a politician thinks of the next election. A statesman thinks of the next generation*—Edelman was fond of the New Deal, especially the Wagner Act. Like many other Jewish socialists, the first vote he cast for a nonsocialist was for Franklin D. Roosevelt in 1936. From then on, his loyalty to the Democratic party never wavered.

Business leaders regularly condemned what they regarded as "New Deal radicalism" and "un-American unionism," and the *Baltimore Sun* was downright shrill in its denunciations of FDR, the New Deal, and the labor movement. But Edelman had the firm support of union members. And the overwhelming majority of Baltimore's voters had pledged their support to FDR in 1936 and would do so again in 1940. Edelman's pro–New Deal and prounion campaign in 1939 therefore struck a responsive chord.

On the City Council, Edelman chaired a number of important committees during his long tenure. He championed civil rights, deploring the council's 1958 defeat of an antidiscrimination bill, which, he said, made Baltimore "appear to the world as a bigoted hamlet instead of a great city." After his retirement from the council in 1971, he continued his career in public service, chairing the Maryland Human Relations Commission until 1976. Throughout the entire period, he continued to provide legal services for organized labor and gave generously of his time to a range of humanitarian causes.

Jack Edelman is still spoken of affectionately in the Amalgamated Clothing Workers. Although not a typical Jewish garment worker—he came to Baltimore with more education and more money than most—Jack Edelman early demonstrated a strong commitment to workers' rights. He defended those rights first on the picket line, then in the courtroom, and then at City Hall.

Kaylon strikers get support from the shipyard workers in 1940.

Krestle Manufacturing Company, *ca.* 1937

All told, 18 women spoke out against Schoeneman's. Some were married, some were daughters of immigrant families, but all were native born and had at least one year of high school education. They were vest makers, armhole basters, and lapel padders, and they all worked for piece rates. Even the fastest of them could not make more than $8 a week.

Revelations about the garment industry gained public sympathy for the strikers and helped persuade about 70 percent of the clothing firms to sign union contracts. But Greif's refused, and Schoeneman's hastily moved out of Baltimore to the safety of nonunionized Chambersburg, Pennsylvania. ACW women formed a human blockade to stop the company's trucks from leaving the city, but Schoeneman's had already sent much of its equipment to the new location under cover of darkness the night before, some of it packed in the cars of management executives.

As a result of the success of the strike, many of the ACW women joined together to form a new local. Although some wanted the women's local earlier denied them, others agreed with union officials on the need for unity in the union and formed Baltimore's first English-language local instead.

But in spite of the Amalgamated's emphasis on working-class unity, women members continued to receive less pay, to be excluded from the most skilled jobs, and to be underrepresented in the union's leadership positions. Although they made up an overwhelming majority of members, no woman was ever selected to head the union at any level.

Union women joined the struggle with their union brothers, although rarely as equals. But union women like Sarah Barron persevered, for, as she noted more than once, when the battle lines were drawn, you had to stand behind your union. Such women believed the union became a better place for both men and women because of their efforts, in spite of the union's spotty record on equality.

From the New Deal to the Present

Despite the steady decline of the clothing industry in the 1930s, the ACW managed to expand its influence in the industry, and the loyalty of its members remained high. In 1937, the ACW moved from its old headquarters on North Eutaw Street to a more modern building on West Redwood, providing tangible proof of its success. (The ACW is now located at 1505 Eutaw Place.)

The clothing union also became more politicized in the 1930s, allying itself with the New Deal and the party of Franklin D. Roosevelt. With the aid of New Deal labor legislation, the ACW managed to keep most of the men's garment industry unionized throughout the Great Depression. More than any other union in the city, the ACW worked for Roosevelt's reelection in 1936.

ACW members' ties to the Democratic party became part of their trade union culture, and they promoted Democrats who spoke to the needs of all workers. They even encouraged their own to run for office. Jacob Edelman, who began in the shops of Sonneborn's and then became a labor lawyer, was elected to the City Council in 1939, serving until 1971. Thomas D'Alesandro, Jr. also worked for Sonneborn's before he began the political climb that took him to the City Council, to Congress, and to Baltimore's City Hall as mayor.

The loft area of Baltimore's once vibrant industry has now all but disappeared. In scattered downtown shops, women can still be found sewing band uniforms or overcoats, and they worked until the late 1970s at Greif's in the Govans area, but their wages have remained low and their jobs precarious. The ACW, which helped eliminate some of the worst sweatshops in the industry and instilled in Baltimore's garment workers a sense of pride and commitment to all working people, remains on the defensive, besieged by a multitude of problems. The garment industry workforce has become an international one, and Baltimore's once thriving industry a remnant of the past.

Members of the Knights of Labor parade along Baltimore Street, east of Lloyd Street, on Labor Day, 1890. Thousands of craft workers marched in Labor Day celebrations, asserting pride in their work and support for their rights.

Chapter 6

East-Side Union Halls: Where Craft Workers Met, 1887–1917

RODERICK RYON

At last the working-people will have a hall of their own, a home where they can meet and discuss, without being subject to temptations of a bar-room and its bad influences. —The Critic, April 30, 1889

In the 30 years before World War I, when Baltimore's population swelled from 400,000 to 600,000, the city's industries employed one out of every four citizens. Most of them toiled as laborers or operators of plant machinery. But a small, proud group of artisans—Baltimore's craft workers—stood out from the rest.

Laborers did the hauling, lifting, loading, and digging to build a rapidly expanding port and city, and plant workers toiled at repetitive assembly-line chores. Craft workers had far more control over their work and the fruits of their labors—control exceeding that found in contemporary industry.

Rather than work at assigned chores under employer supervision, craft workers made whole products or parts of products. They often owned their own tools, chose raw materials, and decided on the size and design of their goods; and they usually produced them to the final stages of finishing and packing. They alone had the knowledge needed to make the products and the responsibility of training new workers.

City craft workers won Baltimore a reputation as a producer of a rich array of industrial goods. Apparel craft workers made coats, dresses, pants, overalls, garment pockets, and buttonholes. Metalworkers crafted iron molding, machine parts, and boilers. Those working in food industries made cans, meats, bread, and beer; construction workers produced bricks, cut stone, doors, and floors. Publishing employed craft workers who made newsprint, printing plates, and bound books. No one trade ever dominated the rest.

But whatever their skills, craft workers shared a common culture with strong, widely held convictions and values. They believed their know-how and control bred good character, confidence, even manhood on shop floors. They thought their knowledge and status separated them from other workers who stood—in the words of the *Baltimore Trades-Unionist*—"cowed and servile . . . cap in hand, before employers."

Craft workers valued education and self-improvement, as well as service for the greater good of craft, family, community, and country. At the same time, they believed in joint efforts through unions to protect craft work and to educate workers "socially,

Organized Labor in Baltimore, 1880–1915

In the late nineteenth and early twentieth centuries, most labor associations of east-side Baltimore craft workers were affiliates of either the Noble Order of the Knights of Labor or the American Federation of Labor.

The Knights, organized in secrecy in 1869 in Philadelphia, promoted the solidarity of all labor. Under the banner "An injury to one is the concern of all," not only native white craftsmen, but African Americans, immigrants, women, and semi- and unskilled workers joined the Knights. Over a million workers were members by the mid 1880s.

The Knights proclaimed the dignity of industrial labor to members and the public alike. It expected that the wage-earning, profit-based system of production would die out and gradually be replaced by a worker-owned, democratically managed system.

To pave the way for the new order, assemblies sponsored educational programs for workers and set up cooperative factories where workers owned and sold their products and gained valuable experience for a transformed system of production.

National leaders counseled against strikes, which they regarded as a waste of funds and energy. They recommended, instead, consumer boycotts and arbitration of industrial disputes.

East-side Baltimore craft workers flooded into assemblies after 1881 when the Knights relaxed secrecy rules, and again in 1886 when leadership began to agitate for shorter hours throughout industry. The workers joined craft assemblies representing particular trades or signed on with mixed assemblies or the citywide District Assembly, both composed of skilled and unskilled workers from various trades.

For a few years, local assemblies sustained cooperative factories, sponsored citywide boycotts, and publicized the worst cases of worker exploitation through public meetings and articles in the labor press. But the lodges collapsed during the depression of 1893 when unemployment reached 50 percent in such major local industries as construction, iron, and garment manufacturing.

As companies slashed wages and replaced craft workers with machines and unskilled labor, weakened local assemblies, often unable or unwilling to strike, acquiesced. As disappointed city workers quit the lodges, national leadership also folded before 1900.

Twenty independent clubs of craftsmen formed the Baltimore Federation of Labor in 1881. Eight years later, it affiliated with the American Federation of Labor (AFL), newly organized in Columbus, Ohio. Federation locals believed the wage system would endure and relied on the strike as the craft worker's most effective tool for higher wages and shorter hours, the so-called bread-and-butter issues of the labor movement.

Exclusion was a hallmark of Federation locals. National charters of unions in printing trades and construction, both employers of many Baltimoreans, barred African Americans and women, and every AFL union discouraged membership of the semiskilled and unskilled.

Willing to strike even during depressions, city unions weathered the depression of 1893 and grew rapidly after 1900. Companies in the city often negotiated contracts with Federation locals at the expense of less skilled labor, extracting wage increases for craft workers from the pay of nonindustrial labor.

New industries spawned new unions, and the Federation had 100 locals citywide by World War I. Responsible for over a hundred strikes between 1900 and 1917, the Federation played an active political role. The membership lobbied for laws regulating child labor, maximum hours of work, and compulsory education. Officers of Federation unions served frequently on the City Council and city review boards and commissions.

Machinists at the Carroll Park Shops of the United Railway and Electrical Company in 1901. Machinists were the elite among workingmen. Frequently they hired their own helpers, had considerable control over how a job was done, and determined the terms and pace of their labor.

morally, and intellectually," in the words of a carpenters' charter.

All these beliefs helped stir craft workers' pride, prompting them to see the benefits of artisan labor as far-reaching. In homes, the higher wages of craft workers supported families, saving dependents from factory drudgery. In communities, artisans formed society's middle class, believing themselves to be more honest, patriotic, and civic-minded than either the powerful or the impoverished.

But craft work was threatened in Baltimore after 1890. Emerging companies tried to pool capital, place knowledge about production in management hands, and introduce assembly-line techniques of work, innovations that foreshadowed the tediousness of modern industrial work. At work in more than a thousand separate city workplaces, and divided by craft, race, sex, and ethnic origin, craft

workers counted on unions to struggle against these so-called reforms.

In halls and rented rooms, craft workers gathered to devise a strategy for countering management and to nurture the artisan culture. Ritual and ceremony, business and social life, linked worlds of work and family and personal life. These gathering places, often humble little rooms, reassured laborers of craft work's dignity and social worth and strengthened them in their struggles against employers. They were, in a sense, secular churches for congregations of laborers.

The Union Hall District

Imagine standing outside City Hall on any workday 80 years ago. You would see groups of craft workers hurrying toward you. Typographers would be coming from Local 12 headquarters across the street

Top left: Workers at Theodore Ludwig's Shop, 1212 Bank Street, *ca.* 1890.

Bottom left: Workers from Fluskey, Cathell & Co., Boiler Makers, located at Fort Avenue and Lawrence Street in South Baltimore, pose with one of their products, *ca.* 1920.

Above: Coopers at the Kimball-Tyler Company in Highland-town proudly line up with their tools, showing off the fruits of their labor, *ca.* 1910.

at 210 Lexington (*site 1*). Members of the oldest and largest craft union in the city, they might be hurrying to keep an appointment with the mayor. Garment workers, young women in the Women's Trade Union League, with headquarters at Calvert and Fayette Streets (*site 2*), might walk toward City Hall for a meeting with city councilmen. In a city of 40,000 craft workers, most of them voters, and 100 labor unions, public officials often welcomed delegations of workers from nearby union halls.

Some 80 percent of city craft workers lived on Baltimore's east side; a tour of their neighborhoods and union halls might begin at City Hall. If you walk east past municipal buildings to the Jones Falls Expressway (I-83), then along narrow north–south streets to Pratt, you'll come to what was once the east side's union hall district. Blocks here housed

halls for 40 craft workers' unions until 1904 when Baltimore's Great Fire burned out 24 of them, most in two-story, street-front buildings, along with much of the rest of downtown.

If you had been standing at any busy intersection in the union hall district in its heyday, you would have seen the front doors to halls where 20 unions met. After working hours, dozens of craft workers hurried to them on foot or by trolley on their way to union meetings or to spend time in the clubs.

Board a Baltimore or Fayette Street bus, or walk from the expressway to Broadway, and you will pass the sites of six union halls once located amid workers' homes in a two-square-mile section of East Baltimore. Craft workers owned two-story rowhouses or rented rowhouse flats in Oldtown, several blocks east of Jones Falls (now the expressway), on and off

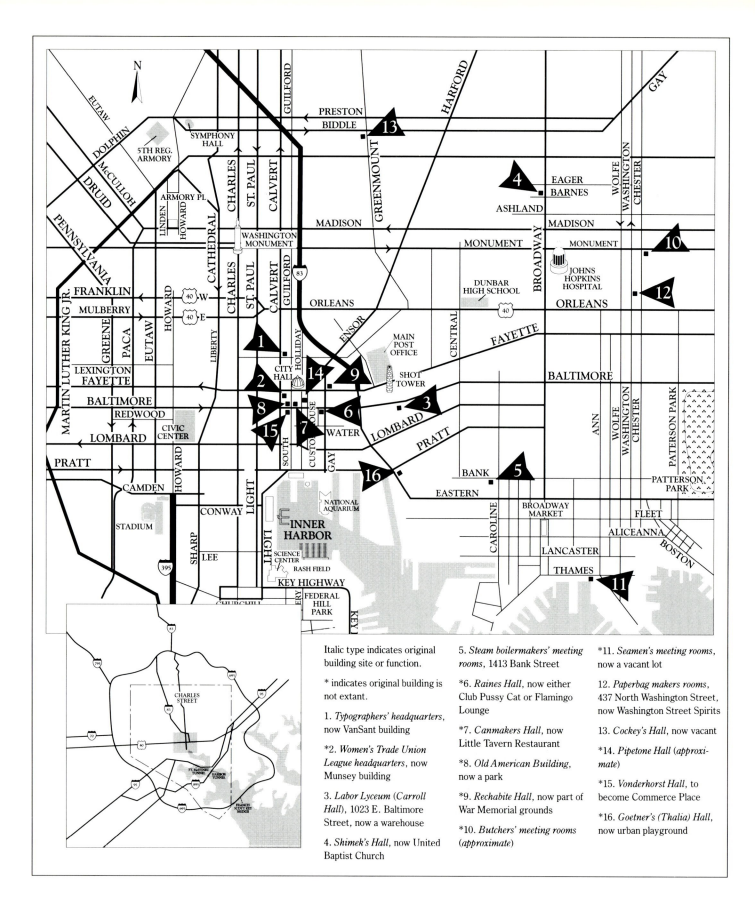

Italic type indicates original building site or function.

* indicates original building is not extant.

1. *Typographers' headquarters*, now VanSant building

*2. *Women's Trade Union League headquarters*, now Munsey building

3. *Labor Lyceum (Carroll Hall)*, 1023 E. Baltimore Street, now a warehouse

4. *Shimek's Hall*, now United Baptist Church

5. *Steam boilermakers' meeting rooms*, 1413 Bank Street

*6. *Raines Hall*, now either Club Pussy Cat or Flamingo Lounge

*7. *Canmakers Hall*, now Little Tavern Restaurant

*8. *Old American Building*, now a park

*9. *Rechabite Hall*, now part of War Memorial grounds

*10. *Butchers' meeting rooms (approximate)*

*11. *Seamen's meeting rooms*, now a vacant lot

12. *Paperbag makers rooms*, 437 North Washington Street, now Washington Street Spirits

13. *Cockey's Hall*, now vacant

*14. *Pipetone Hall (approximate)*

*15. *Vonderhorst Hall*, to become Commerce Place

*16. *Goetner's (Thalia) Hall*, now urban playground

In Search of Old Union Halls

The 16 halls noted in this chapter are all located within a mile and a half of City Hall. To visit them conveniently, you might plan two trips, one close to City Hall and the other farther east beyond the Jones Falls Expressway.

Six of the halls—those of the typographers in the VanSant Building, the garment workers' Labor Lyceum (also known as Carroll Hall), the Bohemian tailors' Shimek Hall, the steam boilermakers' house on Bank Street, the paperbag makers' hall on North Washington Street, and the bookbinders' Cockey's Hall—are the original structures used by union groups. The Great Fire of 1904 gutted the halls clustered on East Baltimore Street from Calvert Street to the expressway, but the two- and three-story street-front buildings that replaced them are similar to the original structures.

The site indicated on the map may be the location of the original hall, but block demolition and new construction sometimes shifted street numbers slightly. At sites designated by street intersections, the record does not always tell us exactly which corner the halls occupied. And unions sometimes moved from corner to corner because the commercial buildings at the ends of residential blocks frequently competed to rent spare rooms. East-side topgraphy—broad thoroughfares and narrow side streets —remains mostly unchanged.

Four of the halls mentioned rented space to a number of trades. Boxers and sawyers used Canmakers Hall. At various times bricklayers, carpenters, caulkers, cigarmakers, machinists, plumbers, plumber suppliers, shoemakers, and steamfitters could be found in the Rechabite Hall. The latter was also a meeting place for the Knights of Labor Mixed Assembly. Vonderhorst Hall was at times the meeting place for blacksmiths and helpers, bricklayers, iron molders, pattern makers, stove molders, and typographers, as well for the Federation of Labor. The brewers, brassmakers, and German Trades Union used Goetner's (Thalia) Hall.

Cockey's Hall was once the meeting place for bookbinders. Located at Biddle Street and Greenmount Avenue, it is now vacant.

The Labor Lyceum, also known as Carroll Hall, at 1023 East Baltimore Street, was home to garment workers' unions, *ca.* 1905.

Contemporary shot of the Labor Lyceum, now a warehouse.

Gay Street to North Avenue. Or they lived in Jonestown, streets south of Fayette Street, or on blocks along Broadway.

For example, the structure at 1023 East Baltimore Street, called Carroll Hall or the Labor Lyceum and now a warehouse, was home to garment workers' unions—men who made pants and overalls and women buttonhole stitchers—in a neighborhood of Russian Jews and Italians (*site 3*). In 1913, about 100 women garment workers marched from the Lyceum along Aisquith and Lexington Streets to a downtown train station where they joined delegations of middle-class women's suffragists on their way to Woodrow Wilson's inauguration in Washington, D.C. to demonstrate for women's suffrage and working women's rights. Parade floats depicted unorganized women

Small Rooms, Large Buildings

East-side craft workers lived close together but worked apart from one another. The small, dispersed plants of the city isolated them from others of the same trade. To talk over pay rates and working conditions, unorganized craftsmen in the 1880s often congregated in market stalls, corner taverns, or a succession of workers' houses in the neighborhood after work.

But those who banded together in unions—the Knights or the Federation of Labor—found the makeshift locations unsatisfactory. They needed places of their own where equipment could be stored and time spent to socialize and debate issues before and after meetings.

Very small or new unions, with perhaps 30 or 40 members, would met weekly in an east-side craft worker's home, often for months at a time. A regular location allowed the group to advertise meetings in the labor newspapers. Steam boilermakers, for example, met regularly at 1413 Bank Street in the 1890s (*site 5*).

Unions of 50 to 100 craft workers more often rented second stories or rooms behind streetfront bars and stores from tavern owners and shopkeepers. The rent was cheap, and as many as six locals shared quarters, meeting on successive week nights and Sunday afternoon. Fraternal and political groups often used the same rooms. Masons, Odd Fellows, and ward Democratic clubs attracted east-side clerks and shopkeepers, as well as craft workers, so union men found themselves in the same rooms several times a week.

Typically, the rooms were packed with chairs and had tables at front and rear, laden with newspapers and pamphlets, tools and equipment. Officers often brought work materials to demonstrate new implements or allow workers to practice on them. Apprentice garment cutters brought bolts of cloth to meetings in order to practice before and after the business of the evening.

Unions with 100 or more members—masons, typographers, and can makers, for instance—rented whole floors of streetfront buildings or bought their own buildings with room to spare in the 1890s. At Raines Hall on Baltimore Street and Post Office Ave-

in east-side sweatshops, ill clothed and huddled in tiny unventilated rooms, next to well-dressed union women who earned good pay in safe, sanitary factories.

Shimek's Hall, now the United Baptist Church at Barnes Street and Broadway, also served as a meeting place for immigrants in the heart of Little Bohemia (*site 4*). Tailors frequented a bar on the first floor and attended Knights of Labor meetings on the second. In the 1890s, Federation of Labor locals, eager to call strikes in garment trades, campaigned for new members among rival Knights' lodges. Organizers often waited at the downstairs bar and accosted tailors after Knights' meetings adjourned.

Raines Hall, where brick-layers met, stood at the corner of Baltimore and Post Office (now Customs House) Avenue.

Rechabite Hall, formerly at 500 East Fayette Street, housed numerous unions, including those of the brick-layers, carpenters, caulkers, cigarmakers, machinists, plumbers, shoemakers, and steamfitters.

nue (now Customs House), bricklayers had enough space for a library of 3,000 books (*site 6*). Can makers met and let rooms to other unions at Canmakers Hall, on the northeast corner of Baltimore and North Streets (now Guilford Avenue) (*site 7*). And typographers rented the Old American Building, a former newspaper office in the 200 block of East Baltimore Street (*site 8*).

If you had walked into any of the larger facilities, you would have been impressed by the fine oak desks, hand-carved podiums, and heavy draperies, typically crafted or donated by members. Many union halls were more lavishly furnished than the workers' homes, signifying the high regard they had for their unions.

Close to Work and Home

The halls were accessible to east-side workers traveling by trolley along Gay, Fayette, and Baltimore Streets, but also drew in workers from South and West Baltimore. Because the halls were clustered together, visitors to the city—national officers of the Knights or the American Federation, for example—easily made the rounds of five or six meetings in one evening.

Proximity had other advantages. Unions sometimes adjourned their meetings so that their members could walk a few doors down the street to another hall to take up matters of common concern. Since the halls were close to newspaper offices, they lured writers and editors who came to hear news about strikes or union elections. In fact, at Rechabite Hall, home to several locals on the 500 block of East Fayette Street, the Federation invited reporters to the president's formal address each year (*site 9*).

Workers frequently rented union meeting rooms near their workplaces in order to exercise a customary craft workers' right: They could walk on and off jobs throughout the workday without permission from the bosses. In their halls they gossiped during

slack periods, played cards at noon, browsed through newspapers after work. Butchers kept rooms across the street from the Northeast Market at Monument and Chester Streets (*site 10*), seamen had quarters at 1741 Thames Street on the Fells Point waterfront (*site 11*), and typographers always located close to newspaper offices.

Women workers in Baltimore factories constituted one-third of the industrial workforce. While most worked at unskilled tasks, those with skills to protect —such as bookbinders, paperbag makers, dress-makers, and buttonhole stitchers—set up flourishing locals near their homes.

They numbered about 10 percent of the craft workers, were younger than their male counterparts (usually in their teens or twenties), and were typi-cally unmarried. Their parents expected them to sandwich housework and care of young sisters and brothers in with their factory work. With little free time to travel, and with citywide trolley lines notori-ous for night-time violence, they wanted union rooms close by.

From flats off East Baltimore Street, Jonestown buttonhole stitchers could walk a few blocks to Labor Lyceum meetings. Paperbag makers lived doors away from their meeting rooms at 437 Washington Street, now the Washington Street Spirits Building (*site 12*). Oldtown bookbinders took only a short trol-ley ride to Cockey's Hall, on the southwest corner of Greenmount Avenue and Biddle Street (*site 13*).

Job Centers

Since most workers rarely heard reliable news about their trades in their own small factories, one of the main functions of union halls was to serve as cen-ters of information and referral for jobs. After work or at meetings in the union halls, workers swapped stories from many work sites: about plants where work orders were down and layoffs imminent, about plants where bosses were short-handed, about em-ployers who had begun to ship work out of the city to nonunion labor. Rumors spread so quickly that clubs appointed investigative committees to visit work-places, call on employers, and write reports that were posted in union rooms.

Craft workers eager for new jobs came to the union

halls to find them. Officers kept lists of openings, and plant foremen—even company owners—went regu-larly to the halls to apprise officers of new jobs or to hire help. Companies that had no separate personnel departments bargained about wages on their shop floors or in union rooms.

Workers who changed jobs frequently gathered outside union rooms early in the morning to barter with bosses for their day's labor. Street space out-side Pipetone Hall at Baltimore and Holliday Streets also drew porters and laborers, who came hoping to sign on for day work when foremen appeared there to recruit craftsmen such as carpenters, masons, or typographers (*site 14*).

Union men who were new to the city came to the halls looking for employment even before they located living quarters on the east side. They showed their union cards to club officers, who then allowed them to examine job lists. Apprentices found their first jobs at the halls when they signed on with crafts-men's assemblies.

Union rules were made and enforced at the halls. For example, to guarantee that work would be spread among many, the clubs had rules limiting the pace at which work should be done. Shop-floor swifters—so-called hell-horses or black legs—caught working too fast were penalized at club meetings. Bricklay-ers even convened special meetings at Vonderhorst Hall at 9 South Street to hear cases and embarrass convicted offenders publicly (*site 15*).

Strikes usually began inside plants, but at the halls unions took charge of them, planning strategy and negotiating support from other unions. The big-ger clubs opened their halls to mass meetings of city laborers convened to support strikers. Work-ing conditions in the turn-of-the-century years—low wages, long hours, and offensive work rules—forced many strikes over the years, and craft workers in every industry joined the walkouts.

Community and Family Values

The routine, week-to-week business in clubrooms played a large part in preserving community and family values, in addition to helping workers maintain and improve their crafts. Unions frequently lobbied for improvements in working-class neighborhoods, petitioning city government for neighborhood institutions.

For instance, unions of German workers regularly defended Baltimore's German-American schools. These public, bilingual schools, located in workers' neighborhoods, were criticized by middle-class reformers as expensive to operate and as un-American. In the 1890s, east-side clubs of native workers, and the Federation of Labor, endorsed the separate schools.

Clubroom resolutions and trips to City Hall on behalf of other issues—free public baths, covers for street sewers, enough trolley attendants to "protect our wives and daughters . . . against loafers and toughs"—consumed as much time in some clubs as wage issues. Workers worried about representation for their neighborhoods if unions disappeared.

Special ceremonies were staged in the clubs to remind workers of their craft heritage. At annual initiation ceremonies, young, old, and retired members convened to hear readings and speeches recalling famous craftsmen, such as Jesus the carpenter and da Vinci the machine maker. The crafts' contributions to history were recited. Well-groomed initiates stood erect before the assembled and swore fidelity to the union and its rules. At especially solemn ceremonies, when sons were initiated, fathers administered the oaths to them.

At other times, whole families came to the halls. Larger clubs, for example, hosted formal dinners on days significant to the craft. Typographers met annually on Franklin Day, January 6, to recall printing's illustrious past. At such occasions, wives and children were reminded of craft work's contribution to the family. Craft work guaranteed husbands and fathers money enough to house their families in good east-side rowhouses, not tenement slums. Unions of craft workers, orators claimed, rescued men from bars, made them sober, temperate hard workers.

Creating a role for themselves beyond work, unions made their presence felt on holidays and family occasions. When city workplaces closed on July 4 and craftsmen joined neighborhood or downtown parades, many first assembled with families in union rooms for a solemn occasion: the reading of the Declaration of Independence by a union officer

or most senior member. At Baltimore Street halls, workers' families viewed annual Labor Day parades from union headquarters. Some clubs bought and distributed coal at cost to members' homes throughout the winter months.

Burial funds made up of craft members' contributions were maintained by clubs to provide members and their families with dignified funerals. At a member's death, specially selected committees visited the widow and presented condolence resolutions along with funds from special collections.

A Threatened Way of Life

New equipment and machinery placed by employers in many city factories after 1890 greatly worried craft workers. Canners installed machines to solder cans, thereby displacing hand can makers. Contractors began to substitute plane-cut stone for granite carved by union stone carvers. Publishers, newspapers, and print shops installed Merganthaler Linotype machines and fired hand typesetters.

The displacement of skilled workers by equipment signaled dangers worse than sporadic wage cuts or longer hours. It foreshadowed an economy characterized by tedious labor, permanent low wages for workers easy to replace, the collapse of craft unions, erosion of the workingman's status as breadwinner, and loss of the knowledge and competence that forged worker pride and dignity.

With their way of life threatened, craft workers tried to sabotage employers' reforms. Sawyers and box makers, claiming breach of agreement, sued local companies that introduced nailing machines in 1890. Some clubs required foremen, who were often responsible for hiring new workers, to join. Club constitutions dubbed them club "servants" who were obligated to enforce rules with what printing tradesmen called "the proper fraternal spirit."

Unions converted club space into practice rooms. Between meetings, club officers pushed chairs to the wall and made space for equipment. They needed places to hone old skills, make themselves so efficient that bosses would find them irreplaceable, or practice on new equipment so that employers would depend on craft workers, not novice workers, to operate it. City typographers sent members to New

Labor Radicalism

Millions of America's farmers and workers grow poorer while a few capitalists amass fortunes, argued economist Henry George in his widely read treatise, *Progress and Poverty*, in 1879. To many Baltimore craft workers, local events proved the poverty-amid-progress theory.

Bankers and outside corporations organized trusts—conglomerates of wealth that enriched local stockholders, the wealthy Baltimore classes that ran east- and south-side factories, but lived in mansions in the affluent north and northwest. As industrial productivity tripled between 1870 and 1900, local owners reaped great profits, while workers suffered wage cuts. Between 1880 and 1900, wages declined in every major city industry, and depressions threw thousands out of work in 1873 and 1893.

George's classic work circulated widely in the city, along with other radical analyses of the widening gap between rich and poor. Some argued for inflation. Greenbackers in the 1880s and Free Silver Populists in the 1890s claimed that a shortage of money held down both prices and wages. It strangled small producers and left rural masses too poor to afford industrial products.

Place the public, not capitalists, in charge of the government, they argued, and it would soon be the poor people's servant, not their master. The nation's money supply would be enlarged, and government would own and operate national railroads. This would eliminate stockholders' profits and manage railroads in the public interest.

To consider issues of inflation and government ownership, east-side assemblies sponsored public debates. In 1891, the Knights of Labor convened a statewide convention of farmers and laborers to consider political strategies to curb big business.

Radicalism critical of the large profits of urban industry also had a following. George's supporters set up Single Tax clubs to agitate for huge levies on private property—taxes on the unearned wealth of capitalists to be used by the government to alleviate social misery. City anarchists, who were students at Johns Hopkins University, argued that workers ought to weaken all forms of government, capital's natural and inevitable ally.

Local Socialists included both students and professors, as well as German and Russian immigrants versed in European economic theory, including Marxian socialism. They spoke up for an end to the wage system of compensating labor, industrial ownership by the public at large, and worker management of factories. Labor would no longer be meted out a pittance by capitalists but would be rewarded with its full share of industrial wealth.

Socialists formed a citywide chapter of the Socialist Labor party, a group founded in 1876 in Philadelphia to disseminate socialist ideas in trade unions and run candidates in elections. After English translations of Marx's *Capital* appeared in 1886, advocating working-class solidarity, Knights' lodges convened educational meetings to debate socialism.

After 1900, economic radicalism was less studied and publicly debated, as moderate reform movements gained a following in both the local Democratic and Republican parties. But it nevertheless still surfaced, influencing women's suffrage and urban reform movements, elections, and trade union programs. The revolutionary Industrial Workers of the World, a new Socialist party, and the Eight Hour Day movement, which embraced a long-standing aim of radical trade unionists, all had a following in the ranks of Baltimore labor until World War I.

York to study linotype machines and eventually installed practice machines in their rooms.

Since national unions, not manufacturers, owned most of the written material on work tools and machinery, education committees sent away for pamphlets and how-to-do-it manuals. As a result, an excess of equipment and reading material forced a few unions to hunt for roomier quarters.

Clubs also tried to publicize the virtues of craft-made goods. Can makers organized special committees to investigate alleged poisoning by food from machine-made cans. At Canmakers Hall, just blocks away from downtown offices, the union displayed badly corroded, acid-laden machine-made cans next to safe handmade ones. Boot and shoe workers gave public lectures about their products in east-side halls. The Federation of Labor advertised union-made goods with displays of union labels that traveled from hall to hall. The Labor Lyceum exhibited craft-made Baltimore products in 1911, complete with a short motion picture and music to advertise craft ware.

From Superiority to Unity

White craft workers often had a sense of superiority and status because their wages were higher than those of other workers and they had more autonomy than others on the shop floor. Factory laborers and machine operators often worked for them, taking *their* orders and directions.

Male tailors in large plants passed on pants and coats to teenage girls to finish; native white carpenters and masons watched over the Italian ditch and cellar diggers who began construction projects; construction craftsmen were assisted by African Americans hired to wheelbarrow bricks and carry heavy beams to them. Throughout city plants, black porters and domestic workers transported materials and cleaned craftsmen's workplaces.

Because foreign-born workers, blacks, and women so dominated Baltimore's semi- and unskilled labor force, the white craftsmen's feelings of status were heightened, reinforced by nativist, racist, and sexist prejudices. The isolation of union hall life, the retreat it afforded from heterogeneous workforces of city shop floors, buttressed feelings of superiority. Workers' social exchanges—pranks, loud guffaws, and ethnic jokes—along with the presence of dirty spittoons, empty liquor bottles, and smoky air, stamped many halls as white, male, and even "native only" gathering places, mirrors of neighborhood geographic and social segregation.

But sentiments about the common interests of labor, stirred by worries about the craft workers' future, challenged these elitist notions. Craftsmen saw industrial monopoly—what typographers called "syndicates of wealth"—or the pooled capital of larger businesses as behind the plants' new machines. The syndicates, not small employers, had the money for new machinery, bigger facilities, and unskilled labor forces.

White craftsmen began to suspect this common enemy required the unity of labor for a common defense. As companies introduced plans to de-skill labor, east-side Knights' lodges broadened weekly educational programs to include more than skills training. In programs often open to the public, they featured talks, presentations, and debates, which exposed audiences to remarkably radical analyses of labor's dilemmas. Members and guests alike argued public ownership of property, equal distribution of wealth, and the union of all labor.

Knights and Federation locals invited prominent teachers and professors to explain the controversial doctrines. Richard Ely, a labor economist from Johns Hopkins University, was a frequent speaker and joined Typographers Local 12 as an honorary member. English Fabian socialists, guest teachers from England at the local Bryn Mawr School, spoke often at local clubs.

Knights officers encouraged members to study these new ideas. One local even purchased pamphlets that excerpted Karl Marx's *Capital*. And the ideas spawned new organizations, which met in union halls to further programs of worker solidarity. At Canmakers Hall, the Workingman's Education Society held lectures about worker unity. At Rechabite, a chapter of the Single Tax Society endorsed reforms espoused by Henry George. The Socialist Labor party, whose aim was to enroll all male industrial workers, met at Goetner's Hall (also known as Thalia Hall) at 915 East Pratt Street (*site 16*) but sent speakers to other lodges as well.

While charters of Federation locals explicitly

excluded the unskilled, Baltimore assemblies of Knights explored programs of broad labor organization and labor unity for a few years. Since Jim Crow ordinances segregated whites and blacks in virtually every public facility, a few west- and south-side assemblies close to black neighborhoods enrolled African-American workers. The lodgemen hailed this show of tolerance. "This very assembly makes a negro feel he is a brother and honors him with important office," one proclaimed in 1889.

The year before, east-side lodges tried to form a citywide organization of labor, including black unions, at Canmakers Hall. It failed, but Knights and Federation locals occasionally convened integrated mass meetings of labor to protest state and national violence against black and white workers.

The ideology of labor unity began to erode even craftsmen's sexist values, which were so powerfully nurtured by a culture that upheld the family wage and female dependency. Proclaiming the rights of all to organize, east-side assemblies gave money to citywide locals of women, while Knights and Federation clubs endorsed women's suffrage. East-side garment workers formed mixed industrial locals of skilled and unskilled workers before World War I.

The Decline of the Craft Worker

"More oil refineries, more glue factories, . . . more foundries . . . stinks," complained Baltimore writer H. L. Mencken in 1923. "Like bringing the cow in the parlor, the carpet is ruined and the milk is no better." But it was not so much the number of new plants that was a problem. It was the relentless determination of old and new manufacturers to reorganize work so that the craft worker became a victim of change.

The depression of 1893 touched off a wave of industrial mergers and sell-outs—purchases of local companies by outside companies and banks. Giants like American Can, Bethlehem Steel, J. Schoeneman garment makers, and the Pennsylvania and B & O Railroads, with access to large amounts of capital, dominated most industries by World War I. So many were managed from outside that Baltimore came to be called Branch Office City.

In new plants that housed hundreds of workers, large companies experimented with the then-popular techniques of scientific management. Managers separated craft jobs into a series of movements, often concurrent with the introduction of new machines, assigning each worker several tasks to be done repetitively. Personnel departments hired workers, dispatchers provided tools and equipment, planning departments acquired and disseminated knowledge of work processes. Detailed supervision and incentive pay encouraged a fast work pace among thousands of operators.

Militant struggles by craft unions lasted into the war years, but innovation and new technologies took their inevitable toll on craftsmanship. Can making by hand, box making, and horseshoeing were demolished trades by 1900. Machine tenders replaced many craftsmen in the confectionary and garments trades by 1910, and construction craftsmen used an assortment of precut materials by World War I.

Thereafter, industries with scant need for craft workers opened so many Baltimore plants that artisans in the surviving craft trades constituted no more than 15 percent of industrial workers by 1940. New industries, such as electronics, chemicals, and auto and airplane plants that initiated production by assembly-line processes at the outset, prodded older ones to reform. In the 1920s, programs of vocational education in public schools ended unions' monopoly on worker training in the trades. Large city garment firms set up a plantwide division of labor at the end of the decade.

The labor movement's divisions and the suburbanization of industry also contributed to the erosion of craft workers' power. While many Baltimore Knights signed on with Federation locals when the Knights of Labor fell apart in the 1890s, sawyers, box makers, and dressmakers, among others, had no locals to join. And after World War I, unions functioned less and less as institutions of working-class neighborhoods.

The opening of the Hanover Street Bridge in 1918 and the city's annexation of eastern suburbs in the same year prompted plants to relocate in southern and eastern sections of the city. Shop floor, home, and union hall—once separated by blocks—now were separated by miles. Greater distances discouraged participation of craft workers who had once frequented halls almost daily and relied on them to better neighborhood life.

In the 1930s, the reorganization of work and industry spawned a reorganized labor movement. The Congress of Industrial Organization (CIO) unions soon formed powerful locals on Baltimore's new east side, Highlandtown, and beyond into Baltimore County. Enrolling skilled and unskilled workers in massive steel and shipbuilding industries, they mostly relegated issues of how much a worker had to say about production to history. Instead, they beat the drums for wages, benefits, and recognition.

Here and there, nevertheless, the spirit of the craft workers' culture and struggles still surfaced and survives today. Although unions negotiated contracts in corporate and union offices, they still rallied workers in union halls to stand fast against industrial employers. Rituals, such as carrying the flag in parades, stirred civic pride and affirmed the responsibilities of workers as citizens. Whole families joined in Labor Day festivities, and workers' benefits programs—adequate health and life insurance— upheld the roles of workers within their families and within the life of their communities.

Acknowledgment: The author acknowledges the Faculty Research Committee, Towson State University, for its support in the preparation of this chapter.

The 1700 block of Thames
Street, Fells Point waterfront,
ca. 1930. The intermingling
of commercial activity and
residences has given the community a lively, cosmopolitan
air over the centuries.

Chapter 7 — Fells Point: Community and Conflict in a Working-Class Neighborhood

LINDA SHOPES

The home-staying Polish woman usually takes pride in keeping her domain clean. If, as is often the case, the home consists of a crowded one- or two-room apartment, occupied by six or eight people, and located two floors above the common water supply, household cleanliness must mean an expenditure of labor and time that may well be termed heroic. —1907 housing report

Standing at the foot of Broadway, you sense immediately that you are in a historical area (*site 1*). The port alive with activity, the old houses, storefronts, and warehouses, the mix of people and land uses, the sheer density all suggest an earlier time, before automobiles and suburbs. Walk along Thames Street, turn into one of the narrow side streets, and imagine it lined with the homes and shops of tailors and blacksmiths and shoemakers, with small grocery and drygoods stores, with boardinghouses and taverns and coffeehouses.

Imagine the air filled with the sounds of a half-dozen different languages. Picture the streets filled with sailors and laborers looking for work along the waterfront, with housewives shopping for the day's food, with children seeking relief from crowded homes, with craftsmen and merchants going about their business. This was Fells Point until well into the twentieth century.

What you also see in Fells Point today is a neighborhood that has undergone profound change. All around you are elegantly restored nineteenth-century rowhouses, their formstone removed and the original brick cleaned to a mellow reddish brown, their architectural details carefully preserved. Along the waterfront, new structures intermingle with nineteenth-century factories and warehouses converted into condominiums, restaurants, bars, and shops. Younger professionals now live next door to older people with strong ethnic roots.

The historic character of Fells Point is part of its current appeal. Residents and developers alike stress the area's early importance as a center of shipbuilding and trade, as well as its historically significant buildings. As one recent advertisement put it, "Fells Point . . . an extraordinary place that captures the authenticity of historic old Baltimore, with its eighteenth century–style architecture and winding brick walkways." Yet these descriptions ignore the fact that Fells Point has also been Baltimore's oldest working-class community, whose residents have often been in conflict with the city's wealthier, more powerful citizens. Moreover, the process of reclaim-

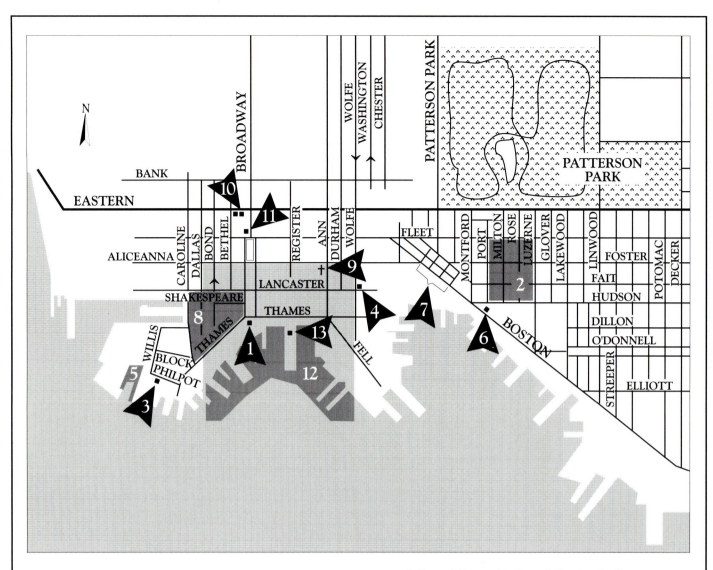

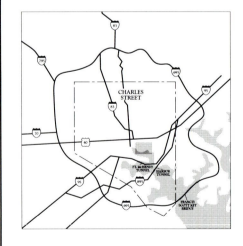

Italic type indicates original building site or function.

* indicates original building is not extant.

1. Foot of Broadway

*2. *David Stodder's shipyard*, now part of Canton

*3. *Frederick Douglass home (approximate)*

*4. *William and George Gardner's shipyard*, now Belford Instrument Company

*5. *Chesapeake Marine Railway & Drydock Company*, now Allied Chemical Company property

6. American Can Company building

*7. *Last cannery building* in Fells Point

8. *"Slum" block*, 1907

9. St. Stanislaus Kostka Roman Catholic Church

10. Polish National Alliance Club and Kosciuszko Permanent Loan and Savings Association

11. Polish Home Club

12. District designated historic, 1969

13. Recreation Pier

1628–1632 Shakespeare Street, *ca.* 1914. These compact rowhouses have been home to generations of Fells Point residents, the narrow streets a playground for neighborhood children.

ing Fells Point as a historic area has transformed its history; increasingly, it is losing its working-class character and becoming home to the prosperous.

This chapter reveals something about working-class Fells Point and the conflicts that have characterized it over the centuries. It also explains some of the contradictory forces at work in the community today.

The next chapter, "Radicalism on the Waterfront," focuses specifically on the seamen who historically have called Fells Point home.

Early Settlers: Laborers and Mariners

By 1800, the waterfront along Fells Point was restless with the business of shipbuilders and merchants.

Frederick Douglass, orator, abolitionist, and statesman, in 1844, when he was 27 years old, six years after his escape from slavery in Fells Point.

Here lived the men who actually built the ships, sailed them, and loaded and unloaded their cargo, along with the craftsmen and shopkeepers who supplied them and their families with their daily needs. The shipyard owners and merchants, however, chose to live in the more fashionable district just north of the basin, now known as the Inner Harbor.

In 1800, Fells Point had a larger proportion of laborers and mariners than any other area in the city. It also had the most renters and the least valuable housing. Houses were typically small, two-story frame structures on small plots of land.

Matthew Taylor, a grocer who lived on Thames Street in 1804, might well have been aware that Fells Point was downtown's poor relation. He might have observed that only about two-fifths of his neighbors owned their homes; that fully one-third of them owned nothing of value—neither house, property, nor personal effects; and that only one-fifth were prosperous enough to own rental property.

He might also have noted that almost half of Fells Point property was owned by people who lived elsewhere, including some of the wealthiest downtown merchants, and that most of this property provided neither a home nor a place to work for his neighbors. It was unimproved land held as a speculative venture.

And if Taylor needed further evidence of Fells Point's disadvantaged position in relation to the rest of the city, the 1800 yellow fever epidemic surely provided it. More than 400 of his neighbors died of the disease that summer, victims of overcrowding, poor sanitation, and weakened resistance. Unlike more prosperous Baltimoreans, they were unable to flee the city for a healthier environment, nor were they able to afford what medical care was available.

Politics in Fells Point—oppositional, fractious, at times militant—reflected the interests and style of its residents. Throughout the late eighteenth and early nineteenth centuries, Matthew Taylor and his neighbors elected fellow workingmen to represent them on both the City Council and in the state legislature. In doing so, they opposed the directives of party regulars, who generally cast their vote for the city's elite.

Worker representatives took the democratic ideals of the American Revolution seriously and spoke to the interests of the laboring classes. They favored the expansion of voting rights to those without property and the lowering of property qualifications for public office. Unlike many of the wealthy merchants, they also supported local manufacturing, which created jobs, and they discouraged foreign imports by endorsing high tariffs.

As was typical for the times, Fells Point residents occasionally took their politics to the streets, instigating several riotous demonstrations during the late 1700s and early 1800s. The specific events that triggered these sometimes violent disturbances were often trivial, but they reflected the underlying political and economic tensions of the day. The demonstrators were asserting their rights as citizens publicly to disagree with those in power. The militia, which recruited heavily in Fells Point, generally sympathized with the crowd and did little to control it.

Racial Tensions: Free Blacks and Slaves

In the years before the Civil War, free blacks and slaves played a significant role in the life of Fells Point. The majority were employed in the shipyards and along the docks where they joined whites as caulkers, stevedores, draymen, and laborers. Few if any, however, were able to become carpenters—this privileged position in the shipyards was reserved for white workers.

Slave labor was especially profitable to owners of larger establishments, such as David Stodder, who, with 17 slaves, was one of the largest slaveowners in Baltimore. The famous frigate *Constellation* (now berthed in the Inner Harbor and open for tours) was built in Stodder's shipyard, just east of Fells Point in Canton (*site 2*), probably, in part, by slaves. Slaves not only worked without pay for their masters; owners like Stodder could also count on their wages when they were hired out to others. For slaves, along with free blacks, provided a marginal labor force that could be called into service when demand was high and laid off when work was slack. And, since black workers could be hired at lower wages than white workers, a racially divided labor force tended to depress the rate of pay for all.

The most famous slave to live in Fells Point—perhaps the community's most famous resident ever—was Frederick Douglass. Originally from the Eastern Shore of Maryland, Douglass lived in the 1820s and 1830s as a servant with Hugh and Sophia Auld, relatives of his master, in a house located on the south side of the 1400 block of Philpot Street, currently vacant land owned by the Allied Chemical Company (*site 3*). After escaping from Fells Point into freedom in 1838, Douglass went on to become a famous abolitionist, author, orator, and ambassador to Haiti.

In his autobiography, Douglass described the blistering heat of Fells Point summers, the lively slave community, and the religious faith that sustained many, including Douglass, in the face of the demoralizing reality that they were slaves for life. He also noted that life was generally less harsh for the city slave than for the plantation slave. "A city slave is almost a freeman, compared with a slave on the plantation," he observed. "There is a vestige of decency, a sense of shame, that does much to curb and check those outbreaks of atrocious cruelty so commonly enacted upon the plantation." Douglass attributed this restraint to the force of public opinion, obviously more powerful where neighbors lived close by and could easily monitor each other's behavior: "Few are willing to incur the odium attached to the reputation of being a cruel master."

Yet Douglass also described how the institution of slavery brutalized even the kindliest of masters. Mrs. Auld first appeared to him as "a woman of the kindest heart and finest feelings." But when she became a slaveholder, "the fatal poison of irresponsible power was already in her hands, and soon commenced its infernal work. That cheerful eye, under the influence of slavery, soon became red with rage; that voice made all of sweet accord, changed to one of harsh and horrid discord; and that angelic face gave place to that of a demon."

As a young man in the 1830s, Douglass worked as a caulker, a trade virtually monopolized in Baltimore by African Americans at that time. He worked at William and George Gardner's shipyard on the northeast corner of Lancaster and Wolfe Streets, now the location of the Belford Instrument Company, where he experienced the mounting racial tensions of the pre–Civil War years (*site 4*). He was repeatedly harassed and beaten by white workers in the shipyard, who feared black workers' competition for jobs and resented having to work with them. After a particularly brutal beating, Auld wanted to have Douglass's assailants arrested. But nothing was done because no white witnesses would admit having seen the assault, and the testimony of African Americans was not admissible in the courts.

Racial tensions again surfaced in the shipyards in the 1850s and 1860s. As early as 1838, black caulkers had organized the Caulker's Association, which contracted wages and working conditions with the powerful shipwrights association. Though many shipbuilders were satisfied with this arrangement, others disliked the power of both the caulkers and their fellow shipwrights.

Beginning in the late 1850s, a time of general eco-

Women shucking a small mountain of corn outside a packing house along the waterfront.

nomic instability, some shipwrights hired less skilled white men to caulk their ships at wages lower than those paid to blacks. Many of these white caulkers were immigrants, eager for work and not so reluctant as native Baltimoreans to do work that had been customarily stigmatized as "Negroes' work."

African-American workers who refused to give up their jobs were assaulted by their white replacements. Other white shipyard workers then refused to work with black caulkers and joined the attacks against them. Initially supported by their employers, the newspapers, and the police, black caulkers were finally pushed out of their jobs as employers gradually gave in to the demands of white caulkers.

In response, a group of African-American social, religious, and political leaders in Baltimore—the caulker Isaac Myers prominent among them—raised $10,000 in the black community to establish their own Chesapeake Marine Railway and Dry Dock Company west of Wills Street, on a site now occupied by Allied Chemical Company (*site 5*). Founded in 1866 and operating for almost 20 years, the company was nearly unprecedented as a black-run business in post–Civil War America. It also precipitated Myers into local and national prominence as a black labor leader.

Cannery Workers

By the mid nineteenth century, the canning industry joined shipbuilding and trade in shaping the day-to-day life of many Fells Point residents. Beginning in the 1830s, dozens of canneries started to ring the Baltimore waterfront. By the later decades of the century, canning was the second-largest industry in the city, making Baltimore the canning center of the United States.

At first, oysters were the principal food packed, with fruits and vegetables filling in the summer months when oysters were not available. By the 1880s, tomatoes, corn, beans, and peaches had become the major foods canned.

Before the twentieth century, a key group of workers in the industry were the hand can makers, skilled tinsmiths who made about 60 cans an hour by hand. The can makers were a powerful group: Their skill, the strong bonds they had developed over years of

living and working together in Fells Point, along with the canners' urgent need for cans when raw food was ready to be processed, gave them strength and solidarity.

During the late nineteenth century, the can makers struck each year during canning season, demanding and generally getting a wage increase. In 1879, can makers organized the Can Makers Mutual Protection Association (CMMPA), Local Assembly 1384, of the Knights of Labor.

Partly to break the power of the can makers, canners began in the early 1880s to introduce machines that automated parts of the can-making process. One machine was even advertised with the slogan "It Never Strikes." The CMMPA resisted these machines by striking, organizing a national boycott of machine-made cans, and threatening to destroy the actual machines.

Despite these protests, the can makers were fighting a losing battle, victims of the canners' desire for control as well as the increasing cost-effectiveness and efficiency of the new technology. By 1900, machines had all but displaced the can makers, and can making became a semiskilled industry, detached from the sense of power and autonomy skill had imparted. The American Can Company, at the intersection of Hudson and Boston Streets, was the largest of the new can-making factories, employing hundreds of workers, including women and young people (*site 6*).

During the early twentieth century, some older skilled can makers continued in their trade until retirement, kept on by a few sympathetic can-shop owners. Others used their tinsmithing skills to become stove and roof makers. Still others, especially younger men, entered new lines of work, for example, becoming machinists, hat makers, policemen, and saloon keepers.

In the early years of the canning industry, oyster shucking employed about 10 percent of the black men in the city, who frequently worked as brick makers or hod carriers when oysters weren't in season. When fruits and vegetables came to dominate the industry, however, canners hired women and children to do the work of food processing, including peeling tomatoes, snipping beans, cutting spinach, and capping strawberries.

Isaac Myers: Nineteenth-Century African-American Leader

American citizenship with the black man is a complete failure if he is proscribed from the workshops of this country, if any man cannot employ him who chooses, and if he cannot work for any man whom he will. If citizenship means anything at all, it means the freedom of labor, as broad and as universal as the freedom of the ballot.

These words were spoken by Isaac Myers in 1869 to the 142 delegates assembled in Philadelphia for the third national convention of the National Labor Union, an early federation of trade assemblies. Myers, representing the Colored Caulkers Trades Union Society of Baltimore, was one of nine black delegates invited to the convention in an effort to unite white and black workingmen. Throughout his adult life, Myers, a member of the small group of black elite in late-nineteenth-century Baltimore, struggled to attain greater economic, political, and educational rights for his fellow blacks.

Born in 1835, Myers was freeborn, like most Baltimore African Americans of his time. But while most had little education and worked as unskilled laborers, Myers received a common school education and, at age 16, was apprenticed to a ship caulker. At 20, he was supervising the caulking of some of the largest clipper ships built in the city. Five years later, he left the shipyards to work in a wholesale grocery as a shipping clerk and chief porter, thereby gaining valuable business experience.

In 1865, Myers was back in the shipyards. That year, racial hostilities led the black caulkers to respond aggressively. Fearful for their jobs and even their lives, they tried to establish their own shipyard. Myers emerged as the leader of the 15 black men who organized the Chesapeake Marine Railway and Dry Dock Company.

Within four months, the group had raised the then-enormous sum of $10,000 by appeals to local black churches. With this sum, they leased the Philpot Street yard and railway from James Miller (no one would *sell* such property to black men at that time), capitalized it at $40,000, and employed some 300 black workers.

Several lucrative contracts from local merchants and the federal government ensured the quick success of the Chesapeake Company. Within five years, the directors were able to pay off the entire debt and, so plentiful was the work, they were also able to hire white caulkers and carpenters.

The company operated for 18 years. In 1884, financial difficulties—caused by increasingly obsolete repair facilities and an increasingly competitive labor market—forced the directors to close down the business.

Meanwhile, Myers had accepted the first in a series of government appointments that were to occupy him for almost 20 years: as a messenger in the Baltimore customs office, as special agent of the U.S. Post Office, and as a U.S. gauger. He was appointed to these positions because of his active support of the Republican party, which, as the party of Lincoln and of Emancipation, enjoyed the support of most black citizens. Myers was, however, one of very few African Americans in the nation to be so rewarded. The vast majority of government jobs—an important source of employment and political influence in the era before civil service—were reserved for white men.

While loyal to the Republican party all his life and a staunch advocate of civil rights (in those days, this meant resisting efforts to disenfranchise blacks, for example, and advocating the inclusion of African Americans on juries), Myers believed that racial equality could best be achieved through economic opportunity.

Black workers had enjoyed a range of occupations in early-nineteenth-century Baltimore, perhaps more so than anywhere in the country. In addition to the caulking trade, they outnumbered whites as hod carriers, barbers, and brickmakers. They worked as tanners, coopers, butchers, blacksmiths, machinists, wheelwrights, plasterers, painters, and in other skilled and semiskilled occupations.

Nevertheless, as conflicts in the shipyards demonstrated, white hostility to black labor, especially skilled black labor, was increasing by midcentury. While national labor leaders recognized the need for unity among black and white workers to prevent, for example, the common practice of using blacks as strikebreakers, they left the actual working out of this relationship to union locals.

In Baltimore, as elsewhere, local customs of segregation generally meant that trade unions excluded blacks. They were excluded not only from the better-paying union jobs but also from union-sponsored apprenticeship programs. In addition, some white labor leaders favored the formation of a radical third political party to develop policies more favorable to the working class. This was viewed warily by the more conservative Myers, who believed trade union activism should remain separate from politics and who was unwilling to turn his back on the Republican party. He also recognized the potential for racism in a white workingman's party.

Thus Myers, while supporting such white organizations as the National Labor Union, determined that black workers needed their own unions to advance their economic interests. In 1869 he began an ambitious program of organizing black workers in Maryland. The same year, he called into existence the Colored National Labor Union (CNLU) and became its first president.

For two years, he spoke, wrote, and toured the country, urging the organization of both black labor unions and black cooperatives, as well as practical education and self-help programs. But from the outset the work of the CNLU was hampered by slim financial resources and, frequently, white harassment. In addition, the organization was split by internal dissent between those like Myers, who favored economic improvement through trade unionism, and others who urged more traditional civil rights activism, primarily through the Republican party, as the means of achieving equality. By the early 1870s, the organization was dead.

Myers continued to maintain an interest in the cause of black labor. In 1875, he organized the Colored Men's Pro-

gressive and Co-Operative Union in Baltimore to secure admission of blacks into local white unions and apprenticeship programs, as well as to promote civil rights. In 1888, he organized a Maryland labor fair to display the talents of black artisans.

Until his death in 1891, at the age of 56, he also remained a leader in local black religious, educational, and political activities. For 15 years, he was superintendent of the Sunday school at Bethel A.M.E. Church. He also worked with local activists to establish a black high school and to open teaching jobs in these schools to black men and women.

Finally, though he opposed the efforts of more militant black leaders in Baltimore to seek an independent political base outside the Republican party, he continued to agitate within the ranks for more party leadership positions and patronage jobs for black men.

The Chesapeake Marine Railway and Dry Dock Company, founded in 1866 by Isaac Myers and other members of the local black community, was located west of Wills and south of Philpot Streets. Established to provide employment for black workers who were repeatedly harassed in white-dominated shipyards, the company was nearly unprecedented in the United States as a black-run business in the mid-nineteenth century.

THE CHESEPEAKE MARINE RAIL WAY & DRY DOCK CO. of BALTIMORE, MD

Instituted Feb. 1866. — Incorporated Aug. 1868.

CAPITAL $100,000.

LITH OF E. SACHSE & CO. BALTIMORE.

OFFICERS for 1866.
G. WASHINGTON PERKINS, Pres!
EDW. SYTHE, 1st Vice
W. SORRELL, 2d
ISAAC MYERS, Secretary.
JOSEPH THOMAS, Treasurer.
L. CORNISH, Cashier.
S. DORRITY, Sup!

OFFICERS for 1868.
JOHN W. LOCKS, President.
GEORGE MYERS, 1st Vice.
REV. W. WILLIAMS, 2d
ISAAC MYERS, Secretary.

JOSEPH THOMAS, Treasurer
JOHN H. SMITH, Cashier.
SAMUEL DORRITY, Sup!

OFFICERS for 1867.
JOHN W. LOCKS, President.
JOHN H. SMITH, 1st Vice
EDW. SYTHE, 2d
ISAAC MYERS, Secretary.
JOSEPH THOMAS, Treasurer.
CAUSEMAN H. GAINES, Cashier.
S. DORRITY, Sup!

In the early twentieth century, many Polish immigrant families in Fells Point "followed the crops" in an annual cycle of labor. In the late spring, women and children would migrate to farms in the surrounding countryside to pick the ripening fruits and vegetables. Later in the summer, they would return to Fells Point and work in packing houses, preparing the crops for canning. Then, in late fall and winter, they, along with the men of the families, would migrate to the Gulf Coast to work in the shrimp and oyster packing plants, returning home in the spring to begin the cycle again. From 1909 to 1911, Lewis Hine, employed by the National Child Labor Committee, photographed some of these families. His pictures were designed to arouse public opinion against child labor. They remain a testament to the vitality, dignity, and disciplined work of these Polish families. The captions that accompany the pictures are from Hine's notes.

Top left: "A street full of Baltimore immigrants lined up and ready to start for the country to the berry farms. Wolfe Street near Canton Avenue [now Fleet Street]."

Bottom left: "Mrs. Lessie and family (Polish). They all work in fields near Baltimore in summer and have worked at Biloxi, Mississippi for two years." This farm was located in northern Anne Arundel County.

Top right: "Group, showing a few of the workers stringing beans in the J. S. Ferran Packing Company. Those too small to work are held on the laps of workers or stowed away in boxes." Ferran's was located at the foot of Wolfe Street.

Bottom right: "Johnnie, a nine year old shucker. Man with pipe is a padrone [locally called a row boss] who had brought these people from Baltimore for four years. 'I tell you, I have to lie to employees. They're never satisfied. Hard work to get them.' He is the boss of the shucking shed." The packing house was in Dunbar, Louisiana.

Where the Tomato Skinners Worked: Baltimore's Canneries

In the early 1900s, the U.S. Bureau of Labor investigated wages, hours, and working conditions among working women in Baltimore. The following description of cannery workers in a Baltimore plant is taken from its report, which was published in 1911. The bureau hoped that publicizing these conditions would lead to improvements.

In this plant, the place where the tomato skinners worked was a shed-like part of the building on the waterfront, having one side entirely exposed. In dry weather this feature has an element of comfort, for the workers get much air, though it is tainted by the odors arising from the harbor. In wet weather, . . . the workers were entirely unprotected, those nearest the outer side of the shed getting thoroughly wet. As the shed itself leaks, the workers even on the inside farthest removed from the open water front, suffered no little discomfort. . . . In cases of chilly weather, the discomfort must reach a danger point, apparently, for there is no provision for reducing the exposure.

But even when there were no showers to drench the workers, the equipment was inadequate and the supervision so faulty, that the resulting conditions were distressing and disgusting to a degree. The vat for steaming tomatoes was in the same shed and kept the women and children in a cloud of hot humidity. The floor was covered with a slippery mixture of tomato pulp and skins, for the provision for carrying away refuse was wholly ineffective. Some of the women and children wore rubber boots as they stood at their skinning troughs, some were barefooted, and others wore coarse shoes, but the skirts of all the workers were wet, some of them up to the knees.

The odors arising from the souring mass of tomato pulp and skins on the floors, augmented by the juice dripping from the tables and benches, the clouds of steam from the nearby vats, together with the addition of an oppressive and distinguishing odor whose origin could not be determined, produced an environment that was distinctly discreditable and called for attention on broader grounds than the health and comfort of employees.

Such carrying away of waste as was done the women had to do. . . . Many of the workers eat their lunches in this room.

Men brought supplies of tomatoes from the vats to the skinning tables, but the women and the children carried the 40-pound buckets of skinned tomatoes over the reeking and slippery floor from the skinning shed into the room where the product is weighed, canned, and cooked. . . .

While the peelers' and cutters' room in this establishment was not so evilly environed as the tomato-skinning shed, it was far from intelligently managed. The women and children brought and carried away all supplies, and the supply court was about 50 yards from the peeling room. As the cutters and peelers, as well as the tomato skinners, are all piece workers, they can not afford to take time from their weary occupations to keep the immediate surroundings clear of waste and refuse.

Sore hands and cut fingers—sometimes unswathed, sometimes wrapped in perilously dirty rags—were common sights in this establishment.

Canners believed women were better adapted to work with fruits and vegetables. As one canner put it: "Women and larger-sized children were preferable. . . . [Cannery work] is unsuitable for men as the spectacle of able-bodied and strong men sitting down all day hulling peas, peeling tomatoes, peaches, etc., is not a very elevating one; nine times out of ten, men who are willing to do such work are lazy and shiftless." Perhaps a more important reason was that women and children could be hired at lower wages than men. Only in the 1950s were the tasks of food preparation generally automated; in earlier years, the canners required thousands of hand workers.

Most of the women working in the canneries were immigrants who lived in the immediate area. Working 12 hours a day, five or six days a week, and with the help of her children, a cannery woman might earn $4 or $5 a week in the early 1900s—about half the earnings of other working women. And cannery work was highly seasonal. Many canneries ran about six months of the year, beginning with spinach in April; continuing with strawberries, peas, and beans in May and June; and concluding with peaches and tomatoes in September. A cannery woman averaged an annual wage of about $125.

Typically a woman cannery worker's day began at 5:00 or 6:00 A.M. when the cannery whistles blew, signaling the arrival of crops. The women would work two hours or so, then return home to make their families' breakfasts and get children off to school. They would then go back to the canneries and work until all the food was packed. Sometimes this meant a short day of 6 to 8 hours, sometimes a long one of 12 to 15.

Cannery work was uncomfortable and exhausting. Canneries were cold and wet. Cooking steam filled the air; refuse covered the floor. Workers sustained frequent hand injuries and suffered skin rashes from handling the acidic fruit and vegetables. Yet cannery women accepted these conditions in order to earn a few dollars to help support their families.

They also had few other choices. Most of these women were married or widowed, and so they had responsibilities for families and homes. They welcomed work close to where they lived, which enabled them to leave the canneries for a few hours during the day to take care of domestic tasks and allowed them to keep an eye on their children while working.

As immigrants, most also knew little English and were unfamiliar with the pace, rules, and techniques of other kinds of factory labor. And so the drudgery of cannery work was undoubtedly relieved by the informality of the workplace, the social interaction it allowed among family members and neighbors, and the security of working in a familiar environment.

There are no operating canneries in Fells Point today, although elderly residents remember when Boston Street was lined with packing houses. Many recall bringing their mothers and grandmothers lunch and pots of coffee during their school lunch hours and then returning to the canneries after school to help them for a few hours. Others recall accompanying their mothers to work as preschoolers when other family members were unable to care for them.

The last remaining cannery building in the area, along the 2200 and 2300 blocks of Boston Street, which was used most recently by the Volunteers of America, was torn down in 1988 to make way for North Shore at the Anchorage, a development of upscale townhouses (*site 7*). You can get a feel for what canneries looked like by visiting the Baltimore Museum of Industry at 1415 Key Highway in South Baltimore, located in a nineteenth-century cannery building originally owned by Sandy Beech Platt.

The Immigrant Community

From the mid nineteenth century to the recent past, the majority of Fells Point residents have been immigrants, their children, and their grandchildren. At first, Germans dominated the area. Later, they were joined by Czechs, Ukrainians, Poles, and other ethnic groups. In the face of extremely difficult circumstances, through hard work and personal discipline, these men and women made Fells Point a satisfying place to live. Here they purchased houses, raised families, worshipped God, and created a network of neighborhood associations.

The Polish community is a good example of the immigrant experience in Fells Point. Poles began to settle in the area in the 1880s, outnumbering all other

ethnic groups 40 years later. They came to this country with little money and few industrial skills. The men frequently found work along the docks as stevedores or oyster shuckers, while the women typically worked seasonally in the canneries.

Poorly paid for their labors, with few other choices, and anxious to save for a better future, these Polish immigrants frequently crowded into unsafe, unhealthy houses. According to a 1907 housing investigation of a predominantly Polish block bounded by Broadway, Thames, Caroline, and Lancaster Streets, three or four households lived in houses intended for one family (*site 8*). Apartments were badly in need of major repairs, poorly lit, and inadequately ventilated and had no indoor water or toilets. "An eight-room house contained seven families comprising thirty-six persons," the study reported. It continued:

One of the apartments in this house, consisting of one room, was occupied by six people; the room had an area of 220 square feet, but had only 12 square feet of window space. A family of seven occupied two rooms in the same house but as one room, a tiny triangular place, was used as a tailor shop, the other larger room served as kitchen, bedroom, and living room.

When they stepped outside, residents of these houses saw storage shacks, chicken coops, wood sheds, and privies occupying almost every open space, and water or sewage running through the streets. Yet this same report goes on to describe how, even in these tenements, Polish families created physical and psychological order for themselves:

A remembered Saturday evening inspection of five apartments in a house in Thames Street, with their whitened floors and shining cook stoves, with the dishes gleaming on the neatly ordered shelves, the piles of clean

Polish immigrants arriving at the B & O terminal in Locust Point, *ca.* 1895. The North German Lloyd shipping line, working under an agreement with the B & O, carried grain and tobacco to Europe and returned with immigrants, many of whom took the train directly to points west; others ferried across the harbor and settled in Fells Point.

Joe Podles's family ran a corner grocery in Fells Point in the 1930s. Neighborhood stores like this one served an important need in the days before refrigerators and freezers were typical household items. They were also an important part of the network of local institutions that knit people together.

WAR! Baltimore Poles reacted with shock and grief when Hitler invaded Poland in September 1939. Many feared for their homeland, as well as for the family and friends still living in the old country.

clothing laid out for Sunday, and the general atmosphere of preparation for the Sabbath, suggested standards that would not have disgraced a Puritan housekeeper. The home-staying Polish woman usually takes pride in keeping her domain clean. If, as is often the case, the home consists of a crowded one- or two-room apartment, occupied by six or eight people, and located two floors above the common water supply, household cleanliness must mean an expenditure of labor and time that may well be termed heroic.

The effort to create an orderly, purposeful life extended outside the home into the larger community. In 1879, Father Piotr Koncz and a group of parishioners founded St. Stanislaus Kostka Congregation. The church they built, still located in the 700 block of South Ann Street, was dedicated two years later (*site 9*). It soon was joined by a parish grammar school, convent, orphanage, and cemetery. St. Stan's, as it is now affectionately called, has been a social as well as spiritual center of the Polish community for more than a century.

Similarly, a sense of belonging grounded in a round of familiar, shared, day-to-day activities and social relations was fostered by the Polish-language newspaper, several political and business associations, dozens of social clubs organized around the Polish National Alliance and the Polish Home, and small ethnic entrepreneurs—shopkeepers, grocers, barkeepers, photographers.

The south side of the 1600 block of Eastern Avenue is suggestive of the dense web of community institutions created by Polish people in Fells Point. It is dominated by the Polish National Alliance Club and the Kosciuszko Permanent Loan and Savings Association (*site 10*). Right around the corner, just south on Broadway, is the Polish Home Club (*site 11*).

For Polish residents of Fells Point, the greatest source of stability and pride has been homeownership. Several members of a family often worked long hours and saved relentlessly to get the few hundred dollars needed to buy a two-story rowhouse on Dallas or Durham, Lancaster or Shakespeare Street. Over a lifetime they would transform a rundown house into a comfortable place to live, installing electricity and indoor plumbing, plastering and paneling crumbling walls, insulating it against the cold with storm windows and formstone.

To help fellow Poles finance the purchase of a house, more prosperous members of the community established some 20 Polish building and loan associations in Baltimore, many of them in Fells Point. These efforts were obviously successful. In 1929, 60 percent of Polish families owned their homes. More recently, about 75 percent have been homeowners.

For several generations, then, Poles, as well as their German, Czech, Ukrainian, and other ethnic neighbors, have made Fells Point a thriving neighborhood of hard-working people. But the community is now being destroyed by rehabilitation and development. Perhaps residents' strong roots in the neighborhood explain their particularly acrimonious resistance to this change.

Whose Neighborhood Is It?

Since the 1960s, Fells Point has been contested terrain as opposing groups have sought to direct changes in the community to conform to their own competing interests. The contenders include older and longtime residents trying to protect their homes and their community of familiar people and places; newer residents attracted by urban living and the cosmopolitan quality of the neighborhood; historic preservationists charmed by the waterfront location and age of the area and wanting to rehabilitate old buildings to their original styles; the city encouraging upscale development in the hopes of attracting prosperous residents and successful businesses that will enlarge the city's tax base; entrepreneurs seeking to capitalize on the area's emergent trendiness; and developers who see opportunities for power and profit.

The sources of these conflicts lie as far back as the early 1960s when Fells Point was experiencing several changes. Residents were getting older, and their children were moving to Baltimore's burgeoning suburbs. The economic base of the community also was eroding. Much of the port-related industry and trade was abandoning the area for the outer harbor, which could accommodate modern modes of shipping more efficiently. Local industries were cutting down their workforces and, in some cases, closing up shop.

Interview with Helen Christopher

Helen Christopher is a lifelong resident of Fells Point. She ran Helen's Corner, a tavern at Broadway and Thames Street, for about 40 years until the early 1980s, when she sold the place. It is now called The Admiral's Cup. The interview that follows is excerpted from the Fells Point Gazette, *March and April 1983.*

"My mother was 12 and my father 17 when they came here from Poland. They were from the same small village. I guess that they came here for the same reason that most Polish people were coming here in those days—everyone thought that the streets were lined with gold. All you had to do was get to America and you'd be rich.

"Of course, that was not the case. People came here and worked as hard or twice as hard as they had in Poland. My mother's mother, a widow, worked and brought all of her family over here.

"My mother went into domestic service and my father worked in a slaughterhouse down here. He worked like a dog. At that time you didn't work eight hours and go home. He got a dollar a day. Many a night he'd come home with his back bleeding from the weight of carrying those heavy carcasses around all day.

"My father got into the tavern business because he had a sister who already owned a tavern—Mrs. Hepner's on Broadway, near where the butcher shop used to be. She loaned him the money to buy this place. Polish people are savers. You don't find many who don't own their own home. Even at that time, they'd get the four or five hundred dollars together to buy a house. They didn't want to be renters.

"My parents were always very busy people. My sister and I helped as much as we could. When they had free lunch on the bar, my father would get up early, go to the wholesale fish market and buy a hundred pounds of fish, unscaled. He'd bring them home and clean them.

"They were both up by five o'clock, frying the fish and getting the bar ready for the day. They cooked ham and black bread for the bar—that was served every day. Friday was fish day. Saturday night they'd sweep the sawdust off the floor and wash it down with lye water. They worked so hard—from five o'clock 'til midnight every day.

"The bars were very old-fashioned. The men dressed in old-fashioned ways. Women didn't come in the bar. If they *did* come in, they sat and talked to the lady of the house back in the kitchen. There was one exception. The old fish lady used to come over for her quick shot every now and then in cold weather. She was entitled to it. She froze in that market. Can you imagine scaling fish in that cold every day? Her hands would get so red that you wouldn't believe it.

"You couldn't beat sailors in those days. They drank to get drunk and have a good time. I guess that my mother and father didn't mind. They were tough, strong people and that was the bar business. They were here to sell booze and that's what it was for. Those men didn't drink to get a glow on. They drank to get drunk and forget their troubles and how lonely they were.

"My mother was tough. She knew that a drunk wouldn't attack a woman like he would a man so, if there was trouble, she'd get out from behind the bar, grab him by the collar, and out he'd go. The police used to come in and commend her on the way she ran the place. Yes, she was a tough cookie.

"My mother said that years ago she had heard that an expressway would be coming through here—back in the 40s. We were really convinced that the road was coming through. . . . [I]f your city councilman or mayor said that you had to sell and get out, that's what you did. People felt that they couldn't argue with the decision-makers. You accepted your fate.

"It wasn't until some of the newcomers came here to live that some opposition to the destruction of the neighborhood got organized. Many different kinds of people converged here at the same time, the late 60s and early 70s, to fight the road. Luckily for all of us, the plans were changed. They showed us that you could buck City Hall. Well, I never believed that up until then."

Helen Christopher presides over her bar at Broadway and Thames Street. For many newer residents of Fells Point, Mrs. Christopher has been an important link with the neighborhood of years past.

Housing, too, was deteriorating. At the same time, artists and intellectuals, as well as historic preservationists, were increasingly attracted to Fells Point, as much by cheap rents and the lively character of the neighborhood as by historic houses.

Baltimore City was also experiencing enormous economic and social changes during the early 1960s (see Chapter 11). Judging Fells Point a decaying and expendable inner-city area, Baltimore officials announced plans in 1966 to route Interstate Highway 83 (I-83) through this community and adjoining Canton. This meant condemning several hundred homes and forcing dozens of mostly elderly Fells Point residents

to relocate. The plan led to the first battle in the struggle for control of the neighborhood.

Fells Point residents, old and new, along with their Canton neighbors, organized to fight I-83 in a way unprecedented in recent Baltimore history. After a decade of stalling tactics, lawsuits, countless meetings, hearings, protests, and sheer persistence, they were successful in their fight. In 1977, the city finally lifted the ordinance condemning 78 Fells Point properties in the road's path, thereby signaling the end of plans to cut the road through the neighborhood.

Yet the victory over the road did not preserve Fells Point as a working-class neighborhood. The tactic

Prevas Brothers lunchstand, a fixture at the Broadway Market in Fells Point for decades.

that finally stopped the expressway was the designation of the area bounded by the harbor, Aliceanna, Wolfe, and Dallas Streets—an area in the immediate path of the proposed expressway—as a historic district (*site 12*). But this designation did not necessarily benefit the area's longtime residents.

It is illegal to raze buildings in a historic district, yet historic designation also makes property more desirable and increases its value. For example, in 1970 the median value of owner-occupied houses in Fells Point was $5,000. By 1980, it had risen 336 percent, to $16,800. In the historic district, property values of owner-occupied houses rose a spectacular 526 percent, from $7,000 in 1970 to $36,800 in 1980. (During the same decade, property values in the rest of the city rose 289 percent.)

As a result, the historic designation created enormous pressures for the neighborhood's working-class residents. It raised property taxes by as much

as 500 percent, forced renters with low or fixed incomes to move as landlords raised rents or sold what had become "hot properties," and created expensive requirements for rehabilitation. The experience of Rose Urbanski, formerly of Shakespeare Street, is a dramatic example of the road fight's failure to preserve Fells Point for its longtime residents.

In 1966, Mrs. Urbanski's house was condemned to make room for the road, but she refused to move from the home she had lived in for 45 years. During the next 10 years, her house was bought by the city for under $10,000, rented back to her, declared a historic property, uncondemned, and then offered back to her for $41,000. This figure included both the repurchase price and the cost of repairs necessary to restore some presumably historic features of the house, including removing its formstone facade and refinishing the floors. Although the city later explained that some of these repairs were not mandatory, the events were so disturbing to Mrs. Urbanski that she decided to move.

Other longtime residents who accepted the city's modest purchase price of $5,000 to $10,000 and moved when the houses were condemned have seen their former homes rehabilitated to historic status and selling for ten and even twenty times what they had been paid for them. Ironically, the area designated as a historic district includes a portion of the community surveyed as a slum in 1907.

Its identity as a historic urban neighborhood has also increased the attractiveness of Fells Point to younger, professional, upper-middle-class men and women, whose way of life, tastes, and values often differ sharply from those of the working-class neighbors they are increasingly displacing. Fells Point has been changing from a blue-collar neighborhood in which families are defined by several children and stay-at-home mothers to a more prosperous community of single individuals or two-career families with fewer children.

Between 1970 and 1980, the median income of Fells Point families more than doubled, from $6,900 to $15,200. At the same time, the number of children in the neighborhood decreased by almost half and that of professional residents and single-person households increased slightly.

These social changes have had a subtle impact on the texture of day-to-day life in Fells Point. Neighborhood schools have become underused and neglected. Small shopkeepers, catering to older, ethnic tastes, have lost business. Neighborliness has eroded.

Marie Pabst Zalk, a Fells Point resident for over 90 years, expressed the sense of loss experienced by many in the face of these changes in a 1979 interview with the neighborhood newspaper:

Yeah, historical. It's historical the way it is now. It's laughable. It wasn't historical when I lived here. It was a community where you lived and let live. . . . [We] bought our homes and they're comfortable and [we've] lived according to the way [we've] wanted to live. . . . I believe in progress but I don't believe in condominiums and all $40,000, $50,000, and $80,000 homes down here. Who's gonna come down here and live in an $80,000 home! Not the kind of people who are living down here now!

Yet capitalizing on Fells Point's historic quality is only part of a much larger process transforming the social character of the neighborhood. Redevelopment along the Inner Harbor has catalyzed similar activity along the entire waterfront, making Fells Point a prime area for investment, especially in the abandoned or underused industrial sites along the waterfront. The search for tourist dollars and the pleasures of a consumer-oriented lifestyle pursued by the prosperous have supported the sort of upscale development characterizing both the downtown and Fells Point. And the amenities of urban living are undeniably attractive to some well-off individuals and couples.

Residents who learned the art of bucking City Hall during the road fight have resisted the encroaching development. They have vigorously protested increased traffic, lack of parking, lack of recreational space, out-of-scale building heights, rising taxes, the expansion of the historic district, and the proliferation of bars that attract a rowdy clientele from other neighborhoods.

Sometimes these protests have been successful. In the early 1980s, the community saved the Recreation Pier at the foot of Broadway from becoming first a theater complex and then a fish market (*site 13*). More recently, community protest helped close down a popular—and noisy—waterfront nightspot. The city—dedicated to redevelopment but forced to recognize the resistance of the community—has taken steps to preserve the human scale and residential character of the neighborhood. Local ordinances now restrict the height and massing of new buildings, require public access to the water, protect some open space, and recommend the creative reuse of original structures. Tax-assistance programs are available to low-income homeowners.

In the early 1980s, the city also involved the community in a complex planning process designed to get community recommendations for the formulation of an urban renewal plan. Yet this process ultimately broke down as insoluble conflicts arose between those whose primary goal was maintaining Fells Point as an economically diverse neighborhood and those for whom redevelopment was the first priority. The final plan itself was more explicit in its recommendations for redevelopment and his-

Renovating Brown's Wharf, just west of Broadway, along the 1600 block of Thames Street, in 1988. These facilities for nineteenth- and early-twentieth-century shipping—an important source of employment for the working class—have rapidly become complexes of bars, eateries, and shops—important places of consuming for the middle class.

toric preservation than for maintaining and improving the community already in place. Continuing debates about waterfront land use led to an additional study in the late 1980s. Its recommendations maintained the previous limits on density and scale and the commitment to public access to the waterfront. While developers complained about the plan's limits, it did little to alter the existing direction of change.

Fells Point Today

Historically preserved houses, high-priced condominiums and inns, marinas, expensive restaurants, and chic shops have been turning this traditional working-class community into an upper-middle-class residential and recreational area. In the process, a historic community and a satisfying way of life for generations of residents have been seriously compromised.

Many residents with an appreciation for a diverse, lively community have moved from Fells Point, finding its increasingly upscale style uncongenial, its rents or taxes too high, the struggles of the past two decades too demoralizing. Others have chosen to remain. They continue their efforts at asserting some local control, working to keep development on a manageable scale and maintain opportunities for housing and services for the less prosperous.

While Fells Point's cohesive immigrant community is surely a thing of the past, perhaps the neighborhood can still be a place where working-class men and women can create self-sufficient, meaningful lives. The process of resistance, while taking a toll, has also been energizing, creating alliances among diverse people and at times a new sense of community. And the economic downturn of the early 1990s has slowed "development fever," giving residents time to gather their forces and consider new strategies for directing change in ways that might meet at least some of their needs. Perhaps as some recommend, developers can be required to contribute to community development funds, which provide services for neighborhood residents. Perhaps tighter zoning laws can restrict development. Perhaps programs that encourage modest small businesses and light manufacturing can be developed.

It remains to be seen how the conflicts currently shaping Fells Point will be resolved and what will become of Fells Point and its centuries-long tradition of dissent.

Acknowledgment: The author would like to acknowledge Jennifer Multhopp, librarian at the Fells Point branch of the Enoch Pratt Free Library, and Thomas Hollowak, historian of Baltimore Polonia, for their invaluable assistance in developing this chapter.

Dr. Beryl Warner Williams: Activist in Education

ANDREA KIDD TAYLOR

Beryl Warner Williams was born in Bangor, Maine, in 1913 into one of very few African-American families in that predominantly white city. Her father had worked since he was 9 years old at many jobs and was a steward on the railroad. "My mother was the first woman to vote in Maine, you know, when women first got the vote. She got up early in the morning, voted, and went to work."

Dr. Williams's mother was also determined that her girls would get the best possible education. She talked a reluctant school department into letting the girls take college preparatory courses, and she provided Beryl with private music lessons. She got 11 African-American women in the community together and formed a mothers' club to help young people go on to higher education. The first girl they helped would become the first African-American woman to graduate from the University of Maine.

Dr. Williams was the second African-American student to graduate from the University of Maine. She would devote her life to helping other African-American students gain access to higher education.

At the university, Beryl majored in mathematics, with a minor in music and English. "I began working my freshman year playing the piano for the physical education department and played all the way through at 35 cents an hour. . . . I made it through." In her first two years, there were no other African-American or Indian students at the university: "At that time the Jews on the campus were said to be in quotas, but I couldn't be much of a quota as one person. . . . I was on the deputation team which went to the country grange halls to talk about going to college. I know I was a strange sight (being black), but I said it was important to go to college—black or white."

But when Dr. Williams graduated with a teacher's certificate, she found that African Americans and Indians were not permitted to teach in Maine. With the help of the Methodist church, she got teaching jobs in New Orleans, in Florida, and in South Carolina. Dr. Williams decided to go back to Maine and get a master's degree in mathematics, but mathematics teachers were routinely expected to coach football—a job requirement that effectively excluded women. So she took jobs teaching English and music.

In South Carolina, Williams met the man she would marry, a psychologist. They moved to North Carolina, and after World War II she was able to find a job teaching mathematics in the engineering school.

In 1948, the new president of Morgan State University conducted what would be called the "great raid" at North Carolina A & T, bringing several faculty members to Morgan State. He asked Dr. Williams's husband to set up a new

psychology department at Morgan. Dr. Williams herself taught part-time in the English Department at Morgan and part-time night-time adult extension classes in Annapolis. From 1954 on, she taught English and mathematics full-time at Morgan.

In 1963, at the request of President Jenkins, she began to set up Morgan's first Division of Continuing Education. Dr. Williams coordinated evening, summer, extension, and weekend university classes. The Division of Continuing Education also ran a Women's Center and programs for retirees. "At that time Morgan didn't realize that continuing education was a coming field, and it was a great struggle to get it going, but now after my retirement it's doing very well." She also developed two evening student organizations with national affiliations, allowing students to travel around the country and to gain experience in working with people of different races and national backgrounds.

Dr. Williams took continuing education studies in English and education at Johns Hopkins, but, she recalls, "Johns Hopkins, you know, was prejudiced in the earlier years, and I never finished there." In 1972, the University of Maine awarded her an honorary doctoral degree in recognition of her work in adult and continuing education—in Baltimore, at Morgan, and around the nation.

Dr. Williams worked for equal opportunity in employment and housing throughout the 1950s and 1960s and as coordinator of the state committee working on integrating public accommodations. She soon became involved in integrating the United Methodist church, which then had a black Washington conference and a white Baltimore conference—they finally came together in 1965. She served on the board of the Metropolitan Baltimore YWCA and in-

Dr. Beryl Warner Williams

volved that organization in the civil rights movement—even though this, some said, would upset the husbands of some board members. Through the League of Women Voters, she went to libraries to show people how to use the new voting machines. She worked with the Cooperative Women's Civic League, a black group later affiliated with the Women's Civic League of Baltimore, and with many other organizations working to improve conditions in the neighborhoods and the city. Dr. Williams played an important role as a parent in the effort to integrate the Baltimore school system in 1954. From the time her son first entered the public schools in 1948 to the time he graduated from Baltimore City College in 1960, she was continuously active in the PTA, either as local president or as citywide board member. She remembers when her son started public school "in a small two-teacher school at the corner of Cold Spring and what is now called the Alameda. I walked him to school in 1948 and saw holes in the floor, with mud underneath. I said this would never do, so I became PTA President."

At the time, there was no music teacher, no art teacher, and no physical education teacher for the African-American students. "I worked with the public library at Bellona and had someone come down and talk to the children once a week, and show pictures and books. We got a sewing machine for the girls. . . . We got the parents of all the children to work together . . . ordinary working parents, a few of them parents of foster children. We had a very close group and we took the children to Fort McHenry, to Washington—to all kinds of places so that the children could have those experiences."

In 1974, Dr. Williams was appointed to the school board by Mayor William Donald Schaefer. She served as a member under three different superintendents until 1984. She tried to expand the outreach of the school board. "I tried to become familiar with the schools throughout the city, visiting many of them, understanding their differences. . . . I was concerned about the whole city."

Desegregation of the school system was a major issue during Dr. Williams's tenure on the school board. "We had the sense always that integration would not be an easy thing. I met with parents from all over the city to try to help them understand that we were all interested in the same thing—that our children got a good education in the Baltimore schools."

As a member of the school board, Dr. Williams remembers, "We were concerned that there be participation in the schools of children of more than one race. And in some instances children were bused from one area to another to effect that. At that time, busing seemed the way to go."

Williams is currently on the board of the Park Heights Street Academy, which was started 12 years ago. "The idea was that it would be an academy for neighborhood children of the Park Heights area, which as you know, is really neglected and impoverished—depressed—and needs many, many things. It is the only senior high school—even though it's a private high school—in the area. There are some junior high schools, but Park Heights got children who literally walked in off the streets because they had dropped out of school. . . . The children generally are 13 or 14 to 21—and they have fairly high ability. One student that I know went on to the Naval Academy, another went to medical school, some are now working with computers. . . . Park Heights meets a real need. . . . It has very good ratings and small classes, and is now part of a national coalition program with schools such as Walbrook and Bryn Mawr." She notes that the idea for the street academy came from the National Urban League.

Dr. Williams retired from Morgan in 1981 at age 68. "I could have continued until age 70 but I felt there were some young women in my area who ought to take the leadership." Williams then turned her attention to a multitude of new activities, among them the Baltimore Women's Fair, which she ran for two years. "We included all the black and white women's organizations—I mean all the way from the League of Women Voters, the health organizations, groups both pro and con abortion, women in political groups, women in law, the American Association of University Women, the Women's International League for Peace and Freedom—just all kinds of women."

Dr. Williams notes that although the Women's Fair is no longer functioning, it contributed to setting up the Baltimore Women's Commission and the Maryland Women's Commission, as well as many interorganizational links among women's groups.

Dr. Williams continues to be active in many organizations, serving on education committees and advisory boards for projects such as the Maryland Education Opportunity Center. "These are all activities trying to help people move ahead. I'm not a rocking-chair type and I don't intend to be. Right now I'm a student in the gerontology program at Morgan, in undergraduate as well as graduate classes.

"At my fiftieth high school reunion, one of the members of my class came to me and I said to him—his name was Epstein—"You've done pretty well up here in Maine." He owned all the movie houses; he owned a real estate business. When he was a child, his father had arrived as a Russian immigrant with a bag—and went around selling pots and pans—and here he was now owning most of the city. He said, 'You didn't do badly yourself, even though you went away.' But we both knew that we had had a struggle, being Jewish and black."

Betty Hyatt: Community Leader

JIM SIZEMORE

"I've always been interested in architecture and history, and I was already part of the Fells Point Preservation Society." Betty Hyatt is sitting in the attractive living room of her Washington Hill co-op as she speaks. "When I came back [to Baltimore], I saw the beginning of the serious blight. I was a member of and did social work for the Methodist church in 1961. About 1968, the church got involved in an organization called Fells Point Home Renewal. They were interested in trying to purchase from the city some of the vacant houses.

"I became involved in that, [but] this just whet my appetite. The Fells Point Home Renewal project fell apart for lack of leadership and, about 1970, there was a movement to declare the area that's known as Washington Hill—which is from Chester Street to Central Avenue, from Orleans Street to Fayette Street—to declare that an urban renewal area.

"In those days, urban renewal really meant destruction. Just tear it down and build new. With my interest in the historic preservation of the area, we—a number of the residents, some of the churches, and the very beginnings of the South East Community Organization—some of the staff people there helped organize us into what is known as Citizens for Washington Hill. I became the president and we took over the planning process." Betty smiles at the memory.

"At that time the city would come in once every other week—or whenever they decided to have a meeting—and you'd have a bank of officials, and you'd have the landlords, and some of the commercial property owners, and nobody could agree on an urban renewal plan. It was a farce. And we really wanted it to happen.

"So we took over. It was the election and we packed the house and elected our own people. And then we told the city that we didn't want them to come back until we invited them, but they were obligated to give us a planner so we could sit down and work out a land-use plan.

"That's basically what we did. We spent from April to September doing that. That was 1971. In March of 1972, an urban renewal ordinance was passed by the community and then passed by the City Council.

"But it took a year for us to establish a relationship with the city and get them to understand that we were not a bunch of kooks out here. They didn't understand that community people had valid ideas and understood their needs. We were willing to sit down, we were willing to compromise, we were willing to negotiate—we were willing to do all those things necessary to come up with a good plan. And we really did. We were able to do what they had not,

which was to come up with a land-use plan and a plan of action.

"In Washington Hill what we did was to develop a job description—as president that's what I helped do—and then advertised for a director. And I applied. I mean, I knew more than anybody who could come in there. I had the basic skills. Over the years, working with the church, I had done a lot of organizing. It wasn't hard to transfer those skills to organizing people around housing issues.

"The very first thing that we were confronted with was a housing development that had been planned by that early Fells Point Home Renewal group. This was a whole block of buildings that was already being demolished. We planned to do some housing there. Can you believe it—for $15,000! With marble foyers! Balconies! Absolutely lovely!

"One of the things we did was work with the developer to make sure that whatever was done fit into what we already had. And I guess I have some very strong opinions about things. One of the things I tried to impress upon people—and it was the people I was working with as well as the developer and the city—is that if you're gonna build city houses, don't try to make them like suburban houses. Don't turn them with their backs to the street and have some courtyard they all face. Because in essence you're saying to the community, 'We don't care about you. We're gonna set up our own little world out here.'

"But the major thing we did was this cooperative I live in. That was the renovation of 90 buildings, 216 units, all contiguous. Two blocks of Baltimore Street, a block of Fairmount Avenue, and two blocks of North Broadway, from Baltimore to Fayette. What we were looking for was a means to provide homeownership because we knew that stabilizes a neighborhood. All around us was low-income housing and to stabilize we needed to have that working-class individual buy into the neighborhood. Eighty-three percent of Washington Hill was owned by absentee landlords. Now there aren't any absentee landlords."

Hyatt described the workings of the cooperative. "You buy a membership in the corporation and the right to use a unit. When you leave, you get equity and your membership share. We did our homework. We looked at other cooperatives and determined what to avoid.

"One thing, we knew we wanted individual furnaces. That's the only way you can get people to take responsibility for not using more than they need. And we wanted good kitchens, more than public housing. We [also] wanted them to be free and clear of government regulations. Whatever we've done we've done with government money, but with few government restrictions. That's kind of our philosophy." Betty laughs. "[We] try to get as much out of the government without having to give back any more than we had to.

"I was born and raised in this area, right at Fayette and

Betty Hyatt

Broadway. Lived here all my life except for about nine years. My husband was from South Carolina. We lived down there on and off. Then I left him and came back here," she says, looking back.

"One hundred fifteen units of housing for the elderly, 175 units of rental housing, 100 units of new housing, 216 units of the cooperative, and on and on and on. A little bit here and a little bit there and it really adds up. And it is diverse. To me, that's exciting. If it's diverse, it will last. If it's all one big housing project, it could just fall apart."

Barbara Mikulski: The Senator as Community Activist

"In 1969, I was a struggling social worker with a social conscience. I had a master's degree in community organizing and social planning, and I was busy trying to decentralize the local welfare department. Then I got a call about a highway project that was going to destroy the neighborhood in East Baltimore where my family settled when they first came to this country. I also knew that there was an expressway coming through the west side of Baltimore that was going to take the first black homeownership neighborhood in Baltimore City. It seemed that this highway was going to take the homes of a lot of people in a couple of neighborhoods—the Poles, the Italians, the Greeks, the blacks—and give them almost nothing in return. It would have even leveled Federal Hill.

"Now, in terms of Federal Hill, they were going to give us a snazzy turn-off into the Inner Harbor so that when you rode through you could kind of look at the dead fish. They had all kinds of multicolored charts and graphs and slide shows about how great it was going to be. But a lot of us didn't think it was such a great idea. We didn't think it was fair to take houses from old people who had come to this country in search of the American dream and who had lived through the sweatshops and the Great Depression. We didn't think it was fair to take the homes from the black community that had fought at Hiroshima and Pork Chop Hill. The *only* way they were ever to get loans in the segregated city of Baltimore in the 1950s was through the VA mortgage system. Somehow we didn't think it was fair to take the homes from those folk and give them no relocation benefits and no assistance at all. We didn't think it was right to destroy healthy neighborhoods so that suburban commuters could get in and out of the city faster. We didn't believe it when we were told this was going to be good for us. We were told, 'Don't worry, honey, we'll take care of you because it's going to be for everybody's progress.'

"We were so ignorant we even liked the Inner Harbor

Senator Barbara Mikulski in her Fells Point district

the way it was. Only we didn't call it the Inner Harbor. We called it the Port and we called it the waterfront and it meant jobs where we worked. We liked tugboats and freighters because they meant commerce and industry. We didn't think that paving it and sealing it off from downtown was an improvement. Whenever we raised these questions, we were told, 'Don't worry, the planners have it all figured out.'

"In fact, this highway was going to be an absolute model of good planning. It had a design concept team. The design concept team was going to combine the best, the very best of architectural, engineering, sociological, and technical design elements. There was even going to be citizen input and community participation. We found out that meant we could choose what color the grid was going to be and what kind of stone we wanted the guard rail made out of.

"We talked to the planners, the architects, and the politicians. We organized the neighborhoods and we challenged the cost–benefit analysis. We ran bake sales so that we could rent the buses to take us to Annapolis, to City Hall, and to Washington to protest the very public policies that were going to happen to us. While we were doing the bake

sales, that design concept team had $5,000 in audiovisual equipment alone—to educate us. So with the mimeograph machine that we borrowed from the Holy Rosary Holy Name Society, we began a neighborhood movement. We formed the coalition with our brothers and sisters in the west side and then formed very lively community organizations. In the west side, it was called the Relocation Action Movement (RAM). Over in East Baltimore we formed the Southeast Council Against the Road (SCAR). Then we formed the coalition called Movement Against Destruction (MAD). Through that, we began to organize and fight in our own behalf.

"Just about everything that visitors to Baltimore see, whether it's the downtown, the Inner Harbor, Fells Point—which I always knew as the Foot of Broadway—Federal Hill, northeast Baltimore where they organized to fight off the blockbusters in the 1960s, and just about every part of Baltimore that is now being called 'vitalized' is here because of a community organization and a citizen protest movement. Make no mistake about it. The Urban Renaissance came because the people got their act together and took control of their own lives.

"We talk about how Baltimore has been revitalized, but I tell you that Baltimore has always been vitalized. When I look back at my experience in Baltimore and think of my own education as an organizer and a planner, I think there are some critical questions that are overlooked. There is a tendency in planning as in any difficult profession to emphasize professional and technical skills. There is an image of planning as a value-free profession made up of technical experts who only make recommendations based on objective data. I don't believe there is such a thing as a value-free profession, and I wouldn't want to meet a body of value-free people; show me somebody who doesn't have anything to believe in and that person is either a fool, a liar, or a crook. All of us have values, and I'm glad that we do. We may have values that are people-directed and egalitarian. Or, we may have values that are elitist, racist, and sexist. What we need to do is to confront our values and really ask ourselves what they are."

(This account was excerpted from a speech given by Barbara Mikulski to the American Planning Association in 1979. The transcript was edited by Elizabeth Fee.)

Lucille Gorham: Activist for Housing

DONNA POGGI KECK

Born in 1931 in Halifax, North Carolina, the oldest of five children, Lucille Gorham always had the responsibility for getting her brothers and sisters off to school in the morning, home in the afternoon, and seeing to it that their school work was done. "I then had to start dinner. Technically, I was their mother and their mother's housekeeper." Married herself at age 18, Gorham had eight children from two marriages before she was 30 years old.

She moved to Washington, D.C., with her parents and siblings when she was 4 years old, arriving in Baltimore with her family when she was 8 years old. The family lived with her grandmother for two years until her mother was able to get an apartment. "For one year we lived on public assistance," Lucille remembers, "but then my mother got full-time work as a domestic and went off public assistance. We grew up with her working."

Early in her life, Gorham experienced personally the effect of public policy decisions. When her family's house in East Baltimore was purchased by the city for construction of a public housing project, the family moved one block north on the same street.

Their second house was purchased by the city a few years later and sold to the Johns Hopkins Medical Institutions, which converted it to housing for married medical students. As a result of this second relocation, Gorham's mother became separated from her sisters and brothers.

A *third* relocation was prompted by the construction of another public housing project. Each time her family was forced to move they were promised an opportunity to move back. But, Gorham says, "No real effort was made to accomplish that."

In 1967, the city approached Gorham's community with a large-scale urban renewal plan for Gay Street in East Baltimore. The plan called for the demolition of most residences and construction of new housing, all subsidized by federal funds.

"I didn't feel good about it," Gorham recalls. "I thought about what it had done to the three communities we had lived in. Those were very tight neighborhoods. My grandmother lived next door, my aunts lived across the street, all the neighbors knew each other. My grandmother held keys for all the kids in the neighborhood. You lose those people when you move and have to make new friends. By the fourth move, the emphasis on community had gone. We had to keep our own keys. There was no one to report to when we came home from school."

It was then, in 1967, that Gorham began attending community meetings, and she has never stopped. Community residents were meeting with city planners to develop a plan for upgrading the neighborhood. At that time, upgrading meant the city would buy or demolish houses, relocate the families that lived in them, and build new housing, which might or might not be available to those who were displaced.

A neighborhood group was formed called Citizens for Fair Housing. Nathan Irby, later a state senator for East Baltimore, was elected chairman. Three weeks later, Irby stepped down, and Gorham, a young mother of eight, was elected chairwoman. "I was a nervous wreck. I had never wanted to be chairman of anything. I am an extremely bashful person. I don't do well talking to the public, but I agreed. Mr. Irby said he would give me help. He always sat in the front row and always gave me certain signals with his eyes that I could follow."

Lucille brought all her children to community meetings. "The youngest sat on my lap and the others on each side of me. If there was something that they couldn't go to, then I wouldn't go. Until they got to be teenagers, I dragged them around with me."

The greatest accomplishment of Citizens for Fair Housing, according to Gorham, was "that we *created* an organization." The committee worked hard with the elderly black homeowners, who at first did not want to lose their homes, but who in the end agreed to the urban renewal plan. Gorham and her committee members worked with the City Relocation Office and developed a certificate that

Lucille Gorham

people being relocated from the area were given. A copy remained on file with the Relocation Office so that, when new housing was available, these people had first priority. "It worked," Gorham says. "The certificates were later used in other urban renewal areas."

To support herself and her children during this period, she worked in the Community School Program at Dunbar High School. "That was my first job. I was only on public assistance a short period of time—about six months." Her next job was working with Keeping All People in School (KAPS). "During that time, there was a lot of federal money around, so there were always ways that you could earn a little money."

In 1971, Gorham was hired as the paid director of Citizens for Fair Housing with funds provided by the city. Her job was to work with community residents and city officials to implement the Gay Street Urban Renewal Plan and address other community issues. Two years earlier, the City Council had approved the plan, which called for comprehensive redevelopment of a deteriorating neighborhood.

Over the next 10 years, six different housing complexes were built, including subsidized rental developments, public housing, elderly housing, homeownership units, as well as playgrounds and parks. In recognition of her accomplishments in this area, she accompanied former Baltimore Mayor William Donald Schaefer and another community leader on a trip to West Germany in 1974 to discuss Baltimore's experience in community development.

In 1978, Gorham switched her attention from Gay Street, where renovation was well under way, to Middle East Baltimore. Community and city attention was turning to this neighborhood, located immediately east of Gay Street and surrounded by the powerful and imposing Johns Hopkins Medical Institutions. Since the neighborhood was showing signs of deterioration—boarded-up vacant buildings, high crime, trash, and rats—the new Middle East Community Organization was formed.

But working in this neighborhood in the 1980s presented an entirely new set of problems. "The disappointment to me in Middle East is just getting people involved," Gorham says. "You can talk to them on the street and you can handle their complaints, but they don't come to meetings." The most active participants in the Gay Street and Middle East areas had been elderly homeowners. "Now they are older and have all kinds of aches and pains."

Meanwhile, the younger generation of people, who would be interested in community activities, are busy working or going to school. "Those that are home have so many children and so many problems they don't have the time. We also have a lot more drug addicts and alcoholics. We have a lot of idleness among both young and old in Middle East," Gorham notes.

But her commitment to renovating buildings and improving housing for the poor is as strong as ever. "I think everybody should live, at least once in their lives, in a decent house. It did so much for my children when we moved from Dallas Street to a newly renovated public housing unit on Chase Street. Their whole attitude changed. They began talking about what they were going to do when they grew up, and it was always positive."

At age 60, Gorham sometimes appears tired, but she works just as hard as she did when she was 18. The nervous, bashful mother of 25 years ago is at the center of yet another visionary effort—working with the Middle East Partnership. Consisting of a team of community-based organizations, neighborhood residents, and city officials with support from the Johns Hopkins Medical Institutions and James Rouse's Enterprise Foundation, the Partnership has launched a comprehensive attack on abandoned buildings, deteriorated rental properties, and low homeownership. It has also initiated badly needed social services, including counseling for teenaged parents and literacy training for unemployed and underemployed residents.

In a series of articles published in the *Baltimore Sun* in April 1988, commemorating the twentieth anniversary of the death of Martin Luther King, Jr., and the ensuing riots, a reporter pointed out that the residents of Gay Street were in effect prisoners in their new homes. Because of crime on the streets, many are afraid to walk around in their own neighborhood or to allow their children to play outside. When presented with this dilemma, Gorham observed, "Well, we dealt with the housing problem. I guess it's the job of the next generation to deal with the economic problems and the drug problem."

Willa Bickham and Brendan Walsh: Stirring Things Up

LINDA ZEIDMAN

In 1968, Willa Bickham and Brendan Walsh founded Viva House in a rowhouse at 26 South Mount Street. "That banner up there probably sums up the purpose of it," says Bickham, motioning to the house next door some 20 years later. "It says what the works of mercy are: feed the hungry, shelter the homeless, and then it lists the works of war: destroy crops, rape and kill, and so on. We felt it made sense to do both things—fight hunger and oppose war—at the same time."

"When we got this building," her husband Brendan explains about the adjoining rowhouse, "we mushroomed into a food pantry. Anywhere between 130 and 150 families come by for a three-day supply of food every month. Then three nights a week we serve dinner to about 100 people a night. So that's the hospitality aspect." In the past, Viva House has also served as a shelter. "There are about 90 Catholic Worker houses like this across the country," says Bickham. "One in New Zealand, one in Mexico and Australia. They basically do the same thing."

"Nobody gets paid a salary for working at Viva House," Walsh explains. "Willa and I take turns working at paid jobs. I teach and Willa works as a nurse. So when you have no salaries at Viva House, you have essentially no overhead. I would say that 95 cents out of every dollar that we get goes directly for the food programs. Different groups come and help do the meals or else do the cooking of the meals, too. It's real simple."

Who are the hungry who come to Viva House for food? "I've been doing this for a long time, but it still just blows my mind to see the people who line up before dawn for a bag of food," Bickham says.

"There are older people. There are Vietnam vets who lost their minds if not their legs or both. There will be a woman with her three or four babies. There will be groups of families that come into the soup kitchen. The alcoholic men still come and the druggies still come and our glue sniffers still come—people who are really down and out. The single men—most of these men are living on the streets and hang around the neighborhood and come to the soup kitchen."

Viva House is located in a working-class neighborhood on the west side of town bordering on Union Square, which is being gentrified. "We chose this house when we were searching for a central place because we knew that we could have black people and white people in the same house," Walsh points out.

"If we were on the other side of Baltimore Street, it would be hard to get white people to come, because some people don't go to a soup kitchen if blacks go there or if there are not enough other whites going there. That's still pretty prevalent today. That old thing of 'I'm white and I'm poor, but I'm still better than a poor black person' still goes on."

The Monroe Street area, a few blocks west of Viva House, has had a lot of racial violence, Bickham adds, "and yet a lot of it is the violence of overcrowding. Things may, in a drunken brawl, come down to a black–white issue, but in the neighborhood we still do live together."

Describing the homeless who came to Viva House for shelter, Walsh recalls, "When folks came here and we would ask what happened they would say things like, 'I got behind on my rent.' They would come to a shelter mainly to try to save the next check and use it as a rent deposit, and then use the following check as the first month's rent and start the process over again.

"I would say a good quarter of the population in this city does not have money to pay their own rent, so they double up or they play the game of going from this house to the next as they get the threat of eviction. It's not the image that the media give of people who have this great job and then they lose the job and here they are homeless—a thunderbolt. It's more like the grinding thing of every day not being able to get the rent and then having to move all the time."

"A lot of the people that we've known for years have died in the streets, and it's hard each time to see one of the folks die," Bickham observes, recalling one especially tragic incident related to designating the community as a historic area. "Union Square Park had just been renovated for a quarter of a million dollars. Benny would get chased out of the park all the time, and he used to say, 'We get six feet of space to park our cars. Why can't a man have just one little foot of space to park his body?'

"He was a laborer, in his forties. He had come from West Virginia and had been here most of his life. We knew him probably about 10 years. Whenever he was drinking, he would stay in the street. When he wasn't drinking, he'd come here. Then one day he was missing. We knew that he had been on the street—the alcoholics in the community, they know where people are, and they watch out for each other.

"They kept looking and looking and finally one of the guys found him and ran up to get Brendan to come. A block away from the park was where Benny froze to death. It was just up the next block, right behind Mrs. Whitely, the chief preservationist—right behind her house in an old abandoned building."

Gentrification in the neighborhood began in 1970 when

"one family had exerted much influence and convinced the city to declare Union Square Park and approximately 40 blocks 'historic.' Mencken's house (and perhaps the square) is historic, but the rest had nothing to do with history or historic preservation," Walsh notes. "It was more bankbook preservation. Actually it was a tax break for the rich. A person who renovated a house got an accelerated depreciation on income taxes.

"But that was in 1970, and I guess everybody—us particularly—was so involved in the Vietnam thing, we never thought much about the historic preservation issue. Then in 1976 they introduced this bill to declare from Fulton Avenue down to Schroeder Street and from Pratt Street over to Baltimore Street historic. We organized and held the bill up for a year to make the city do impact studies. The area was composed of poor whites and blacks. We were saying that what would happen with historic preservation is that their homes would become prime properties to buy and sell, which means that the poor would be put out as the gentry moved in."

"Brendan and I came to Baltimore [in 1967 and 1966, respectively] independently—he from New York and I from Chicago," says Bickham, a former nun. "We were working over around the McCulloh Street/Pennsylvania Avenue area, Brendan [formerly a seminarian] with a church and me with the Joseph House Community Center."

Bickham explains what makes Viva House different from the Catholic missions. In addition to the daily work of feeding, clothing, and sheltering, "we spend as much energy letting people know that they do not cause their squalor or misery. We talk about capitalism, militarism, sexism, and racism.

"We have been arrested more than 15 times for resisting that which keeps the poor poor: the military buildup; the nuclear weapons; the wars in Vietnam, El Salvador, Nicaragua, Northern Ireland; the cutbacks in public housing, welfare, and decent jobs.

"When our neighbor froze to death because her gas and electricity were turned off, we confronted Baltimore Gas and Electric at the front door of their office building. We raised quite a raucous protest.

"I feel good," Bickham concluded, "about the fact that we've done our share of agitating. We have no solutions, but we can make the problem visible. You know, other people may be good planners, and other people can have other talents, but our sort of talent is to raise the dust a little bit and see what happens."

Willa Bickham and Brendan Walsh

Striking Baltimore seamen
awaiting assignments at the
NMU Hall, 1702 Eastern
Avenue, *ca.* 1941.

Chapter 8

Radicalism on the Waterfront: Seamen in the 1930s

LINDA ZEIDMAN & ERIC HALLENGREN

They were a motley group and truly international in character—whites, blacks and browns; Scandinavians, Portuguese, Spanish, Hawaiians, Philippinos—all of them seasoned American merchant seamen.
—Charles Rubin, seamen's union organizer

Like the name, the colonial-style furnishings of the Admiral Fell Inn at the corner of Broadway and Thames Streets (*site 1*) suggest that this renovated hotel and restaurant was originally built to lodge ladies and gentlemen visiting eighteenth-century Fells Point, when it was a small shipbuilding community with cobblestoned streets. In fact, the building, originally called the Anchorage, represents an entirely different history. It was constructed in 1892, more than a century later than the current decor would imply, as a boardinghouse for merchant seamen, a portion of Baltimore's most poorly treated and hardworking population. One hundred years ago, the rooms of the Anchorage would have been crowded with cots, rather than the four-poster beds that one finds now; and sixty years ago, the quiet lobby where guests leisurely read the morning newspaper would have been packed with arguing seamen.

The Anchorage holds an important place in the history of worker protest. In the 1930s, during the Great Depression, it was a center of radical activity, an important institution in the lives of seamen engaged in strikes on Baltimore's waterfront. The Anchorage was the site of what some historians call the Baltimore Soviet, named after similar organizations formed by workers in Russia during the Bolshevik revolution.

This chapter takes us to 1934 to learn about the Baltimore Soviet and to the fall and winter of 1936 for the story of the seamen's strike that helped establish the National Maritime Union, a champion of seamen's rights.

Homeless, Rootless, and Eternally Unmoneyed

Historically, shipowners and ship captains maintained a legal authority that restricted seamen's civil rights. A ship captain could convict and sentence a seaman for a crime without further review by a civil court. Originally, captains were given the power to court-martial because a ship at sea was far from law-enforcement agencies. The popular view of seamen as rough and violent gave the captain's unregulated power added legitimacy.

Most seamen were law-abiding and hardworking, but they told stories of hair-raising encounters with

The Anchorage hotel, at the left, established by the Port Mission, was an alternative to roominghouses that encouraged seamen to drink and boardinghouse owners who frequently provided prostitutes, *ca.* 1930. Located at the corner of Broadway and Thames Street, the Anchorage is now the Admiral Fell Inn.

Seamen's quarters. The original caption reads: "With the plumbing out of whack, crew members had to use a hose to flush urinals. The rope lashings on this urinal were not intended for decorative purposes, but to keep it from vibrating. This picture is reminiscent of the '30s, before the NMU was built."

the true proletariat of the Western world, the homeless, rootless, and eternally unmoneyed. [Men with] no stake in the system beyond this month's voyage . . . [who] have been all over the world and seen none of it beyond its dull ubiquitous Sailortowns, . . . have become a part of it nowhere. Four out of five of them have no wives and three out of five have no addresses.

Cattle Are the Best Off

Shipowners used as much space as possible for cargo, and they often crowded seamen in sleeping quarters, in the ship's forecastle ("foc'sle"). Andrew Furuseth, president of the International Seamen's Union (ISU), characterized sailors' quarters as "too large for a coffin and too small for a grave." Six-foot-two Joe Curran wrote, "I had a top bunk under a dripping steam pipe, and I learned to curl up like a pretzel so the scalding water wouldn't drip on me when I slept."

A report by a physician compared the minimum air space allowed for cattle in cowsheds and for humans in military barracks, boardinghouses, and seamen's quarters. It concluded that "cattle are the best off in this respect and seamen the worst."

The food served to seamen was, in the words of a British marine officer, "badly cooked and badly served, and . . . usually more fit for pigs than humans." One Baltimore seaman, Dan Goodman, remembers seeing the uneaten food from his luncheon plate scraped back into the pot to be served at dinner.

The cramped, foul sleeping quarters and the poor-quality, inadequate food often made seamen ill. The surgeon general of the U.S. Marine Hospital Service confirmed that "seamen suffer in a startling manner from diseases, most of them springing from the inadequacy of pure air and healthful conditions in which to eat and sleep."

Always seeking to maximize their profit margins, American shipowners skimped on measures that affected the safety of the crew. The owners were notorious for understaffing ships and hiring the cheapest, most inexperienced workers. Charlie Rubin claimed that "all the written safety rules and regulations could be used as toilet paper as far as the shipowners were concerned." Wind, sun, water, and salt corroded vessels and equipment, but shipowners

their shipmates that reinforced the popular stereotype. Charlie Rubin, a seamen's union organizer who met his wife in Baltimore and who wrote *The Log of Rubin the Sailor* largely from his correspondence with her, describes one ship where the sleeping quarters were "a mess, with clothes, broken bottles, spilt wine and drink-crazed maniacs all over." Joe Curran, a union militant and first president of the National Maritime Union, had two big scars on his back, the result of an attack by an ax-wielding shipmate who had gone mad.

The extent to which seamen were seen by the public as unsavory and undesirable can be judged by this description in *Fortune* magazine in 1937:

Seamen's quarters. The original caption reads: "The picture . . . reveals the overhead leaking over a top bunk, making it necessary for the occupant to rig a piece of canvas above himself in order to keep from being drenched."

Seamen's quarters. The original caption reads: "The mess room is too small and hot to be comfortable so after work is over, the crew has to sit around in the bare sailors fo'c'le."

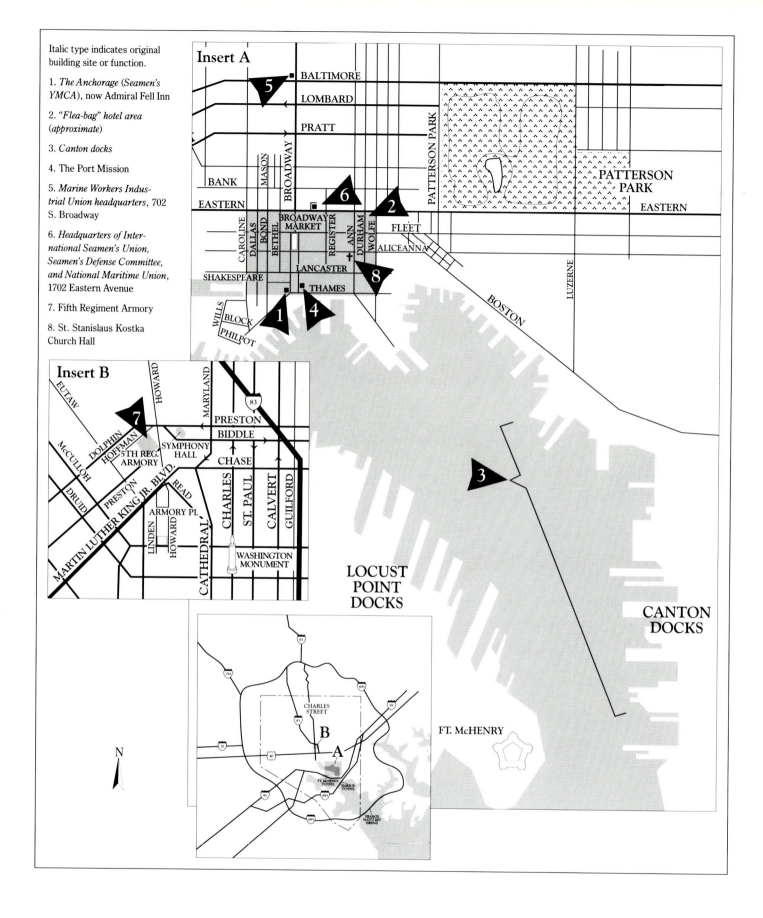

Italic type indicates original building site or function.

1. *The Anchorage (Seamen's YMCA)*, now Admiral Fell Inn

2. *"Flea-bag" hotel area (approximate)*

3. *Canton docks*

4. The Port Mission

5. *Marine Workers Industrial Union headquarters, 702 S. Broadway*

6. *Headquarters of International Seamen's Union, Seamen's Defense Committee, and National Maritime Union, 1702 Eastern Avenue*

7. Fifth Regiment Armory

8. St. Stanislaus Kostka Church Hall

Insert A

BALTIMORE
LOMBARD
PRATT
PATTERSON PARK
PATTERSON PARK
BANK
MASON
BROADWAY
EASTERN
EASTERN
CAROLINE
DALLAS
BOND
BETHEL
BROADWAY MARKET
REGISTER
ANN
DURHAM
WOLFE
FLEET
ALICEANNA
SHAKESPEARE
LANCASTER
THAMES
WILLS
BLOCK
PHILPOT
LUZERNE
BOSTON

Insert B

EUTAW
HOWARD
MARYLAND
83
PRESTON
BIDDLE
SYMPHONY HALL
CHASE
McCULLOH
DOLPHIN
HOFFMAN
5TH REG. ARMORY
MARTIN LUTHER KING JR. BLVD.
PRESTON
READ
CHARLES
ST. PAUL
CALVERT
GUILFORD
DRUID
LINDEN
HOWARD
ARMORY PL.
CATHEDRAL
WASHINGTON MONUMENT

LOCUST POINT DOCKS

CANTON DOCKS

83
795
695
CHARLES STREET
81
695
95
70
40
95
FT. McHENRY TUNNEL
HARBOR TUNNEL
B
A
695
FRANCIS SCOTT KEY BRIDGE

FT. McHENRY

N

Seaman at work in a ship's firehold, 1944. Excessive hours and the use of inferior coal, which made cleaning the fires difficult, led seamen to support NMU demands for better working conditions.

supplied paint only for the crews to mask, rather than fix, the problems. Not surprisingly, accidents at sea were common.

First-Class Prices for Third-Class Food

On shore, the world of the seaman was only a little more hospitable and secure. As a result of their reputation, seamen were unwelcome in most parts of the cities where they docked. Since they needed temporary housing, they kept to areas immediately surrounding the port.

Fells Point was no different from any other so-called sailortown. It was rough and expensive but, after a stint at sea, this environment provided distraction, entertainment, and the camaraderie of like-minded men.

A seaman disembarking ship would possibly find his way to a boardinghouse or cheap fleabag hotel

Advertisements on this East Baltimore Street coffee-house give a picture of a seaman's life in Baltimore's sailortown, 1942.

The shape-up, *ca.* 1930. Seamen looking for work formed a semicircle around the shipping agents (known as "crimps"), who could easily scan the crowd and hire cronies or men waving bribes.

on Aliceanna or Thames in Fells Point (*site 2*). Often seamen of the same nationality boarded in the same place, especially when the owner was a fellow countryman. Boardinghouses and hotels for black seamen were segregated from those for whites.

Boardinghouses were often overcrowded, with three to six men to a room. The owners were generous suppliers of liquor and prostitutes, but seamen paid a high price for both. They also paid "first-class prices for third-class food" at local restaurants. Seamen frequented pool halls and houses of prostitution, as well as gin mills where they could find cheap liquor. They enjoyed drinking, spending money, and sometimes brawling.

The Crimping System

Boardinghouse owners frequently functioned as "crimps"—shipping agents who hired seamen for the shipowners. Many seamen spent more than they could afford and were frequently in debt to these boardinghouse owners when it was time to ship out.

As both the seaman's debtor and his employer, a crimp could control when a seaman went back to work simply by refusing to carry the debt any longer. With this control over the supply of labor, crimps had an advantage bargaining with shipowners as well as seamen. Crimps played an important role in setting wages and determining working conditions.

Crimps were in charge of the "shape-up." For example, seamen milling around the docks in Canton (*site 3*) looking for work, would form a semicircle around the crimp when the time came to select the crew. In this way the crimp would be able to scan the faces of the seamen and call on those he wanted to hire. Dan Goodman remembers that "when you raised your hand [to get the attention of the crimp], you'd better have a five-dollar bill in it."

Under Christian Influence

Aware that the boardinghouse system encouraged drunkenness and prostitution among seamen, a number of religious and charitable organizations pro-

Racism on the Waterfront: *The Log of Rubin the Sailor*

The Marine Workers Industrial Union (MWIU) and the National Maritime Union (NMU) were among the first advocates of equal treatment for black and white seamen. While many organizers were eager to recruit blacks and were strongly committed to desegregating the industry, they often encountered opposition from rank-and-file seamen and their employers.

For their part, black seamen were wary of promises made by the new unions. The small number of existing unions for black seamen provided a modicum of protection for members, even if these unions legitimized the segregated division of labor on the waterfront. The policies of white unions worked to keep blacks out of safer, better-paying jobs. Black seamen wanted assurances that the new unions would behave differently.

The difficulty of black and white cooperation is illustrated in the following passage from The Log of Rubin the Sailor, *written by Charlie Rubin, a seaman and organizer for the MWIU and NMU.*

One day a fine-looking Negro came into the office. He was a fireman on the Merchants and Miners line. Paul Palazzi, the Firemen's agent, was out, so I talked with him. He had heard that we had rotary shipping—first registered, first shipped. He believed the M & M Company was ripe for organizing and he offered to give us a hand, but first he wanted our assurance that if the company was organized and he or any of the other Black firemen quit the ship, they could be registered and shipped on any other ship or company.

This Negro worker was really asking me if we were a democratic union. Had we actually licked the racial problem and could we guarantee him and other Negro workers the same privileges we guaranteed white workers?

"Listen carefully," I replied. "I'm going to give it to you straight. Our policy and our aim is a racially integrated union. Have we accomplished it? No. Have we improved on what it was before we started organizing a rank-and-file union? I can honestly say yes."

"I see you are trying to pretty up your reply. Why not say it? The answer is no," he retorted.

"Please give me a few minutes to explain something," I pleaded. "When I say 'our aim,' the word 'our' doesn't include the whole organization. I am talking about the guys who started it—the rank-and-file movement. Most of them are very progressive and some are Communists. The racial question is as important to them as the pork-chop struggle is—it's one and the same, and—"

"Why," the Black fireman interrupted, "why are you suddenly so interested in Negroes?"

"Because the founder of the Workers' Organization, Karl Marx, stated a universal truth when he wrote that you can't organize and improve conditions of white workers as long as Black workers are enslaved! This truth is almost a religion with most of the early organizers."

"Then why not practice it?"

"Why not? From where do you think we recruited the tens of thousands of seamen in our organization, from Timbuctu? Or from Communist Russia? They are Americans coming from every section of the country, including the deep South. They bring into the union all their prejudices and misinformation and that rotten racist superior attitude. It's up to us who see the wisdom of Marx's saying to educate and make true union brothers out of them."

"Why aren't you doing it then?"

"Why? Because we don't have the power to cram it down their throats. We have to show them and to prove that it's in their own interest—their own bread and butter; their own pork chops are at stake. Unless we organize the whole industry—Black, white, Red, and Brown—and really and truly give them all equal rights, we will never have security. We are succeeding, but not as fast as we would like to. I don't want to make excuses, but we are pioneering in race relations. Racism has been like a disease eating into the vitals of our democratic institutions. As far as I know, we are the first union that's making a real effort, and, believe me, we are having a hell of a tough time doing it.

"I'll tell you frankly, at this stage we will not be able to ship you in most ships as firemen, unless some damn good rank and filers or Communists are aboard and carry the ball where it's most effective—on the job. There is nothing I would like more than having men like you help us in this fight. But that's asking too much sacrifice from one who has done nothing but make sacrifices. I have given you the score, that's all I can do now."

After some hesitation, he [the black fireman] said: "I do believe you are trying to do something, but right now I need a job, whatever it is, whatever it pays. I can't afford staying ashore for a cause that many before you, including Lincoln himself, weren't able to get far with, except on paper."

He offered his hand. We shook hands—and he left.

vided alternative housing for them. In 1881 the Port Mission was established at 813-15 South Broadway (*site 4*) to encourage seamen to join a church of their choice and provide them with room and board.

On April 27, 1892, the Port Mission Women's Auxiliary built the Anchorage, now the Admiral Fell Inn, "to maintain under Christian influences a boarding house for seamen, a home-away-from-home, a social and recreational center where the seafarer might find safe refuge while in port." In 1929, the YMCA took over the management of the Anchorage, and from that time it was also known as the Seamen's YMCA. At that time it contained 106 rooms and accommodated 165 seamen.

Although seamen frequently boarded at the Anchorage and other charitable institutions, their dislike for them was well known. They found the managers paternalistic, condescending, and overly zealous in promoting religion.

Divide and Conquer

Shipowners and crimps knowingly used ethnic and racial distinctions to keep workers apart, a goal often easy to achieve. Ships' crews were selected with the maximum possible ethnic and racial diversity in mind. Spanish-speaking seamen might be hired as firemen, jobs usually reserved for the Irish, or Asians might be assigned to the deck, traditionally the province of Scandinavians. Even among African-American seamen, crimps could count on antagonisms between native-born blacks and those from the West Indies to distract seamen from joining forces to challenge pay and working conditions. Thus seamen's job grievances were often transformed into complaints and attacks on seamen of different races or nationalities.

The more skilled seamen of the engine department, who operated and maintained the ship's power plant, looked down on the less-skilled deckhands, who were responsible for navigation and the maintenance of hull and deck equipment. Seamen in these departments in turn felt superior to the blacks, who worked exclusively as stewards in the ship's kitchen or did general housekeeping.

Waterfront Radicalism

Yet the experience of seamen also brought them to-gether at times to change conditions. Their shared isolation from family and normal civic life fostered a sense of fellowship among them, as well as a desire for integration into a community, in contrast to the persistent condition of rootlessness.

When seamen were stirred to action, they proceeded with a determination and openness to radical solutions that reflected the special character of a seaman's life. Seamen's opportunity to travel often opened them to unconventional explanations of social and political events. It also fostered a sympathy and awareness of problems faced by the people of other nations.

For example, many seamen who witnessed British police firing on native demonstrators in India questioned the benevolence of colonial policy. Others were struck by the irony of picking up a cargo of grain to be shipped to Britain from a port filled with starving people. Charlie Rubin noted the grief of people mourning Lenin's death in the Soviet port of Batumi. Their sorrow contradicted the popularly held American view of the Soviet people's hostility to their leader.

Outsiders even in their own country, and with little in the way of personal ties or material belongings to lose, seamen were willing to consider alternatives that others might consider too radical or even revolutionary. Seamen were also accustomed to hardship and were not afraid of, or deterred by, the deprivation or violence that was often part of a strike or other labor-organizing activity.

The New Red Union

A number of important events outside Baltimore had a profound effect on Baltimore's waterfront. The first national organization of seamen, the International Seamen's Union (ISU) formed in 1895 under the American Federation of Labor, did little to better the condition of seamen. Like other AFL affiliates, the ISU organized only skilled workers, often establishing separate locals by craft. Shipowners were able to break strikes called by the ISU in 1921 and 1922 by using craft rivalries and racial and national prejudices to foster disunity.

In fact, the ISU contributed to making conditions worse. In the 1920s, the ISU failed to oppose

Mother Geier

The waterfront, pictured in the popular imagination as filled with rough seamen, sleazy gin joints, and flophouses, sometimes shows a different face. These excerpts from an article that appeared in the Baltimore Sun *on November 25, 1936, during the seamen's strike of that year, paint a more complex view of life on Baltimore's waterfront.*

Heart of Water Front Is Sad for "Mother" Geier Is Dead

———

Usually Boisterous Seamen Mourn
Loss of Friend Who Trusted Sailors and Fed Them
When They Were Broke

———

"Mother" Geier died yesterday and the heart of the water front was sad. . . . Mother Geier ran a restaurant and seaman's rooming house on the Northwest corner of Broadway and Shakespeare Street for the past twenty-seven years and it was a haven of seamen—whether or not they had any money.

A robust, white-haired, laughing woman who came to this country 36 years ago, Mrs. Paulina L. Geier ran Geier's restaurant with her husband, August Geier. She was 60 years old when she died yesterday of heart trouble.

FOUR CHILDREN

Her husband came to this country in 1899 and sent for his wife a year later. They raised their four children and ran their lunchroom, which gradually gained strong favor with the seafaring men.

It was nothing for a man fresh from a ship, and broke from the night before, to roll into Mother Geier's, confess empty pockets and eat her substantial grub. Mr. Geier always tended to the kitchen end of the business.

Many stories are told of men coming back after many years to pass varying amounts of money across the counter in payment of bills contracted when times were bad. Mother Geier never kept any books and many times failed to recall the debt—but when the original credit was given, Mother was wont to say, "Now don't forget!"

FED STRIKERS

Word of Mother Geier's death got around about 2 P.M. yesterday and there was a decided change in the mien of the striking seamen. Her death was announced at a meeting of the International Seamen's Union and immediately yarns of her beneficence spread through the meeting room at 1702 Eastern Avenue.

In the seamen's strike of 1921 she fed hundreds of seafaring men; in 1930 she fed 700 men twice a week, and took the men without overcoats inside while they waited for their grub.

And now with another strike in progress 25 men are fed there daily. "Not stew," one sailor said, "but regular meals with dessert."

WILL SEND FLORAL CROSS

And the seamen—with little money as a result of the strike—are going to send Mother Geier a blanket of roses and lillies and a floral cross.

Skimming quickly through his list, Fred (Blacky) Nassar pointed proudly to the names and contributions collected between 6 and 9 o'clock last night. It amounted to $40.

"See that, Old John gave $5; old John Swain, he's about 80 and he's a ship's carpenter who's on strike. He had 50 cents this afternoon. He played two-horse parley; won $25 and gave me $5."

So that was the water front last night. And today they're all going to file up the narrow stairway to the second floor of 808 South Broadway for a last visit with Mother Geier.

the reintroduction of the "fink books," an employment record shipowners required seamen to carry. In these books, ship's officers identified so-called troublemakers. By not pressing rank-and-file demands to hire from union halls, the ISU tacitly cooperated with the corrupt practices of company agents and crimps.

In April 1930, in New York, a handful of seamen, longshoremen, and other waterfront workers challenged ISU leadership by forming the Marine Workers Industrial Union (MWIU). While the inspiration for the MWIU and many of its leaders came from the Communist party, the majority of the union's rank and file were not party members.

The MWIU's popularity was based on the problems it addressed that the other unions ignored: a single union to replace the many, often competing unions of waterfront workers; and strikes, sit-downs, and job actions in defense of fairer hiring practices, job assignments, wages, and working conditions. The MWIU also opposed discrimination against African-American seamen and favoritism to seamen of particular nationalities. Many seamen strongly agreed with the MWIU's criticism of capitalism as an unjust system that meant low wages and little respect from society for the work seamen did.

The MWIU chapter in Baltimore, headquartered at 702 South Broadway (*site 5*), became strong and militant. Good organizers made use of the size and concentration of the waterfront district to do a lot of recruiting, and Washington, D.C., was close enough to provide a target for demonstrations over seamen's grievances.

A seaman could sign up for an initiation fee of $1 and dues of 50 cents a month because there were few paid staff members. Unlike other waterfront unions, which hired staff members to implement decisions made from the top down, the MWIU was run democratically by a system of ship and dock committees.

The Baltimore Soviet

During the Great Depression, wages fell, hours of duty rose to 12 per day, and shipowners replaced seamen with inexperienced "workaways" who accepted a wage of $1 a month plus room and board on ship. More than 1,000 seamen were unemployed in Baltimore in the mid 1930s, compared to 300 in 1930.

Government relief efforts began on January 1, 1934, with money from the federal Emergency Relief Act. The Seamen's YMCA, which had taken charge of running the Anchorage in 1929, was the distribution site, and several former employees of the YMCA were put in charge of administering the relief money. These administrators targeted the YMCA as the sole provider of food and shelter for seamen, thereby assuring the YMCA of income when other business establishments in the area suffered from the seamen's decreased buying power. The former YMCA employees also used their authority to break up union meetings and political discussions held in the building.

Early in January, a delegation of Baltimore seamen, led by members of the MWIU, marched into the Emergency Relief Act offices in Washington, D.C., to protest these practices. Calling the former YMCA employees "grafters" and "hypocritical tyrants," the delegation demanded that the Waterfront Unemployed Council, composed of members elected by seamen, take charge of the relief effort in Baltimore.

While Emergency Relief officers tried to mediate the conflict, the Waterfront Unemployed Council took over the YMCA, threw out the state-appointed employees, and began to administer the relief money. This action was supported by maritime workers, as well as by some small businessmen, mainly restaurant and hotel owners whose businesses depended on revenues from seamen and who objected to the YMCA's monopoly over relief money. The Waterfront Unemployed Council had promised to send relief recipients to businessmen who provided decent food and accommodations in return for their support.

Given the support the Waterfront Unemployed Council received from waterfront workers and the community, and the potential threat of a riot on the part of the large number of unemployed seamen, the federal relief agency urged local officials to exercise restraint in dealing with the occupation of the YMCA. The police were not called in to oust the demonstrators, and the Waterfront Unemployed Council remained at the YMCA for almost four months.

During that time, they administered the relief money so efficiently that relief benefits were larger

Striking ISU members on the picket line, 1936.

than those in other cities. Seamen gained a sense of dignity and took pride in programs they administered through elected representatives. One seaman commented that "for the first time in years, the seamen in Baltimore began to live like men."

You Can't Find a Scab in Baltimore

Buoyed by their successful takeover of unemployment relief, the seamen turned their attention to hiring. On February 10, 1934, 700 seamen voted to support an MWIU proposal to form the Centralized Shipping Bureau (CSB), which would assign seamen to ships on a rotating basis without regard to race, nationality, or ethnic origin. The CSB would be run by a United Front Shipping Committee elected by the seamen. In response, 95 percent of the seamen in the port boycotted crimps and hired out only at the CSB. The newspaper of the MWIU declared, "You can't find a scab in Baltimore."

The seamen's actions antagonized shipowners and local and state officials, who saw the connection between generous relief benefits and seamen's increased militance. Shipowners bombarded Emergency Relief offices with letters challenging the government's relief policy on grounds that in Baltimore "federal relief was actually encouraging communism, mutiny through intimidation, voluntary idleness, and even violence."

Shipowners hired goons to attack seamen, an attempt to intimidate those who supported the CSB. Under cover of night, shipowners brought in busloads of scabs, many imported from ports as far away as New York. The ISU helped supply the scabs because they feared the success of their rival union more than the shipowners did. Finally, a boycott of shipping facilities in the port by the shipowners succeeded in undermining the influence of the CSB.

All these developments, added to pressure by

Striking ISU members in the soup line, 1936.

Emergency Relief mediators, forced the seamen to grant some concessions. In May 1934, seamen ended their occupation of the Seamen's YMCA building and agreed to work two days a week for the relief money they were to collect. In return, they retained the right to unionize and participate in relief decisions, but the tradeoff was a face-saving one at best. The seamen effectively gave up their bargaining chip when they left the Anchorage Building.

In Baltimore, seamen's relief money was whittled away by a combination of budget cuts by local officials and then, in 1935, by the termination of the federal program. MWIU leaders in Baltimore and other ports were blacklisted, while police raided union offices and arrested seamen carrying MWIU literature. The repression was so effective that by February 1935 the MWIU disbanded. Seamen were left with a "two-front war," to use the words of organizer Paddy Whalen. They were fighting the conservative policies of the

ISU leadership on one flank and the shipowners on the other.

The Fall/Winter Strike of 1936

Seamen once again organized to push the ISU leadership to take a more militant role in the spring of 1936 by establishing the Seamen's Defense Committee (SDC), chaired by seaman Joe Curran. The seamen who joined the SDC agreed with many of the policies of the MWIU, especially the importance of organizing all maritime workers regardless of race, nationality, or job classification.

On October 30, 1936, 400 Baltimore ISU seamen agreed to join a strike called by the SDC in support of seamen and longshoremen belonging to the Maritime Federation of the Pacific who had been locked out of their ships following a breakdown of contract negotiations. Meeting at 1702 Eastern Avenue (*site 6*), the Baltimore seamen voted to use the strike to press local demands for replacing the shape-up by hiring from the union hall on a rotating basis without regard to race or nationality, for an eight-hour day, overtime pay, and no work in port on Saturday afternoons and Sundays.

Pickets from Canton to Locust Point

The first day of the strike saw 800 workers register for picket duty. As pickets went on duty at piers and railroad terminals from Canton to Locust Point, extra details of police were assigned to the waterfront. Strikers faced arrests daily for small or even imagined infractions of the law, often at the instigation of shipowners and ISU officials. But, unlike New York, Philadelphia, and Houston, where hundreds of striking seamen were clubbed and beaten by police, there was no mass violence on the Baltimore waterfront.

But goon squads dispatched from New York did beat strikers, particularly those whose militant roles were well known to local ISU officials and company agents. Individual picketers were sometimes pulled off a line by these squads and beaten with blackjacks and brass knuckles, and any striking seaman leaving a Fells Point waterfront tavern alone at night was an especially inviting target for thugs. One seaman was shot and seriously wounded in the stomach, in classic hit-and-run style.

Bodies of eight striking seamen were found floating in Baltimore harbor during the first three weeks of the strike. Though several had broken beer bottles jammed into their anal cavities, police said such killings were not unusual around the city's docks and did not investigate with any real vigor. The strikers soon learned to travel in small groups for mutual protection.

For their part, the striking seamen often attacked and beat seamen who were not on strike, usually outside bars in and around Fells Point. Though no lives were lost as a result of these attacks, two men had their ears cut off, and one man was taken to the seamen's headquarters on Eastern Avenue, subjected to a mock trial, and forced to run a gauntlet of angry seamen who rained down a torrent of punches after he was convicted of selling out his mates.

A temporary injunction that would have made picketing illegal was issued on November 10. Since the success of the strike depended on discouraging seamen from boarding ships by picketing them, organizer Paddy Whalen appealed to Baltimore's legal community for help. A young lawyer who was just starting practice, I. Duke Avnet, responded.

Avnet cited a law passed by the Maryland legislature in 1935, known as the Anti-Injunction Law. It protected the right of workers to strike and to picket, and it clearly prohibited an injunction without a hearing. Since a hearing had not been held, Avnet won an immediate order to dissolve the injunction. Meanwhile, new walkouts swelled the ranks of strikers to 2,800. Another 2,000 longshoremen worked only sporadically because the lack of steam aboard struck ships prevented the use of steam-driven loading and unloading equipment.

Speeding Up Broadway

From the beginning, the 2,400 members of the two Baltimore locals of the International Longshoremen's Association (ILA) followed national leadership and refused to support the strike. The longshoremen union's officials opposed the Maritime Federation of the Pacific (MFP), the union that started the strike, because it recruited longshoremen as well as seamen into an industrywide union. Even appeals from Harry Bridges, head of the West Coast longshoremen, were unsuccessful in changing the stance of the East Coast's longshoremen union's leadership.

Despite official ILA resistance to the strike, however, many rank-and-file longshoremen union members were uneasy about strikebreaking. Seamen knew their only hope for success was to persuade these longshoremen to take action independently of ILA leadership. From soapboxes set up behind dockside picket lines in Fells Point, they appealed daily to the dockworkers to join them.

The Baltimore seamen also enlisted the aid of approximately 50 longshoremen from the striking West Coast seamen's union. Arriving after the Thanksgiving holiday, MFP members replaced the seamen on the soapboxes and met with the rank-and-file leadership from ILA Local 829. Their efforts paid off handsomely.

With the help of a mass rally held at the Fifth

Striking Baltimore seaman, 1936. The original *Sun* caption reads: "Meet 'Broken-Nose' Burns. He is typical of the 2,940 seamen on strike in Baltimore. He is 25 and has figured in several rescues in the North Atlantic."

and a full entourage of bodyguards, led by Chowder-head Cohen, a beefy New York thug notorious in union circles for his skull-busting tactics, charged up the steps, only to find the doors locked.

Surrounding the hall were approximately 2,000 seamen, who had come in support of the longshoremen. Recognizing their enemy as he pounded on the hall's double doors, the seamen moved in with loud whoops and jeers. While a cordon of policemen and bodyguards vainly attempted to clear a path, the excited seamen jostled Ryan and Cohen while pelting them with rocks, clods of earth, shoes, and even loose change—anything they could get their hands on. Ryan and Cohen finally made it to a car, but its path was blocked by the crowd, which began rocking the large black sedan in an attempt to overturn it. With much shoving and liberal use of their nightsticks, the police were finally able to force an opening large enough for the car to escape, and the shaken Ryan was last seen speeding up Broadway. A waterfront poet, known only as Forty Fathoms, immortalized the incident:

In Baltimore town
the boys are rough,
Ryan lost his pants
by an ILA hand
and clad in fig leaves
he turned and scrammed.

The Aristocrat of Southern Black Labor

Significantly, the members of the segregated longshoremen's Local 858 did not join the strike. Racial conflict and segregation had long characterized work on the waterfront. The longshoremen union accepted black members, but they were subordinate to whites on the docks and in the union.

At the same time, the job of longshoreman was one of the best available to blacks. In the words of a Gulf Coast longshoreman, the stevedore "was the aristocrat of southern black labor, and was quite conscious of it." Since the union had played a role in maintaining this relatively privileged position, black longshoremen would react more cautiously than whites to appeals from other workers to defy union leadership. And since white unions had a history of discrimina-

Regiment Armory (*site 7*) featuring union leaders Harry Bridges and Joe Curran, the rank and file of ILA Local 829 voted on December 19 to join the seamen's strike. Their action brought to nearly 5,000 the number of maritime workers officially striking the Baltimore port, all of them in support of the MFP and local demands for a union hiring hall, better pay, and shorter hours.

While immeasurably improving the chances for the strike's success, the longshoremen's vote also produced the seamen's most satisfying moment. Having learned of the disturbing events in Baltimore, the longshoremen union's president, Joseph Ryan, made an emergency trip from New York to dissuade Local 829 from supporting the strike. Arriving late at St. Stanislaus Kostka Church Hall on Aliceanna Street (*site 8*) where the strike vote was being taken, Ryan

tion against people of color, they hesitated before committing their support to organizations like the Seamen's Defense Committee (SDC). These were some of the conditions of black longshoremen when Local 858 considered joining the wildcat strike begun by the all-white seamen's Local 829. Given the situation of black longshoremen in the industry and in the union, it is not surprising that Local 858 voted against supporting the strike.

With the black membership in Local 858 voting overwhelmingly to stay on the job, with more than 40 percent of Local 829 voting against striking, and without the emergence of strong leadership among rank-and-file longshoremen following the strike vote, the wildcat strike could not survive the intense pressure to reverse the strike action exerted by national and local officials of the longshoremen's union. On December 21, seamen's Local 829 voted to go back to work. With the loss of the longshoremen went any hope that the strike could be won.

The Midnight March of the Baltimore Brigade
By December 23, the port returned to near-normal operations. Scab activity increased significantly, and seamen began to desert picket lines in increasing numbers. Some even slipped onto ships they had been picketing and shipped out. As the new year of 1937 began, ships were leaving Baltimore harbor with full crews. On January 14, the national officers of two supporting unions ordered all their locals to return to work.

With picket lines dwindling all over Atlantic and Gulf ports, delegates to a national SDC conference in New York decided to concentrate pressure on Washington, where the legitimacy of the International Seamen's Union (ISU) contract with shipowners was being reviewed by the National Labor Relations Board.

Sensing that the recent strike would be seen by the board as a sign of weakness and failure, Paddy Whalen conceived the idea for a show of strength: a march on January 18 from Baltimore's harbor to the U.S. Capitol to press the seamen's cause with the board. The idea caught the imagination of the striking seamen, and they came from every major port on the Atlantic and Gulf to join the march.

Calling it the Midnight March of the Baltimore Brigade, Whalen led hundreds of seamen and supporters from other unions along U.S. Route 1 through a day and night of rain and slush to the nation's capital. There the marchers were joined by several thousand more demonstrators, and pickets were thrown around the Department of Commerce as well as the Capitol. The seamen visited all the principal department heads in government. One delegation even went to President Franklin Roosevelt in the White House.

The success of the Washington march gave the committee an opportunity to claim a moral victory and thus bring the strike to an honorable end. On January 25, Baltimore's striking seamen voted in accord with back-to-work resolutions adopted by the committee in New York, and the port's 87-day strike was over.

With the impetus gained from the seamen's strike and a favorable ruling by the National Labor Relations Board, the committee established itself as the National Maritime Union (NMU) by the spring of 1937. Its constitution committed the union to organizing all seamen "without regard to race, creed and color."

So great was its popularity among working seamen of all classifications and positions that by the end of 1937 the maritime union had challenged the bankrupt ISU in 67 companies and won representational fights in 56 of them. The victory of the maritime union was an added boost to the growing movement toward industrial unionism that was gaining prominence in the organizing efforts of the Congress of Industrial Organizations (CIO).

The men who boarded at the Seamen's YMCA could finally celebrate the victories of the NMU. This union established fairer, nondiscriminatory hiring practices, winning many of the demands of seamen who were members of the MWIU and participants in the Baltimore Soviet.

Acknowledgments: The authors wish to thank Captain Dan Goodman and I. Duke Avnet for their reminiscences of the 1930s, and Bruce Nelson, author of *Workers on the Waterfront: Seamen, Longshoremen, and Unionism in the 1930s* (1988), for his invaluable assistance and generosity in sharing his own research.

Striking Baltimore seaman, 1936. The original *Sun* caption reads: "'Little Joe,' the 'Oscar' of the seamen's strike head-quarters, stirs thousands of the little brown beans 'round and 'round with his bat each day. 'I hit 'em, they catch 'em,' says Joe."

Rail mill at Sparrows Point in the 1920s

Chapter 9   Sparrows Point, Dundalk, Highlandtown, Old West Baltimore: Home of Gold Dust and the Union Card

LINDA ZEIDMAN

The sun always rose over the blast furnaces and set over the plate mill. —Steelworker Ed Gorman

You work in a steel mill, with red-hot molten steel all around you. You watch for spills, listen for noises that indicate trouble. You worry. Will the foreman hire a new man to replace your father, who has been out sick for two days? Your family worries. Will you be able to go to your daughter's graduation next week? You don't know because you haven't been told yet what shift you'll be working.

Everything is fine while the steel stays on the conveyor belt, traveling red hot at high speeds, pressed thinner and thinner by stands of rolling mills. But if it slips off, someone will likely get hurt. You remember stories of steelworkers speared by an errant rod in the wire mill, or others, in different parts of the mill, burned alive in a cauldron of steel.

You're proud of the work you do, but you know it could be safer and better paid. The union organizer told you that a union would mean better working conditions and higher pay. You wonder if you could get the others to sign up. That way, there would be less risk of getting fired.

These were some of the concerns of Baltimore steelworkers in the 1940s—steelworkers who lived in the four communities in Baltimore described in this chapter. This introduction to Sparrows Point, Dundalk, Highlandtown, and Old West Baltimore gives you an understanding of the unionization of the steel industry from the perspective of those who lived it. In fact, it offers a firsthand look at events that were also an important part of a larger story: the unionization of workers all over this country in such key industries as auto and steel.

Sparrows Point: A Company Town

If you had visited Sparrows Point, the home of Bethlehem Steel's Maryland plant, in 1940, the massive buildings of the steel mill and the smokestacks belching white smoke would have drawn your attention first. Behind the buildings and the smoke, you would have noticed a totally different sight—rows and rows of three-story houses, home to 2,000 steelworkers and their families.

In all, about 5,000 people lived in Sparrows Point in a close-knit community that defined itself, the world, even heavenly bodies in terms of steel production. "The sun," said one resident, "always rose over the blast furnaces and set over the plate mill."

The story of Sparrows Point began in 1893 when the Pennsylvania Steel Company built a steel mill and

Top left: The workforce at Sparrows Point in the 1890s. In contrast to steel mills in the Northeast where the majority of workers were immigrants, only one-third of the workers at Sparrows Point were foreign born. Another third were African American, and the other third, native-born white.

Bottom left: African-American steelworkers were given the least-skilled, hottest, and dirtiest work in the mill.

Above: Steelworker, 1920s

shipyard on what was then a farm and peach orchard and founded a residential community named Sparrows Point for the mill's workforce. The plant, called the Maryland Steel Company, produced rails for the growing railroad industry. By 1916, the Bethlehem Steel Company, headed by Charles Schwab, had purchased the Pennsylvania Steel Company along with the mill and company town at Sparrows Point.

Most of the managers and steelworkers who lived in Sparrows Point were white, native born, and of English, Irish, Welsh, or German ancestry. Many came from rural Pennsylvania, Maryland, and nearby Southern states. African-American residents of the company town came primarily from the rural South.

The layout of Sparrows Point reflected the mill's chain of command by locating employees according to their salary, rank, ethnic origin, and race on streets named A to K (*site 1*). The size of the houses and of the front porches got progressively smaller, reflecting the declining status, rank, and salary of those living in the alphabetically named streets.

The general manager's house stood alone on A Street near the bathing beach on the south side of the peninsula. Plant superintendents, other upper-level managers, and the school principal lived on B and C Streets. The business district on D Street separated upper management from the foremen and white skilled workers who lived on E and F Streets. Humphrey's Creek (where G Street would have been located) was the physical barrier segregating African-American workers on the northern part of the peninsula, on H, I, J, and K Streets.

Most of the houses had four bedrooms, but two-room bungalows with outhouses, originally built for blacks, housed immigrants. Single men might rent bunks in shanties, originally intended as temporary housing, in various places on the Point.

The company assigned housing on the basis of a foreman's recommendation. All the housing was rented, and the cost was low compared to prices in Baltimore. The company maintained the housing, painting on a regular schedule and providing materials for repairs. The company built a park and sponsored recreational activities, especially sports events. They subsidized churches by charging congregations only $1 a month rent. Bars were prohibited in Sparrows Point, presumably to keep the workforce sober.

Neighbors shared common living and working conditions, and community cohesiveness was high. Mischievous children had to beware the watchful eyes of neighbors as well as parents. Adults, too, were concerned about the opinions of others.

In addition to low rent, free home maintenance, and generous credit at the company store, the company gave residents first crack at promotions, and members of residents' families were hired for new job openings, benefits unavailable to steelworkers who lived outside Sparrows Point.

The community high schools had shops that trained the sons of steelworkers for jobs at the mill.

Baltimore Steelworkers Remember

The following interviews represent the experiences of two generations of steelworkers. Mary Gorman is of the older generation who worked in the mill before the union was established. Born and raised in Sparrows Point, she married a steelworker and lived there until it was torn down in 1975. In addition to caring for her family and taking in boarders, she worked as a midwife to the company physician and eventually as a matron in the tin sorting mill. McCall White, Ed Gorman (Mary Gorman's son), and Marian Wilson are among the steelworkers who started working after the union had been formed. They were all active union members. Ed Gorman was raised in Sparrows Point, while McCall White and Marian Wilson lived outside the company town. Their stories are a sampling of the varied experiences of the thousands of steelworkers who have worked at the Point.

Mary Gorman

When the open hearths were built, the dirt that came from there was red. Then they put in a terrific large blast furnace and if that gave off, when the wind was blowing into town, you got the black. It was just like little beads—little pebbles. At home you were sweeping and hosing off all the time. You never opened a window there—you had the air conditioners and the windows were caulked. But as clean as you kept the place, you could still wipe that dirt off the windowsills or whatever was around.

When it came to washing and hanging out clothes, you'd have to look to see which way the wind blew. If it came from the open hearth, you were going to get red clothes, so you didn't hang out. If it came from the east side, the clothes would be black. If you had a lovely high windy day, there would be people washing all over town. But otherwise you had to bring the clothes in and put them back in the washer again.

McCall White

I was hired in the mill in the 1940s. When I applied, all the blacks were put into a large auditorium. We were asked our age, where we were from, and what we expected out of the company in the future. If you were known to have a high school background, they wouldn't hire you. If you were from Baltimore, they were reluctant to hire you. You had to tell them that you had a job on a farm and no more than a grade school education, then they'd hire you.

The company would look at a black's size, his physical fitness. My foreman made it quite clear that he wanted blacks with strong backs and no education. I almost didn't get hired because I had a book in my hand that I had brought to read on my way down on the streetcar.

Prior to the unions, in the early 1940s and 1950s, blacks were hired mainly for the hot, hard, physical labor. You were put into the coke ovens, blast furnaces, and the "CB's department"—the "colored boys' department." That's where you stayed. If you tried to transfer, you were given a termination notice.

Wages were much lower, much lower than for white workers. Job classes ran from 1 to 32. Black workers usually stayed around job class 1 and no higher than a job class 4.

Ed Gorman

Working conditions in the old tin mills were hot, dirty, noisy, just about unbearable. The heat was so bad that the men had to wear long woolen underwear even through the summertime to keep the heat off their bodies. They wore wooden clog shoes because the floors got so hot that the leather shoes would just eat up on them. For the most part, there was some spell time between heats, but the average guy worked—the perspiration shone through his underwear and his outerwear.

The men had to take the steel out of a furnace with a pair of hand tongs and then feed it into the tin mills. The tongs would get so hot that they would have to wrap rags around their hands to keep their hands from blistering. In order to cool the tongs, the men would put them in buckets of water. The tongs weighed about 45 pounds—along with the sheet it weighed about 70 pounds. The men had no cleaning facilities, no washroom facilities, so consequently they brought their own piece of soap and a piece of toilet tissue and washed their hands in the same water that they cooled the tongs off on at the end of the shift.

The shifts were basically a daylight shift of 10 hours and an evening shift of 14 hours. There were only two shifts of work. In order to swing over to the next turn, the man that worked the daylight turn on Saturday had to switch over and work a double shift into Sunday. Now when you do that, your bowels—your normal physical make-up—does not work, it cannot function. So in those times it was very difficult for a man to swing over, but that was what he had to do. He had to work that way.

I was born in Sparrows Point and lived there my formative years. Until I went in the service at the age of 19, I thought the sun always rose over the blast furnaces and set over the plate mills. Until I got in the service I thought everyone worked shift work and everyone worked on weekends. I found out when I went in the service that there was an entirely different lifestyle.

Marian Wilson

I went to church one Sunday morning and a girl friend of mine asked me if I would like to go down to Sparrows Point to put in an application to get a job. I said, "Yeah, I think I'd like to go." I didn't know anything about the tin mill at this time. Women were brought into the tin mill at that time I believe because of the type of work—you stood on your feet long hours, you stood in one place and you sorted tin plate. Women were more conscientious, so to speak, about the work. That was the reason that they used women in that type of work.

Anyway, on Monday morning my girl friend didn't show up, so I went by myself. I had an interview with someone there. They told me to get an age statement, and I did, and in two weeks they called me and told me they had a job for me. When I told my mother and father I was going to work, my mother seemed kind of glad, but my father didn't want me to work at Sparrows Point, because he already worked there. He worked shift work, he worked on weekends, and he thought that wasn't the kind of life I should have. He wanted me to stay home. But I went anyway. I went down and they hired me. I was 18, very young.

The first two or three days I didn't know if I was going to make it because the work was so hard. And I was never used to somebody standing over me, watching me— I never knew what this was like. They put you on what they called a probation period, where you work to get your raise, and naturally everybody wants to get the raise, so they work as hard as they can. I wasn't too long in getting my raise, but I had a couple of run-ins with some of the girls and some of the floor ladies.

We had certain rules we had to follow, like about the dress codes—we had to wear uniforms, blue uniforms with white collars and white shoes and stockings. The reason for this was that our supervisor—she was an older woman and she had come from another tin mill somewhere—she liked drama. She wanted everybody to look the same. She would march us up and down the aisles and we all looked alike, you know. As time went on, we resented wearing uniforms. A lot of us wanted to wear slacks because we had a lot of stooping and bending to do. And of course we younger girls liked to look nice, because after work we went out. We would go out and stop up the road, like the men do. It all changed when a few of us got together and decided that we were going to come in our street clothes. I think there were about five of us.

Then we went to the bathroom; if we were gone too long the floor lady would come in and she would look underneath the door, through the space between the door and the floor. And she would bang on the door and tell you, you had to leave if you were there too long. Well, at that time we couldn't smoke, so a lot of the girls would sneak in there to smoke and I guess the floor lady knew that.

I wasn't even there a year when I was called into the office and asked if I knew I had been on seven wildcats, or seven walkouts, or lockouts—they had all kinds of names for them. And I said, "No, I didn't know it was seven." And the man said, "Well, I'm telling you, young lady, you've been on seven sitdowns and we're not going to tolerate another one." Well, I don't think it was three weeks until I was back out again. But I survived all that, and I've been there for 31 years.

My father was a strong union member and I guess that's where I got my background from, because when I went into the steel mill I saw things I didn't like and I'd hear him talk about the same things when we'd eat dinner in the evening. I think you have to have the union, because if you didn't, there would be all kinds of discrimination. Some people aren't capable of taking up for themselves like others. They do their job, but even though they do it, somebody pushes them a little harder. A lot of people can't fight back for themselves—I found that over and over again, especially with women. They don't want to speak up. They'll tell everybody else about it, but they won't tell the person they should tell, like the foreman. They're scared. So without a union I don't know what it would be like because you wouldn't have anybody to turn to. Even though everybody that works in the plant doesn't believe in a union like I do, if we didn't have one, they probably would. In fact, I don't think I would be here if I didn't have a union. I wouldn't have a job today. And I know. I've been the shop steward for the last 15 years, and I know I have saved a lot of people's jobs.

(These accounts are excerpted from oral histories taken by the author for "One Voice," a film and traveling exhibit about the history of Locals 2609 and 2610, USWA, funded by the National Endowment for the Humanities and the Maryland Committee for the Humanities.)

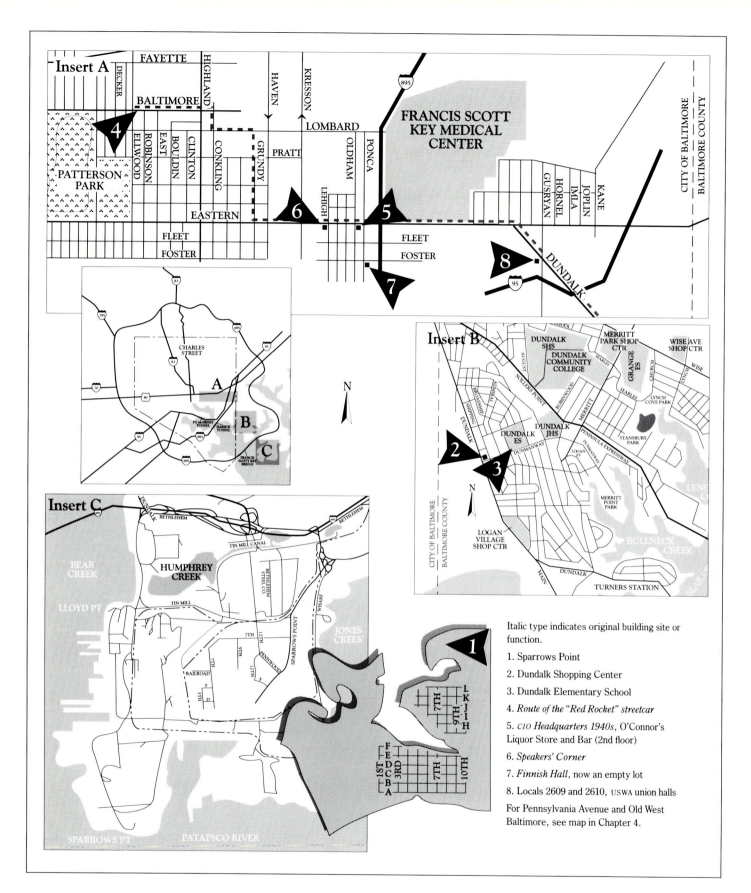

Insert A

FAYETTE
BALTIMORE
4
DECKER
HIGHLAND
HAVEN
KRESSON
LOMBARD
895
PATTERSON PARK
ELLWOOD
ROBINSON
EAST
BOULDIN
CLINTON
CONKLING
GRUNDY
PRATT
OLDHAM
PONCA
LEHIGH
EASTERN
6
5
FLEET
FOSTER
FLEET
FOSTER
7
8

FRANCIS SCOTT KEY MEDICAL CENTER

GUSRYAN
HORNEL
IMLA
JOPLIN
KANE
DUNDALK
95

CITY OF BALTIMORE
BALTIMORE COUNTY

CHARLES STREET
83
795
695
95
70
40
A
FT. McHENRY TUNNEL
HARBOR TUNNEL
B
C
FRANCIS SCOTT KEY BRIDGE
N

Insert B

DUNDALK SHS
MERRITT PARK SHOP CTR
WISE AVE SHOP CTR
DUNDALK COMMUNITY COLLEGE
GRANGE ES
SCHOOL
AUGUST
SOLLERS POINT
SEARLES
SEARLES
CHURCH
WISE
LYNCH
BROADSHIP
ADMIRAL
SHIPPING
DUNDALK
DUNDALK ES
DUNDALK JHS
DUNMANWAY
MERRITT
PENINSULA EXPRESSWAY
LYNCH COVE PARK
STANSBURY PARK
2
3
LOGAN ES
DUNMANWAY
N
CITY OF BALTIMORE
BALTIMORE COUNTY
LOGAN VILLAGE SHOP CTR
MERRITT POINT PARK
BULLNECK CREEK
MAIN
DUNDALK
TURNERS STATION
LYNC

Insert C

DUNDALK
BETHLEHEM
BETHLEHEM
TIN MILL CANAL
695
HUMPHREY CREEK
BETHLEHEM STEEL CO.
BEAR CREEK
TIN MILL
WHARF
SPARROWS POINT
JONES CREEK
LLOYD PT
7TH
12TH
7TH
9TH
FENNWOOD
RAILROAD
12TH
F
5TH
F
D
1
L
K
J
I
H
7TH
9TH
F
E
D
C
B
A
1ST
3RD
7TH
10TH
SPARROWS PT
PATAPSCO RIVER

Italic type indicates original building site or function.

1. Sparrows Point
2. Dundalk Shopping Center
3. Dundalk Elementary School
4. *Route of the "Red Rocket" streetcar*
5. *CIO Headquarters 1940s*, O'Connor's Liquor Store and Bar (2nd floor)
6. *Speakers' Corner*
7. *Finnish Hall*, now an empty lot
8. Locals 2609 and 2610, USWA union halls

For Pennsylvania Avenue and Old West Baltimore, see map in Chapter 4.

Home economics classroom for white girls, Sparrows Point, 1920s.

Home economics classroom for black girls, Sparrows Point, 1920s.

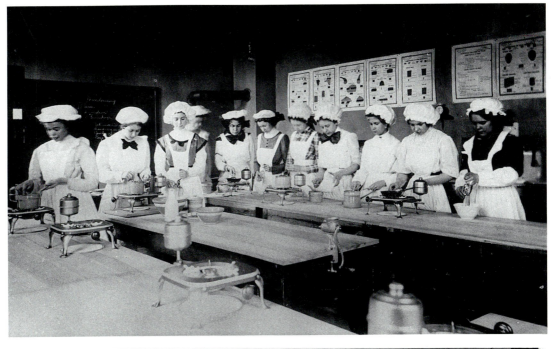

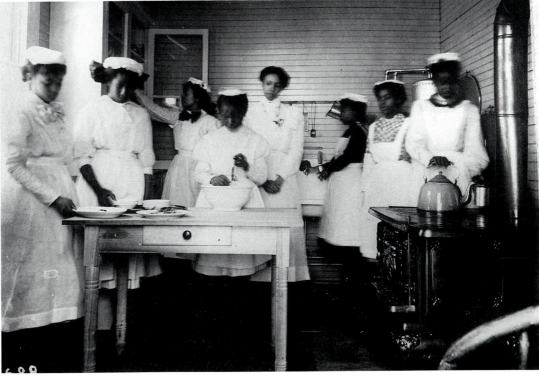

Classrooms for white boys were better equipped than those for black youths. White male graduates would fill the skilled jobs in the mill. Although black graduates were limited to unskilled mill jobs, these were still safer and less back-breaking than those reserved for African-American steelworkers who lived outside Sparrows Point.

In the state's first home economics program, girls learned how to be thrifty, efficient homemakers who could take in extra sewing, laundry, or boarders to stretch a steelworker's limited family income.

In all, residents of Sparrows Point enjoyed privileges that set them apart from other workers, gave them a sense of loyalty to the steel company, and

The general manager's house, the only residence on A Street in Sparrows Point, 1920s.

In the 1920s, white workers in Sparrows Point lived in spacious four-bedroom houses with large front porches.

predisposed them to view union organizing with disfavor or suspicion. Identification with the company and antiunion sentiment were also characteristic of residents of Dundalk, another community where employees of Bethlehem Steel lived.

Dundalk: Ships and Steel

If you had parked your car in Dundalk in the 1950s, during the heyday of steel production, you would have found it covered with a layer of red dust after an hour or two. "Gold dust" is what residents of Dundalk and Sparrows Point called the fine powder that coated windowsills, clothes on the line, porches, sidewalks, and everything else within blowing distance of the mills. Though a bane to housewives, residents appreciated what one foreman told a steelworker: "Remember, as long as that's there, you're working."

Bethlehem Steel established Dundalk in 1916 on the peninsula immediately west of the steel mill. The older part of the community lies between Dundalk Avenue and Sollers Point Road in Baltimore County. Today, its rough boundaries would include the area between Dundalk, Holabird, and Wise Avenues and Bear Creek.

The community was built to house shipyard workers, who formed an increasing part of the workforce at Bethlehem Steel as the company expanded to meet the increased demand for ships during World War I. In contrast to Sparrows Point, residents of Dundalk owned their houses, purchased by payroll deductions. At a time when home mortgages for families with steady but modest incomes were very difficult to obtain, this measure enabled lower-level managers, foremen, and a few of the highest-paid skilled workers to buy houses.

Bethlehem Steel intended to develop Dundalk as a community of single-family dwellings on the model of Roland Park, an exclusive Baltimore City residential community. But when the United States entered the war, the company turned responsibility for the community over to the U.S. Navy. To meet the pressing wartime demand for housing, the U.S. Shipping Board altered those plans by constructing faster-to-build duplexes.

Today, if you walk or drive through the neighborhood around the original shopping center at approximately 2800 Dundalk Avenue (*site 2*), you will find curved streets—with names like Flagship and Midship—laid out in the shape of a boat. The shopping center on Dundalk Avenue had a bowling alley and movie theater, in addition to shops, a bank, fire and police stations. The center faced a park several blocks long where the library and post office were located. The field behind the center, on the grounds of the elementary school (*site 3*), served as a focal point for community activities, like Dundalk's annual Fourth of July Heritage Festival.

By 1920, 2,000 residents lived in Dundalk. In 1924, responsibility for the development of the community was given to the Dundalk Company, a corporation founded by Bethlehem Steel to handle its real estate. Under its influence, the Dundalk population grew to 8,000 over the next decade. Today, homeownership is no longer connected to employment at the steel mill, and the influence of Bethlehem Steel extends solely, although significantly, to the employment it provides for many residents. Dundalk has always been and remains a community of white steelworkers and managers.

Dundalk's attractive houses with well-maintained gardens and tree-lined streets continue to make it a pleasant community. An occasional boat or camper parked in a driveway is symbolic of the prosperity of some of the current residents.

Highlandtown: Home of
Foreign-Born Steelworkers

The communities of Sparrows Point and Dundalk were too small to contain the entire workforce of the steel mill. Besides, many steelworkers found living in a company town distasteful, choosing not to live in Sparrows Point even when housing was available to them. Primarily as a result of these two factors, a significant number of steelworkers always lived in nearby areas of Baltimore City. By the 1930s, all but 2,000 of the 25,000-person workforce lived outside the company town.

Thousands of steelworkers, especially the white foreign born, were attracted to Highlandtown, a community bordered on the east by Interstate 95, on the west by Patterson Park, on the north by Pulaski

Highlandtown, 1930s, where many steelworkers, especially the foreign born, lived.

The "Red Rocket," the street-car that brought Highlandtown steelworkers to work at Sparrows Point.

Highway, and on the south by Eastern Avenue. With a special pass from Bethlehem Steel to lower the cost of the trip, steelworkers paid 10 cents for a 30- to 45-minute ride on a streetcar that took them across the county line to the steel mill.

If you stand at the corner of Baltimore and Ellwood Streets (*site 4*) today, you'll be standing where steelworkers caught the No. 26 streetcar to Sparrows Point. Although it no longer runs, in 1930 it zigzagged through Highlandtown, picking up more passengers at Fairmount, Ellwood, Baltimore, Conkling, Lombard, and Grundy Streets, finally heading east on Eastern Avenue to Dundalk Avenue and the steel mill—the end of the line. The streetcar was nick-named "The Red Rocket" because of the speed it traveled along a special right-of-way constructed for it down the middle of Dundalk Avenue.

Highlandtown is known for its rowhouses with white marble steps. On Saturday mornings, a visitor will be struck by the sight of housewives scrubbing the steps of two-, sometimes three-story buildings on street after street. There are few trees on the sidewalks of Highlandtown, but residents enjoy a reputation for pretty backyard gardens and well-kept, clean alleys.

Today, the corner of Eastern Avenue and Old-

ham Street is the center of the area known as Little Athens, surrounded by Greek restaurants, grocery stores, and coffeehouses. Although fewer Greeks lived here 50 years ago, this part of Highlandtown and the large area to the west of it attracted Finns, Czechs, Poles, Lithuanians, Italians, and other foreign-born workers.

Located close to compatriots, ethnic groups tried to maintain the traditions and values of their country of origin by establishing churches and building meeting halls in Highlandtown. Many of these Baltimoreans worked at Bethlehem Steel and in the other major manufacturing industries located on the eastern edge of the city.

The steelworkers of Highlandtown saw work at the steel mill differently from those who lived in Sparrows Point or Dundalk. In Sparrows Point, where every worker was a steelworker, the dangers of working in a steel mill, the dirty working conditions, the fatigue of a 10- to 12-hour shift with a 24-hour swing shift, all seemed like natural conditions of life and work.

But Highlandtown steelworkers compared their working conditions to those of workers in other Baltimore industries. Unaffected by the benefits and advantages granted residents of the company town at

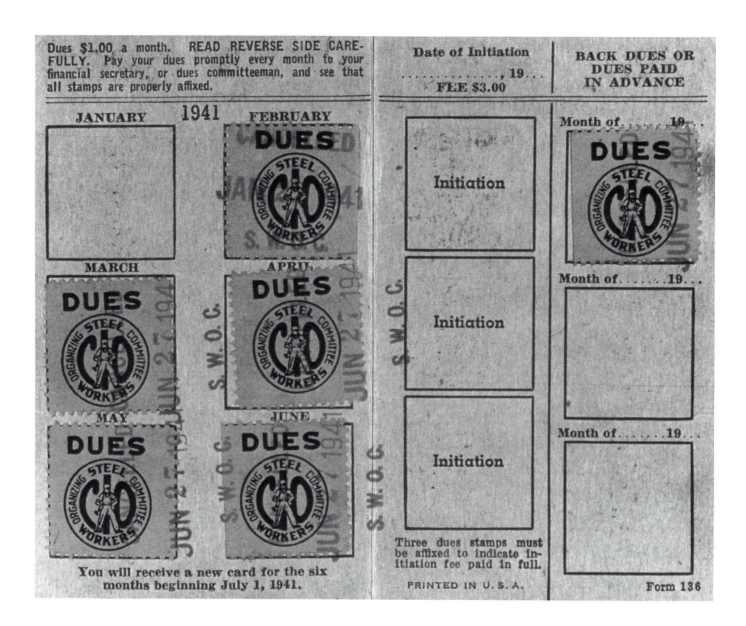

Union dues book

Sparrows Point or in Dundalk, Highlandtown steelworkers were more willing to consider a union as a way of making changes. In fact, in 1941, steelworkers in Highlandtown took the lead in joining the Steel Workers Organizing Committee (swoc) when it came to Baltimore to organize the industry.

Birthplace of a Union

O'Connor's Liquor Store and Bar is located on the southeast corner of Eastern and Oldham Streets (*site 5*). From 1940 to 1942, the years of concentrated steelworkers' union activity in Baltimore, steelworkers congregated at O'Connor's, on the frontier between Highlandtown and Sparrows Point, to hear the

latest news about the union drive, especially on Friday evenings after they cashed their paychecks. The second story of this building was the organizing headquarters for swoc and other cio unions. A secretary who worked in the office remembers how steelworkers would come to her with their pockets stuffed with the dollars collected from their organizing efforts for the day.

In the early 1930s, before the swoc was formed, some steelworkers held secret meetings of the Amalgamated Association of Iron, Steel, Metal and Tin Workers in a storefront several doors to the east of O'Connor's. A union of skilled workers in the steel industry formed in the later part of the previous century, the Amalgamated tried to organize all steel-workers for a brief period in the 1930s.

They met secretly because they knew from experience that union sympathizers were harassed or fired by Bethlehem. The need for secrecy made organizing difficult, and since the Amalgamated committed only modest resources to steelworker organizing, it is not surprising that this effort failed to produce a union.

It was only in 1935, as a result of worker discontent during the Great Depression, that Congress passed the Wagner Act, which granted union members and organizers a modicum of protection. In response, the CIO established SWOC to organize the steel industry, sending organizers seasoned in the struggles of mine workers to steel towns in and near Pittsburgh, Chicago, Gary, and eventually Baltimore in 1940. SWOC would become the United Steelworkers of America in 1943.

Even with the legal right to organize embodied in Section 7a of the Wagner Act, steelworkers in Baltimore and other steel towns were not sure they would be protected. They were cautious, aware that the company hired spies to seek out and report union members and organizers. Union members used their break time to recruit, taking care to talk to other steelworkers only when the foreman wouldn't notice. Members also wore their union buttons under their collars until all the workers in the mill had signed union cards.

A major problem for organizers in Baltimore was reaching steelworkers in Sparrows Point to tell them about the union. Nathaniel Parks, retired steel-worker and former resident of Sparrows Point, describes an inventive way organizers solved that problem:

During 1932, 1933, I can't just remember what year it was, the company never did allow people to come in and talk union at Sparrows Point. It was an island. . . . And it happened that the car pulled up a half a block from this corner. And they had iron poles for the lights, you know—the lights on the street. And a lady got out [of the car] and a man got out, and they walked over to this iron pole, and then she handcuffed him to the pole. And then he started putting in his spiel about union:

what its advantages was, what they were trying to do. And then, the police, they were in a quarrel; they didn't know what to do. They ran around trying to find a hacksaw or something to get him untied from this pole. And he got his spiel before they got him. And then when they put him in this patrol wagon and carried him on the other side of the bridge, he was still with his head out of the window . . . blasting out just about what the union was in for, what the people was in for. Oh, it was really nice to see what was going to happen [with a union] the way the company was treating men on the jobs in those days. . . . I got a regular kick out of it.

While the foreign-born workers did most of the actual organizing, native-born workers in the union movement did most of the public speaking and frequently received most of the credit for the organizing efforts. The foreign-born devoted their energies to speaking to workers of their own country of origin, communicating with them in their native language with references to shared cultural experiences.

If you walk to the intersection of Eastern Avenue and Lehigh Street, you will see a traffic island used during the union drive by soapbox organizers (*site 6*). The speakers were often women. The wives and daughters of steelworkers—unlike their husbands, fathers, or brothers—could not be fired or harassed by company spies who caught them speaking out in favor of a union. Women also organized for the union in the streets and backyards of Highlandtown, campaigning door to door, or telling neighbors over the back fence about the advantages of a union as they hung out the family's wash. Many women employed at the mill as inspectors of tin plate joined the union as steelworkers.

The opposition of many Highlandtown businessmen, civic leaders, and clergy to unionization made it difficult for union leaders to find rooms where union meetings could take place. An exception was the Finnish Hall, which used to stand on the now empty lot located on the southeast corner of Foster and Ponca Street (*site 7*). Union meetings were frequently held here.

In fact, the Finns in Highlandtown were among the leaders of the organizing effort. Their experiences in the steel industry explain their strong union

The Finnish Hall at Ponca and Foster Streets in the 1940s, one of the few meeting places in Highlandtown that welcomed union-organizing activities.

A demonstration by residents of West Baltimore protesting discriminatory employment practices by neighborhood merchants, 1930s.

support. While steel companies routinely assigned immigrants difficult or dirty work, the Finns were singled out for the hottest areas because the company assumed they were used to heat from their traditional use of the sauna. Bethlehem Steel recruited Finns from steel towns in West Virginia and Ohio to work as so-called heaters in the new tin mill opened in 1935. These Finns had already participated in union drives, and they believed that a union could make work better and safer.

The Finnish Hall was a social, cultural, and political center for the Finns of Baltimore. Steelworkers held meetings there and discussed strategies for supporting the union effort. The Finns also welcomed African-American steelworkers to meetings, despite neighbors determined to keep the neighborhood segregated. Sirkka Holm, a resident of the Finnish Hall at the time, describes the reaction of the community and of steelworkers to the union drive:

We had black steelworkers come to the Hall, and as a result—we lived in an area that was quite racist at the time—quite a few windows were broken at the Finnish Hall. I think that the people in the neighborhood could have stood the Finns being radical, but the fact that they had blacks, that was really unforgivable. . . .

And the blacks, of course, didn't trust the whites either, because they had been burned before. But I think the blacks working together with the whites, with the working conditions, sharing the same problems, that was what brought unity into the union.

Old West Baltimore:
African-American Steelworkers

Bethlehem Steel employed more African-American steelworkers at the Sparrows Point plant than at any of its other plants in Pennsylvania or Maryland. One-third of the workers at Sparrows Point were African American, a higher proportion than in most steel mills in the country. Although many black steelworkers lived in Sparrows Point, there was not enough housing for all of them. The thousands who lived outside the company town were barred from segregated communities like Dundalk and Highlandtown. Many of them settled in Old West Baltimore, the community discussed in Chapter 4, located farther from the steel mill and close to the center city.

In contrast to Highlandtown residents, African-American community leaders, including clergymen and some business owners, supported the union effort in the steel industry. Churches opened their doors for meetings. Clergymen announced rallies

from the pulpit, endorsed some union campaigns, and supported some of the boycotts associated with the union drive. The local newspaper, the *Afro-American*, published news of strikes and publicized organizing events.

The union struggle fit into the tradition of protest in Old West Baltimore, where citizens had already mobilized for the continuing battle against discrimination. For example, the "Don't Buy Where You Can't Work" campaign of 1933, protesting the refusal of white-owned stores on Pennsylvania Avenue to hire African Americans, brought some positive results and gave residents experience in picketing and organizing. Also in the early 1930s, such visiting guest speakers as W. E. B. Du Bois brought debates about the merits of industrial, biracial unionism to the attention of various church congregations in Baltimore. With this experience, consciousness, and sense of commitment, the community of Old West Baltimore threw its support behind the CIO and SWOC as part of the struggle for equality.

African-American steelworkers liked the ideas and ideals of industrial unions advocated by SWOC. Across-the-board wage increases, supported by SWOC, would give workers who held the lowest-paid, hardest, and dirtiest jobs in the steel mill a larger net gain in wages than a simple percentage system. Reliance on seniority, rather than favoritism, in hiring and promotion could open the way to better-paying and safer jobs in the steel mill for black workers. Finally, black steelworkers no doubt appreciated the fact that SWOC hired black organizers to persuade workers in Old West Baltimore to join the union.

The support of the African-American steelworkers of Old West Baltimore was essential to the union victory. Of the 15,714 steelworkers who cast their ballots when the SWOC vote was taken in September 1941, 10,813 supported the union. With a voting strength of approximately 5,500, African-American steelworkers at Bethlehem Steel made the difference between victory and defeat.

Nicholas Fontecchio, director of SWOC, acknowledged the importance of black steelworkers' support for the union on the occasion of the union victory. He was quoted in the *Afro-American* as saying: "Had their [blacks'] vote been against us we would have

lost the election. I want it known that we appreciate their support and we are going to work for the common good of all along the policy of the CIO, which frowns on all race, color, or creed discrimination."

Twilight at Bethlehem Steel?

At the foot of Dundalk Avenue, one short block from Eastern Avenue, you will find, side by side, the two halls of the United Steelworkers of America, Locals 2609 and 2610 (*site 8*). The mostly brick building on the corner of Gusryan Street is the older of the two, built in 1952 to house both locals. As the unions grew in size and strength, Local 2610 built the more modern hall next door to it. Across the street from the union halls, you will see the steelworkers' credit union. The growth of union facilities mirrored the increasing importance of the union in the workplace and the increasing prosperity of its members. By the 1970s, steelworkers were getting decent pay for doing one of the nation's most dangerous jobs. In addition, the union contract provided good health benefits, sick leave, and an innovative vacation policy.

In the 1980s, however, steelworkers' financial security and the power of the union to protect hard-won benefits were challenged. Employment at Sparrows Point declined sharply, dwindling to 16,500 production workers in 1980 and plunging to about 8,000 in the late 1980s. These job losses reflect the decline of the U.S. steel industry worldwide, which has been accompanied by reductions in wages and benefits and concessions on work rules and employment practices. The loss of jobs has brought profound changes for steelworkers, the union, and the communities where steelworkers have traditionally lived.

Sparrows Point was one of the first communities to be affected by this economic crisis. To improve the company's competitive position, Bethlehem designed and constructed a computerized blast furnace. It tore down the last remaining houses of the company town in 1975 to make room for the L-Blast furnace—the tallest structure on Sparrows Point today, amid smoke and smokestacks. Sparrows Point is no longer a residential community.

To date, no one has systematically studied what has happened to the steelworkers who have lost their jobs. Data that might provide a picture of changes in

Locals 2609 and 2610, USWA
on strike in 1946.

the communities described here, Dundalk, Highland-town, and Old West Baltimore, are not yet available. We do, however, have the testimony of union leaders and steelworkers who are still employed. They talk about workers who suffered strokes or heart attacks triggered by losing their jobs, and of former steel-workers who now earn money as handymen or by picking up odd jobs. They talk of laid-off workers who wait at home, expecting to be called back, and of those who have gone back to school or retrained themselves for new jobs in the mill or in other indus-tries in the region. They can also name some who left Baltimore to find work in other cities.

The education and retraining that many steelwork-ers have received does not ensure either employ-ment opportunities or pay commensurate with the work they did in the steel mill. The employment pros-pects are worse for African Americans and women who, as the last hired, lost their jobs in greater num-bers and who are more likely to encounter discrimi-natory hiring practices.

At one time, steel work was a good way to make a solid living, although a dangerous one. Now that jobs are scarce, steel is no longer an industry with promise for young women and men looking for work. Steelworkers and their daughters and sons, in com-munities like Dundalk, Highlandtown, and Old West Baltimore, will now have to forge new alliances with one another, devise new strategies for unions, and explore new ways to create a working future.

Acknowledgment: The author wishes to thank the men and women of Locals 2609 and 2610, United Steelworkers of America, and Mark Reutter, author of *Sparrows Point: Making Steel—The Rise and Ruin of American Industrial Might* (1988), for his help and encouragement

George Meyers: Labor Leader

ELIZABETH FEE

"My father and my grandfathers and my uncles were all coal miners," says George Meyers, reminiscing about his life as a labor union organizer and activist. "But when I came out of school in 1930, the Great Depression was already under way. I would have been glad to get a job in the mines—even though my parents insisted I would never work there—but there were no jobs in the mines or anyplace else."

Of German-Irish descent, Meyers was raised by the Irish side of the family. Lonaconing ("Coney"), Maryland, where Meyers was born and grew up, is a small mining town in the nation's oldest mining area. "It's an old Indian name meaning 'where many waters meet,'" says Meyers, who left Coney to travel around the country for three years looking for work. "I never found anything more than one or two days at a time until I got a job in the Celanese Plant near Cumberland making artificial silk.

"Conditions were really terrible," he remembers. The noise affected his hearing, chemicals burned his lungs. (Twenty years later, "the workers in our department began dying off like flies, because their lungs had been damaged.") The day was long and the speed-ups relentless. Since most of the workers had a union background, "it wasn't long before we began thinking about organizing a union."

Two years later, in 1935, a year before the CIO was founded, the union was organized. In 1940, at the age of 27, Meyers was elected the youngest president of what had been the largest (10,000 members) local in the CIO until the automobile industry was organized.

Meyers helped lead a series of successful sit-down strikes in the process of organizing the union. "This was taking place at the same time as the big sit-down strike in Flint," he recalls. "You have to imagine that every day you could pick up the paper and see the big headlines about strikes somewhere or other. It was just such a ferment all over the country. People were afraid to go to bed for fear they would miss something." In 1941, the 28-year-old Meyers was elected president of the Maryland/D.C. chapter of the CIO.

His first contact with somebody from outside the Cumberland Mountains in relation to union work was Paddy Whalen, who would later head the CIO in Baltimore and the National Maritime Union in Baltimore. Whalen, who became mentor and friend, had come with Johnny Samuels to ask the miners of Allegany County to raise money for the seamen's strike in 1936 when he met Meyers.

"There are a million stories about Paddy," says Meyers, who enjoys telling the one about Whalen's "very scientific

approach to taking down Jim Crow" at Baltimore's waterfront.

"The National Maritime Union always worked integrated crews, and we'd go into a waterfront bar and order up a bottle. The bartenders would serve the white seamen and refuse to serve the others because, they said, it was against the law. So Paddy's guys would pick the bottle up and throw it into the mirror . . . and that was the way the waterfront was integrated. After that, anyone could be served with no problem.

"The CIO played a hell of a role in fighting racism when it was the law of the land here," Meyers says. "One of the things we did which I think had a long-range impact was the integration of black workers into industry. There were no black workers at Glen L. Martin, some of the shipyards, at the Celanese plant, the Kelly Springfield plant in the early 1940s. So we had a meeting with Governor O'Conor and demanded that companies start hiring black workers. We went to the press and made a lot of bad noise about it, so our plant, Glen L. Martin, and the Kelly Springfield began to hire black workers for the first time." Other plants followed suit.

George Meyers

Meyers also recalls trying to arrange a union convention at the Emerson Hotel in 1942. "The hotel manager told me, 'The colored will have to ride in the freight elevator. We don't want them sitting around here looking like they own the place.' No hotel in Baltimore was willing to hold an integrated meeting, but we finally found a hotel in Washington.

"The hotel was on its last legs, and Jim Crow was on its way out. They were so desperate that they agreed to an integrated meeting. The hotel made it as a result of that incident because all the progressive organizations, all the labor organizations, starting meeting there.

"That's the part unions played at the time—the unions together with the NAACP. Mrs. Lillie Jackson was a very diligent, fantastic leader. She built up the NAACP to 25,000 from nothing. It was really the beginning of the freedom movement in Baltimore."

A member and then a leader of the Communist party in Maryland during the cold war, Meyers worked for antiwar and pro–civil rights causes. He actively opposed the war in Korea. He was sentenced to four years in prison during the McCarthy era after being accused of conspiring to "teach and advocate to overthrow the government by force and violence at some future date." This charge was directed against every member of the Communist party. He spent 42 months in prison, including a weekend in a holding cell in Richmond with "some guys who were in there for murder. The guards gave them the idea to give me a hard time."

When two brothers charged with murder walked into his cell and began to threaten him with knives, Meyers tried directing their attention to a carnival train that happened to be going by. "The prisoners said they'd worked for a carnival once, so I asked them to tell me how they put those things up so fast—the Ferris wheel, the merry-go-round, and all that. Next thing you know, they were telling me how they did it, and after that they're asking me for advice on how to get out of jail. That was the closest call I had.

"But mostly communists were looked up to in prison because they were sympathetic with the people. Most of the guys in jail were trying to beat the system, but we were trying to change it. They liked to talk to us because they knew we would listen. I learned a lot in prison from the other prisoners."

Meyers, now 78, has served as labor secretary for the Communist party for the past 25 years, traveling extensively in this country and abroad to help organize and unite workers and campaign for international trade union cooperation and peace.

Robert Moore: 1199 Organizer

LINDA ZEIDMAN

"As a kid I had a friend—a white kid—whose father owned a garage up the street from us. One afternoon we were sent to the White Coffee Pot to fetch lunch for his father. We both sat down at the counter to order the lunch, and I was told to get down off the seat. He starts to hop down with me because he thinks we're both being chastised, but the waitress tells him 'No, not you honey. You can sit there.' I thought the woman was being particularly mean. Later on that day my mother screamed at me for going into the place." This was Robert Moore's earliest conscious experience with racial segregation.

Moore associates this event with his decision to join the civil rights movement, which led to his current job as president of the Baltimore and Washington local of District 1199-E, National Union of Hospital and Health Care Employees. The union organizes a low-paid, largely black workforce, and has always had close ties with the civil rights movement.

At the age of 15, Moore joined the picket lines at the Baltimore Gas and Electric and C & P Telephone companies—demonstrations organized by the NAACP and some local churches to end employment discrimination. As a student at Morgan State University, in the winter of 1963, he took part in the movement to desegregate the Northwood Shopping Center, several blocks from the college. He joined the Students for a Democratic Society (SDS) chapter at Morgan, and in the summer of 1964, he dropped out of college to spend four years working with the Student Non-Violent Coordinating Committee SNCC in Atlanta.

Moore returned to Baltimore in 1968. "At that time the resources of SNCC had shriveled to almost zilch. So, many people had to make choices about how they were going to continue to work and support the organization. We recognized that beyond the South there was another kind of struggle had to take place in the cities.

"Whereas desegregation of public accommodations was becoming law, and the voting rights act had been passed, in the urban centers of the North, where people had the right to vote, they didn't have real choices about what to vote for. So, they tended not to vote. There was much unemployment in black communities."

Moore decided "that the next phase of the civil rights movement was in urban areas. And [Baltimore] was home, and I had roots; and I could play a role in this community—more than in some of the places in the South where I had been working."

When Moore returned to Baltimore, he was recruited as an organizer for 1199, part of the union's effort to ex-

Organizing Chart

Robert Moore

pand beyond its New York base. Moore already knew of 1199 as a progressive organization.

"They organized these low-wage service workers who, in large part, tended to be black or minority and women. They tended to be people at the bottom. The labor movement [was more concerned with] industrial workers and seemed to focus more on trades. And people didn't believe that you could actually organize people at the low end of the service industry. I think [1199] was progressive in that sense and in the sense that it very actively supported civil rights activities and seemed to be developing black leadership.

"In many ways the attempt to organize the hospitals in Baltimore came at the right time. The black community was looking for ways to organize for greater power.

"When King was shot, it was the end of a period. It was clear that you had to do something besides just having marches and demonstrations. [In Baltimore] at the time, there had been battles over who was going to be the school superintendent and what the schools were going to be like. There had been the election of a black to the City Council.

We'd come through the first congressional election where Parren Mitchell had just lost by a hair. There was a sense of galvanizing for greater power into organization."

The power of organized black workers was evident in 1199's successful seven-month fight to win recognition at Hopkins hospital in August 1969. "Obviously, a place like Hopkins has a lot of concentrated power in the city," explains Moore. But "when the Hopkins victory came, a number of other victories also came about. Six hospitals were organized, and 25 to 30 nursing homes—and all within a period of about a year. It was a phenomenal organizing drive for the period.

"What made [the victory of District 1199-E at Hopkins hospital] possible was the link between civil rights and the politics of the black community in Baltimore. These poor black workers saw they could organize and have some power."

A visit by Coretta Scott King to Hopkins hospital during the strike "helped to cement and symbolize this progress. Well, she didn't make a speech. She came and stood outside the main employee entrance door to the hospital, and workers and people poured out. Probably close to 1,000 people went through and came around to meet her. She was in a receiving line and shook their hands.

"The hospital management kind of just looked out of windows and lost any opportunity to co-opt. I often wondered why they didn't come out and get in the greeting line too. But I suppose they felt a little overwhelmed by it all.

"[Management] could have gotten on board and said they were for civil rights and admired the work of Dr. King. Being apart, they separated themselves and helped to clarify and draw the line—as opposed to the kinds of things that are happening now, where the lines get blurred where

you think everybody was on board. Since that time, of course, Coretta King has been back and has spoken at Hopkins, and they make it their business to make her welcome."

After more than 18 years working as field organizer, administrative officer, secretary-treasurer, and president of 1199, Moore hopes that his work will have accomplished a goal: "I hope the ability to provide people with an opportunity to have greater power and some control over their lives will lead to a situation where working people, as well as the black poor, will have a role to play in changing the priorities of the country."

Sirkka Tuomi Lee Holm: Finnish Activist

LINDA ZEIDMAN WITH LINDA SHOPES

Sirkka Tuomi Holm, retired secretary and actress, historian of the Finns in the United States, and political activist, was born on August 15, 1920, in Virginia, Minnesota. At age 13 she came to Baltimore where she has lived most of her life. Holm is the daughter of Finnish immigrants: Her father worked in the ore mines in Minnesota and the steel mills of Ohio and Maryland; her mother worked as a cook and maid.

Holm expresses her pride in her working-class origins when speaking of her mother. "You know some people look down on being a servant. But actually my mother was always proud that she was in a skilled trade . . . it's a craft; it's an art . . . you have to know how to clean, and how to cook, and you have to know how to serve dinner, how to react to people, how to answer the door, the telephone."

Finnish halls, cultural centers established by immigrants in areas where they settled, played an important role in Holm's family life. She recalls her mother telling her that when she worked for a family as a live-in cook and housekeeper, she would cook dinner and serve it, "and then she'd throw the dishes in the oven—she didn't do them—because right after dinner [she would] grab a streetcar, go to the Finnish Hall . . . rehearse the play and then take a streetcar getting back to her working place about 2:30 A.M., wash the dishes, go to bed, and then get up in about three hours and cook breakfast." She really loved the theater, as did most of the Finns.

Poetry readings, plays, musical events, and calisthenic competitions took place in the Finnish halls. "We also had Finnish Sunday school at the Finnish Hall. . . . Of course we *spoke* Finnish [at home]—but we were taught how to read and write it. . . . I didn't speak English until I went to school."

The Finnish Hall was also a center of political activity.

Rallies protesting the Sacco and Vanzetti trial and meetings of union organizers showed the Finnish community's concern with workers' rights and fair treatment for the foreign born. These causes identified the Finns as radicals, and many, including Holm's parents, were socialists.

In 1930, when Holm's father was blacklisted for participating in a strike at Republic Steel in Warren, Ohio, she experienced the double stigma of being poor and foreign born. "Relief was the most debasing thing. . . . You were treated . . . like a criminal, especially if you were foreign born. . . . I remember one time when I needed shoes and I had to get a slip from the principal. . . . When I went into her office, she said, 'You dumb foreigners, why do we have to pay to keep you people alive?' And I said, 'Well, my dad can't find work. Nobody will hire him.' She signed the slip and threw it on the floor and I had to pick it up."

In 1933, Holm's family moved to Baltimore where her father found work at the Bethlehem Steel plant in Sparrows Point. In 1943, she joined the Women's Army Corps, and after the war studied drama at the Carnegie Institute of Technology under the GI bill. "Then I went to New York and I stayed in New York for four years trying to break into show biz. . . . I came back here in 1950. . . . I was hoping to get a children's theater started because I love children, and so I became very active at the [Finnish] Hall."

The 1950s also marked the beginning of the McCarthy era, a period of repression for people and organizations supporting progressive causes. These included the foreign born, who were threatened with deportation. Holm remembers: "The first ones attacked were the labor unions because they had led the way for Baltimoreans to start changing their conditions. . . . The attack was in the form of the Taft-Hartley Act, and one of the provisions in that act was to forbid communists (or anyone they deemed a communist) from holding any position of responsibility in the unions. This was ironic, of course, since it was the communists, socialists, and other radicals who organized those very unions."

Sirkka Tuomi Lee Holm

In May 1957, Holm was subpoenaed to appear before the House Un-American Activities Committee (HUAC), which was investigating communist activities in Baltimore and Maryland. She was questioned about her participation in the American Committee for the Protection of the Foreign Born, a national organization that worked against the harassment and deportation of immigrants suspected of subversion. She was also asked about her activities at the Finnish Hall. Holm repeatedly took the Fifth Amendment and refused to cooperate with HUAC.

"The attack in 1957 in Baltimore by HUAC, to which over 20 'unfriendly witnesses' were subpoenaed, was a disgrace to Baltimore. It was televised, and the hysteria and panic that ensued ultimately hurt all Baltimoreans. Over a half-dozen steelworkers were called, and with the exception of one, they all lost their jobs as a result of not 'cooperating' with HUAC. Everyone else who was called suffered the same consequence, including me. My husband, Robert W. Lee, was fired from his job and then my 65-year-old mother, who worked as a cook for a rich family, was fired. No doubt her delicious cheese omelets were tainted with red from association with her daughter."

The hearings lasted three days and were held in Room 556 of the Federal Building, located in the old post office at Calvert and Fayette Streets. "The atmosphere in the courtroom of the HUAC hearings was like that of a lynch mob. When my name was called and I went up to the table to confront the committee, I passed a bunch of women who were wearing red, white, and blue miniature bunting on their dresses and hats and were armed with sunglasses to protect their eyes from the glare of the television lights. They were a cheering section for HUAC.

"The resulting hysteria created not only the loss of jobs for all of us but a continuing attack. . . . [A] woman whose husband had also been uncooperative told me that her son in grade school was on the baseball team and the teacher kicked him off the team so he wouldn't contaminate the other children. Our windows were broken four times, the first time when a friend was sitting by the window and a rock came sailing through and barely missed her. There were a handful of liberal people who questioned HUAC, including a former Sun paper's editor and an Episcopalian bishop, but there were not enough of them.

"In the early 1950s, the ones who suffered most, of course, were the communists who were arrested under the Smith Act. . . . They were not found guilty of trying to overthrow the government but of a *conspiracy* to do so, and no such conspiracy was ever proven.

"The one thing the Sun papers did . . . was to expose the ludicrous behavior of the FBI. One of the defendants was a petite teacher and a kindly, gentle, soft-spoken lady. . . . She had graduated cum laude from Goucher and could have been quite high in social life but believed in working people and their destiny. She lived near Druid Hill Park, and while out on bail, she went out for a walk one sunny day. Four FBI men followed her. The [*Baltimore Sun*] photographer took a picture of her sitting calmly on a bench, basking in the sun, and in the background, peekin' from behind the trees, were the FBI agents keeping a sharp eye on this enormous threat to the American government."

These experiences made Holm keenly aware that "an attack by government on one group of people, such as radicals, will ultimately lead to an attack on all people who question."

A few years ago, Holm moved to a home in New Hampshire with her husband, Taisto. But she still feels it is important to know Baltimore's history. "When you pass Fells Point, remember the seamen and other union organizers; when you go through Highlandtown, remember the steelworkers; when you go by the Federal Building, remember the farce of the hearings . . . and when you go by Druid Hill Park, remember a tiny lady surrounded by four government agents; and after you have said, why how ridiculous that is—remember—it can happen again—make sure it doesn't."

This account was excerpted in part from an interview with Sirkka Tuomi Lee by Matti Manu Paavola on May 5, 1975, on deposit at the Maryland Historical Society.

Dean Pappas: Antiwar Activist

ELIZABETH FEE

One evening in 1968, Dean Pappas, then a physics teacher at Park School, and his friend, a chemistry teacher, sat in the living room making homemade napalm—following a recipe given in the Green Beret field manual. "Do you know what napalm is? It's three parts gasoline and one part Ivory soap chips. You get a big bucket and then you put it in by volume, a quarter of it soap chips, and you pour in the gasoline and then you stir it up so it's sticky. Then you put it into cans."

Daniel and Philip Berrigan, flamboyant Catholic radical brothers in the antiwar movement, had asked for napalm to burn military draft files—real napalm, they felt, would add to the symbolic quality of their protest against the Vietnam war. Those who would become known as the Catonsville Nine in Baltimore's most famous antiwar protest were planning to burn the files of the Catonsville draft board. Pappas had agreed to be the lookout: "They were certainly willing to be arrested, but they wanted to burn draft files first before they got caught. My job was to make sure the coast was clear and the cops hadn't been tipped off ahead of time.

"They went in and took over the office; they gathered every bit of draft files they could and stuffed them into big wire baskets and ran outside. They poured the cans of homemade napalm into the baskets, right in the parking lot. They lit it and then stood around and said the Lord's Prayer. And that was it! Then they waited for the cops—who came a lot later."

A few years earlier, Pappas had been, by his own description, an "apolitical, even somewhat conservative" Yale undergraduate. He had grown up in the New York City Borough of Queens, the son of a Greek immigrant family. "I was a white ethnic, lower-middle class kid from New York who was tracked into science and engineering—a career in physics." As a graduate student at Johns Hopkins, he worked at the Applied Physics Laboratory in the summers. "I got attracted to physics because of 'Sputnik.' I had security clearance and all that. It was part of my patriotic component to be a defense worker. I was working on microelectronics, circuitry that would be used for satellites. I guess I would like to believe that it had a peaceful component but I wasn't too concerned about it being used for weapons. . . . Mostly I thought it was a ticket to a career."

Pappas was attracted to programs—especially folk dancing—organized by the Reverend Chester Wickwire, the university chaplain. Starting with folk dancing, he began to meet left-wingers and people active in the civil rights movement. In 1963, he got involved in the Baltimore Tutorial Project, tutoring inner-city kids. "I was very insistent that I was not going to participate in any demonstrations. It was fine to tutor and stuff like that, but no demonstrations. I was for civil rights in a theoretical way and I had an ethnic consciousness about being Greek—my grandfather was an immigrant and a waiter—so I did understand the concept of a minority group.

"In the tutorial project I got close to the kids and close to the other people working there, and I felt I was part of a community. When George Wallace came to town a year later, I was ready to demonstrate, ready to walk the picket line. It was so stark and so negative that this man—Wallace—would espouse segregation so nakedly. For me, and maybe for a lot of other people, walking a picket line was a quantum jump—in this society it is so much identified as a radical thing to do.

"It was almost a religious experience. It was exhilarating—like entering the locomotive of history. I knew that something really important was going on."

At the Wallace demonstration, Pappas met Eugene Chase, one of the first African Americans to go to Johns Hopkins. Chase was involved with Democratic party politics and was actively registering black voters. He encouraged Pappas to get involved, going door-to-door in the African-American community on the west side of town.

There Pappas met community activists, including Walter Lively, a leader of the civil rights struggle. He met members of Students for a Democratic Society (SDS), a radical antiwar group. He got involved in local efforts to gain community control of the antipoverty program. He joined a support group for the Mississippi Freedom Democratic party, then trying to unseat the regular, conservative Mississippi Democrats. And mostly he lobbied: "Even when we went in the streets, we were trying to get enough attention so that whoever had the power would change things. We believed in the liberal consensus, even though we were operating within it in a militant fashion."

Many people Pappas now knew opposed the war in Vietnam: "They had no question that if you were for civil rights domestically, you had to be for civil rights globally. Thus, the war in Vietnam was an imperialist venture. I didn't accept that at first. . . . There was a lot of resistance on my part. . . . I thought civil rights was fine; it was American; it was home grown. But this other stuff—you know, I thought we were fighting communism.

"In the atmosphere at the time it was hard to be for civil rights and not be against the war. People like Karen Whitman and Gren Whitman, for example, were both very active—folks like that definitely had an antiwar influence on me.

"I guess there are certain pivotal books that one reads. For me, the *Playboy* interview with Fidel Castro was pivotal in showing me the global aspect of what was going

Dean Pappas

on domestically. That and reading the autobiography of Malcolm X. Around 1965 or so I became focused on the war, and I started to become a Marxist. At the same time it was becoming clear that whites were not really to be part of the black movement, so I moved more into antiwar activities.

"I withdrew from graduate school in 1965. Then I went back a couple of years later and got a master of arts in teaching so that I could get certified to teach high school. I put most of my time into civil rights and antiwar stuff, that and my teaching. I always enjoyed teaching physics, which is why I love being a physics teacher.

"In 1967, the Vietnam Summer was a large-scale attempt by the American antiwar movement to really go out and raise consciousness about the war. A lot of people took the summer off. We organized teach-ins, and we developed information packets that would enable people to talk at community meetings about the war. There was a real sense of going to the grass roots, and the massive outreach was very successful.

"Then people conceived of the Pentagon Action as a large demonstration that would have a component of massive civil disobedience. The demonstration would have maybe 100,000 people, and at a certain point in the demonstration, a subset of us would sit down and occupy the Pentagon. People were very excited about this. Jerry Rubin was in my living room talking to about 30 people—the Baltimore committee that would be working to organize it. At that time we got in touch with the Berrigans, who had already participated in a number of sit-ins at army bases and had poured blood on draft files in Baltimore. There was organizational strength in the Baltimore radical Catholic community, but the Pentagon Action was more the mainstream of the antiwar movement.

"We sent down quite a few buses. Probably there were 100,000 in the main march, and about 20,000 to 30,000 occupying the Pentagon itself. It was just so massive that you had no sense of where you were. There were crowds all over the place, and at a certain point everybody just sat down.

"The paratroopers were right behind us. We tried to get as close to the building as possible, and they tried to stop us. For the first time, I really had a sense of the drama of the military and the demonstrators. These guys had guns, the U.S. marshals would point, and they would selectively pull people out. This was a year before Chicago. You definitely saw batons flying. You felt that you were up against military power.

"The mode then was civil disobedience—link arms and sing 'We Shall Overcome.' At that time there was a sense that militant resistance was definitely nonviolent and that was bought as a tactic by everybody. It didn't matter whether you believed in pacifism or not; it had nothing to do with it. The basic assumption was that our tactics might

be militant and they might be disruptive, but they were nonviolent; you might resist arrest by linking arms, but there was no suggestion that you were going to fight the cops. . . . There was none of that.

"Then came King's assassination. And Chicago. Martin Luther King, of course, was an awesome figure. I think everybody felt that King's assassination was a key turning point, even more so than the Kennedy assassination. We were shocked and outraged, and everybody felt we were entering a new era.

"I think the summer of 1968 was definitely when I consolidated my world view. It became apparent to me that the United States was responsible for the cold war . . . at that point I realized that I believed in revolution.

"In Chicago, we were amazed—they were beating us up on TV. Some were delighted: The government was exposing its brutal side and proving one of our main points. A lot of other people who saw police violence on TV for the first time were outraged.

"After Chicago, the trial of the Catonsville Nine gained a lot of support in Baltimore. We had a week of activities based on the trial, punctuated by daily marches on the courthouse. On the opening date of the trial, I'll never forget it, we marched down Howard Street. There were 2,000 people—the biggest local march we'd had on the war. After Chicago, our orientation was "We don't want to get hurt. We don't want the cops to get angry, so therefore if they come near, we'll start chanting 'More Pay for Cops.' As soon as we approached the sidewalk, the police moved aside and pointed to the sidewalk—like they gave it to us.

"It was very clear that people were going to be burning draft cards because you couldn't have a demonstration without some people being seized by the zeitgeist and burning draft cards. The FBI would dash in and grab anyone burning a draft card.

"In the wake of Chicago, the population was on edge, primed for some confrontation, but when we actually got into the steets, our act was so clean. We were scrupulously into dialoguing with people on the side. If somebody was yelling at us, we didn't want to get back into a shouting match with them. In the course of the march and the week's activities, we interacted pretty positively with mainstream Baltimoreans.

"During the height of the antiwar movement, we collected a progressive peace tax. It was graduated, providing detailed guidelines for contributions depending on income. We were able to raise $500 a month, and people saw they were getting something for their money. We had a building with a mimeograph machine—the Peace Action Center at 2525 Maryland Avenue. The tax also paid for a full-time staff person, Gren Whitman.

"New people were always coming in. In 1968, we were surprised at how many people were coming toward us. In 1966 and 1967 the antiwar movement was a minority issue, but in 1968 after Chicago, and especially in 1969, the majority of people seemed to be against the war.

"Success produced its own crises too. It's hard to cope with success when you're used to being marginal. The Baltimore Defense Committee was the premier radical organization in the city because we were so big, and because we worked on a lot of other issues: housing, anti-

racist stuff, the first stirrings of the feminist movement. This was a multi-issue organization, but its main focus was on the war.

"We had masses of people flocking to us who really didn't go over the same material we went through—the same praxis. I'm using the word 'praxis' to mean learning by doing and learning by reading—the double process that goes on in a person's life at the same time. We learned so fast that we assumed that everybody else was getting it right away. That wasn't the case. After 1969, so many neophytes came in and didn't develop politically in any way. They were consumed with moral outrage against the war, and they were often the kinds of people who would start yelling at GIs that they were baby killers. The radical left did not do that—we were very conscious that GIs were a key constituency to organize. So we started coffeehouses and we started newspapers.

"The success I think is indisputable. There was nothing to match the 1960s in terms of the changes, the excitement and the vitality. We definitely were part of the conscience of America. There isn't a single issue you can think of— be it ecology or reproductive rights or school prayer, the Pledge of Allegiance or anything that doesn't relate in some way to what happened in the 1960s. But one of the prices that the American left pays for not having enduring organizations is that we tend to lose control over our own history and how that history is presented to the American public.

"I think people like myself are very representative in a lot of ways—white middle-class guys, pegged for a certain social role, who had their lives turned completely upside down by what happened in the 1960s. I think that happened for a lot of people, and . . . it is passed on. As ahistorical as America is, I think radical traditions do get passed on from generation to generation. As much as people forget."

Ann Gordon: Gay Rights Activist and Community Leader

IRENE REVILLE AND LINDA ZEIDMAN

Ann Gordon, gay rights activist and community leader, remembers the growth of the women's movement and the emergence of feminist politics in Baltimore in the early 1970s. "Reproductive rights issues were the launching pad for a lot of women who became and continue to be involved in feminist politics." That is why the People's Free Medical Clinic on Greenmount Avenue, organized by community activists in the Charles Village/Waverly neighborhood, became an important resource. "There was neonatal health care, birth control and domestic violence counseling and referral available at the clinic. Usually we would take that information and we would plaster laundromats with it and pretty much hand it out on the streets."

The clinic also housed a number of organizations that provided information and support services to women. One of them was the Women's Center, a community-based organization that promoted feminism through education, advocacy, and service. The Women's Center was the precursor of the Rape Crisis Center, now the Sexual Assault and Recovery Center staffed by 16 people who educate the community about rape prevention and provide supportive services to women and children who have been raped and sexually abused.

"Little more than a file folder and a hotline" is how Gordon describes the Lesbian Community Center, which also used space at the clinic. "The Lesbian Community

Ann Gordon

Center provided information and referral services, support groups, political advocacy, and cultural events." For Gordon, the growth of all of these institutions constituted "a real positive effort in the community."

The publication *Women: A Journal of Liberation* also played an important role in shaping feminist politics in Baltimore. "We used a lot of local talent to write articles, essays, poetry; even much of the artwork and photography was produced locally." According to Gordon, it was "the first regularly published women's liberation journal and subsequently spawned many newsletters, quarterlies, magazines, and other journals. The *Journal* was extremely well respected and read nationally and internationally."

The Women's Union, formed in 1972 and lasting until 1978, was also instrumental in defining feminist politics and practice in Baltimore. "Basically the Women's Union was concerned with exploring the politics of patriarchy, class, and race with a very, very local focus.

"The Women's Union held a lot of workshops, teach-ins, and outreach brunches that had a snappy name—

Coffee Break—and some very successful annual women's fairs. We had success with getting people who ordinarily wouldn't come to a meeting to come to the Women's Union.

"It was a socialist–feminist organization that was around a lot longer than many of the other women's unions in much larger towns." Gordon attributes this "to a kind of a self-deprecating sense of humor and flexibility in Baltimore. . . . We don't take ourselves as seriously and we aren't as humorless as activists in other cities that have been inflexible in the face of problems with sectarian political groups."

The problems that threatened to destroy the Women's Union centered on divergent views of lesbianism; the conflict served to define the politics of feminism. "Part of the ideology of lesbianism was that it was the logical extension of feminism—that feminism was the ideology and lesbianism was the practice. This analysis was extremely threatening to some straight feminists, while others simply and strongly disagreed with it.

"I guess taken to its logical extension, every time a

woman made love with another woman a little bit of the patriarchy was diminished in the process. I think the politicized Baltimore lesbian community came to believe this is not true, but it certainly held sway then. But Baltimore is not a place where lesbian separatism developed a following or any clout.

"Many of us who had worked for a long time in the vineyards of the civil rights movement, the antiwar movement, the labor movement, and the left had to hide our sexual orientation. That was painful. When you're exploring the root and the rightness of other issues about society and power and powerlessness, you cannot ignore the internal machinery that allows you to go out into the world and to function as a happy and constructive person. And accepting your sexuality, of course, is an important part of that.

"How the personal and the political fit together has always been a paradox for progressives. Why am I doing this? What enables me to keep doing this effectively? Certainly personal satisfaction and growth have to be a piece of that puzzle. I think lesbians figured that out pretty quick. Now through alternative psychology and the radical therapy movement, I think we all understand how important personal integration and wholeness are, because we've seen too many friends and associates burn out and not be able to continue to be effective in their organizing and political work if their personal stuff—their home stuff—isn't in good shape."

Gordon explains some of the difficulties lesbians had in finding places to socialize as well as some differences in the lesbian community: "The early women's community was helped along socially by the bars, many of which no longer exist. The bars were generally located in low-rent warehouse districts. The bar culture helped politicize the lesbians who came out of the women's movement and the antiwar movement. We learned about class and race discrimi-nation and oppression from meeting African-American and working-class lesbians at those bars because we were the outsiders there."

Gordon sees the women's movement as having a profoundly positive effect on the city as well as the state. "The Baltimore progressive community in the broadest sense . . . has been infused with and enhanced by the energies, experience, and leadership of people who have worked in feminist politics on a very basic organizing level in Baltimore. Many of us are women who have been through the experience of the Baltimore Women's Union. And as a whole the city is nourished and is enhanced by our experiences.

"Feminist political work in Baltimore enabled us to develop a commitment to equality for all women, of all races and classes, and the skills to organize effectively. Transforming political thought into positive action is a direct legacy of working in the women's movement. If the Reaganized Supreme Court continues to erode civil rights and women's right to choose, our experience in organizing communities will be repeated and expanded until we win the right to choose for all women."

In the spring of 1989 Gordon was recognized by the *Gay Paper, The Alternative*, and the Greater Baltimore Business and Professional Association for her work with the Baltimore Justice Campaign, a coalition that successfully passed a Lesbian and Gay Civil Rights Bill in Baltimore City in 1988, and for her work in co-producing the video documentary "Connecting the Pieces: A City's Response to the AIDS Quilt." A civil rights officer for the Maryland Department of Human Resources, Gordon was appointed to serve a three-year term on the Baltimore Community Relations Commission, and chairs the Mayor's Task Force on Gay and Lesbian Issues.

Newly completed rowhouses
in the Poplar Grove sec-
tion of West Baltimore at
Presstman Street and Bloom-
ingdale Road. The section
was developed in the 1910s
and 1920s.

Chapter 10 Flight to the Suburbs: Suburbanization and Racial Change on Baltimore's West Side

W. EDWARD ORSER

Would you like to live in the suburbs of Baltimore where you can enjoy the pure, fresh air of the country and at the same time have every city convenience? —Rowhouse advertisement, *ca.* 1910

If you ride west along the Route 40 corridor from downtown Baltimore's Howard Street to the Beltway, you will be on a seven-mile journey from the tidewater lowlands where the city first began along the banks of the Patapsco's harbor to the ring of westward hills on the edge of the piedmont plateau.

The brick rowhouses along Route 40 look very much part of the urban scene today, but successive sections at some point in the past were part of the suburban frontier of the expanding metropolis. The suburbs offered new housing opportunities with the appeal of the country and the convenience of the city. New transportation technologies in the post–Civil War era opened this suburban dream to a growing section of the populace able to afford it.

Movement outward was not only the result of the attraction of the country; it was also related to changing urban social conditions. Industrialization, congestion, and the presence of social groups deemed inferior or threatening—whether because of race, ethnicity, or social class—helped fuel relocation to the city's edge and beyond.

The suburban rowhouse developments almost always were exclusively white preserves. Their moderate cost appealed to middle-income buyers with both white- and blue-collar jobs.

Developers were quick to respond to this market. Until World War II, they usually opted for the rowhouse, which was efficient to build and produced a quick return on capital investment. Developers Edward J. Gallagher, Ephraim Macht, Frank Novak, and James Keelty filled this niche in Baltimore's expanding housing market, circling the old walking city with the modest brick rowhouses of the commuting suburban metropolis.

As white social havens, the new neighborhoods left behind an expanding population in a black ghetto. In the earlier walking city, blacks and whites had lived in close proximity to one another, though not necessarily in close social contact. The new means of transportation and the physical expansion of the city produced a pattern of clearly defined residential segregation, preserved by law and custom. As a result, by the turn of the century, Baltimore's black population was largely concentrated in two ghettos to the immediate northwest and northeast of the downtown

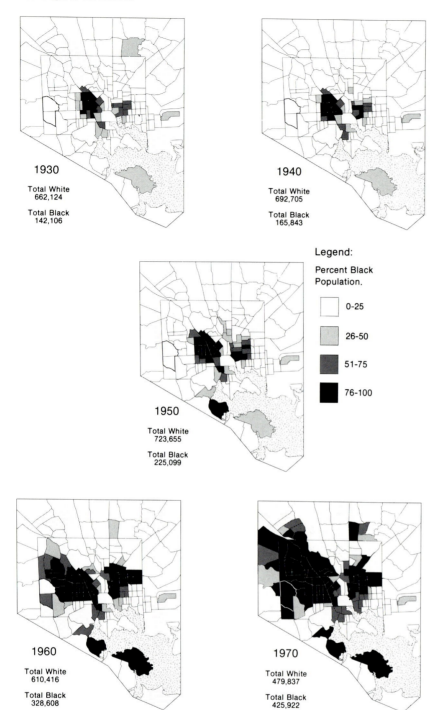

1930

Total White
662,124

Total Black
142,106

1940

Total White
692,705

Total Black
165,843

Legend:

Percent Black
Population.

0-25

26-50

51-75

76-100

1950

Total White
723,655

Total Black
225,099

1960

Total White
610,416

Total Black
328,608

1970

Total White
479,837

Total Black
425,922

Racial composition and
population, Baltimore City,
1930–1970. The census tracts
roughly corresponding to the
Edmondson Village area are
in bold outline on the city's
west side.

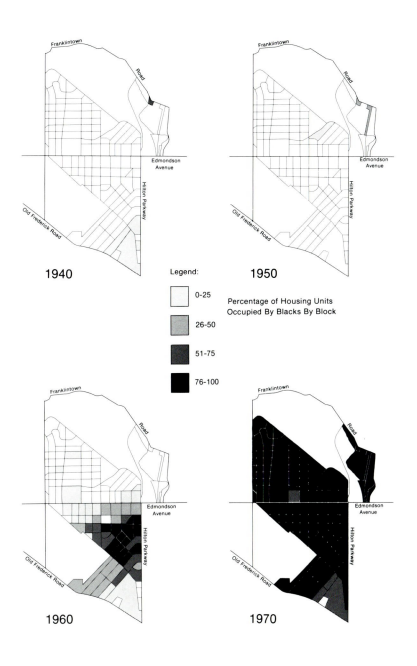

1940

1950

1960

1970

Legend:

0-25

26-50

51-75

76-100

Percentage of Housing Units
Occupied By Blacks By Block

Racial composition of the
Edmondson Village area,
1940–1970.

The Builder

Mr. and Mrs. James Keelty, Sr., as depicted in *St. Bernardine's Church, Silver Anniversary, 1928–1953.*

James Keelty's career typifies the rise of the rowhouse developers in late-nineteenth and early-twentieth-century Baltimore. Born in Ireland in 1869, Keelty was brought to Baltimore by his parents as a child of 10 or 11. Joseph Keelty describes his father's early career: "He was a stone-mason by trade. Being an entrepreneurial type, I guess he decided to build a few houses down on Calvert Street, in the area where Mercy Hospital is [today]."

Next, James Keelty turned to Greenmount Avenue, where he built several houses before selling the remainder of the land to a group that eventually used the site to erect Oriole Park, where Baltimore's minor league baseball team played in the early twentieth century. He then shifted operations to the west side, first building small groups of houses, then complete blocks, and eventually entire neighborhoods.

After modest rowhouse construction projects during the century's first decades on West Fayette and West Baltimore Streets and in the Poplar Grove section, Keelty set out in the 1920s to develop an entire neighborhood. From then until the early 1950s, the James Keelty Company built most of the hillside rowhouse community spanning Edmondson Avenue from the Gwynns Falls Bridge to the crest of the hill where the Edmondson Village Shopping Center was erected in 1947 by Jacob and Joseph Meyerhoff.

Keelty's so-called daylight rowhouse proved extremely popular. He prided himself on the quality of his construction, referring to himself in advertisements as "The Builder." During development of the Edmondson Avenue area, he maintained his office in the community and made himself accessible to residents, many of whom became satisfied homeowners.

Keelty's involvement in the community was also evident elsewhere. He contributed to the cost of the sanctuary of the new St. Bernardine's Roman Catholic Church, built in 1928 as a memorial to his recently deceased daughter. The church's distinctive gold dome is still a major landmark along Edmondson Avenue.

James Keelty died in 1948. His company erected its last Edmondson area rowhouses in 1954, then abruptly sold off its remaining land and left the community it had built. Increasingly, company operations concentrated on rowhouse and detached-house development in the suburban Catonsville and Towson (Rodger's Forge) sections of Baltimore County. Today, the Keelty Company operates primarily in the growing Timonium area of the county.

Looking west along the recently completed Interstate 170 from the Social Security Building at Greene Street, 1979. Franklin Street lines the corridor on the right, Mulberry Street on the left. One of the buildings in Murphy Homes, a public housing project erected in the early 1960s, is visible on the far right.

business district, a process described in Chapter 4. Periodically, the contest for residential space and the persistence of separate housing patterns erupted in episodes of black expansion into formerly white residential areas, followed by white flight and eventual resegregation.

Segregation has a long history in Baltimore's social relations, clearly evident in the nineteenth century and reaching its twentieth-century apex during the 1950s and 1960s. The pressure of black housing needs, the civil rights movement, and the role of blockbusting speculators combined to usher in a period of racial change of unprecedented proportions. Rapid and nearly total turnover occurred in large sections of the city, though nowhere more dramatically than from 1955 to 1965 in the Keelty-built Edmondson Village area, the focal point of this chapter.

The social struggles that grew out of this process are not unique to Baltimore, nor indeed to Baltimore's west side. But the particularly intense form they took there, especially the massive upheaval caused by blockbusting and white flight in the 1950s and 1960s, left an indelible stamp on the area's social geography, as tangible as the brick rowhouses that line the streets. To understand this connection is to understand the racial and class divisions that are the basis of both neighborhood identity and neighborhood isolation in metropolitan Baltimore.

Urban Frontier: The Fulton Avenue Bridge

Well inside the city's current boundaries, in the vicinity of Fulton Avenue, you can see the history of Baltimore's suburbanization in capsule form. This area was the "urban frontier" in the 1880s, represented the west side's racial dividing line in the 1930s and 1940s, and since that time has become a predominantly black area.

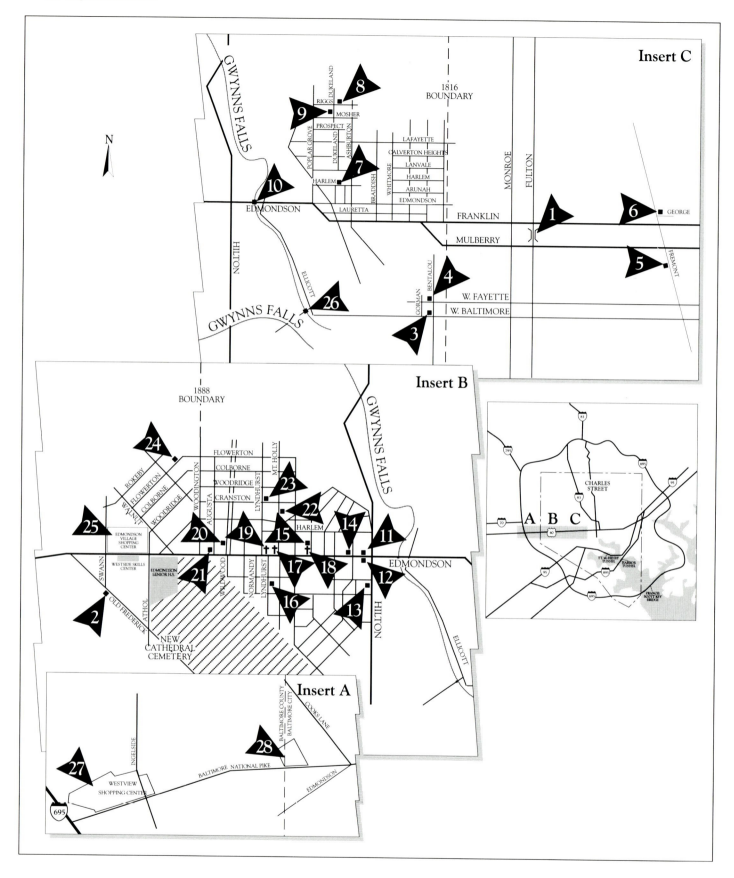

If you stand at the Fulton Avenue Bridge above Interstate 170 (*site 1*), you are at the approximate edge of the city of the 1880s. You could have walked to the city's center, visible to the east and approximately two miles away, or traveled to town by horsecar. The higher elevations of the ridge, visible approximately two miles to the west, afforded desirable locations for the rural retreats of the privileged few. One such country estate along this rural route was "Uplands," the summer home of Baltimore and Ohio Railroad magnate Robert Garrett and his wife Mary Frick Garrett. (Robert was the son of John Work Garrett, who is discussed in Chapter 2). "Uplands" is now the New Psalmist Christian School, at 4501 Old Frederick Road (*site 2*).

But the limited confines of the early walking city became overcrowded. In 1888, annexation extended the city's boundary nearly two miles farther west, opening up the section beyond Fulton Avenue for new development opportunities. Electrification of the trolleys in the 1890s brought potential house buyers to the expanding edge of the city where developers erected the modest two-story rowhouses that still line Franklin and Mulberry Streets, as well as the cross streets.

Several blocks to the southwest, James Keelty built some of his first "rows" on the west side in 1908, along the north side of the 2300 block of West Baltimore Street (*site 3*). In 1911, on the same block of West Fayette Street, he constructed rowhouses with

Neighborhood boys straddle the barrier separating Franklin Street from the exit ramp of the new I-170, 1979. Behind them are rowhouses of the "blind" type (three rooms deep), built around the turn of the century.

Pedestrians at the intersection of Fulton Avenue (Route 1, northbound) and Edmondson Avenue, 1951. Trees adorn Fulton, shading the rowhouses lining the street.

plain fronts, large central windows, and marble lintels—houses that were advertised as having "all improvements, annex taxes, low ground rent" (*site 4*). Sale prices of $1,100 to $1,275 put them within the reach of white middle-income buyers.

These 12-foot-wide rowhouses, like others typical of the era, were of the two-story, so-called blind type, meaning they were one room wide and three rooms deep with no outside windows in the middle rooms, although sometimes the upper rooms had skylights.

As areas of new white settlement extended farther to the west, periodic breaches in the invisible wall of residential segregation led to gradual expansion of the west-side ghetto. By the 1930s and 1940s, Fulton Avenue served as a distinct racial division street, with blacks restricted to the section roughly east of that line. But during and immediately following World War II, an expanding black population created explosive housing pressures. By the late 1940s and early 1950s, the demand for housing finally resulted in black settlement in adjacent white areas to the west of Fulton.

Following a pattern long established in Baltimore race relations, when blacks moved in, whites rapidly moved out. One black resident of the area remembers this episode of white flight:

Black people started moving out of the confined areas somewhere around 1947 or 1948, but what would happen was that whites would evacuate a block or two blocks, and black people would move in. The evacuation would take place first. I remember streets like Fulton Avenue, Monroe Street—they were once totally white, and they went through the transition and changed somewhere between 1946 and 1949—that was the time I was in the service. When I went in, there were no black people and when I came out, they were black streets. . . . But it wasn't integration . . . it was an evacuation.

While the movement of the color line brought new housing opportunities to some, the older section of black homes east of Fulton Avenue deteriorated in the post–World War II period. A 1944 *Baltimore Sun* reporter wrote: "Homes are very badly in need of repair and paint; dead rats lie in the street where they were crushed by automobiles; alleys are littered with debris and foul-smelling garbage; lots where homes formerly stood are covered with a thick layer of ashes."

City officials used such descriptions as a rationale for routing a new east–west urban expressway through the neighborhood. A 1945 report argued, "A trip afoot, making detours into the alleys, will be sufficient to convince most people of the need for cleaning out these slum areas."

After two decades of planning and controversy, demolition did occur in the late 1960s for the one-mile stretch of I-170 constructed in the 1970s. Costing $50 million, this project resulted in the demolition of 971 houses, 62 businesses, and a school. Resettlement of the mostly black, low-income residents in nearby, predominantly black neighborhoods created new pressures and problems in those communities.

The roadway ends abruptly a few blocks west of the Fulton Avenue Bridge. Opponents of its westward extension through neighborhoods and through Gwynns Falls and Leakin Parks joined in a citywide coalition with those fighting expressway development in Fells Point and South Baltimore (see Chapter 7). They eventually won their fight, prompting transportation officials to abandon plans for extending I-170.

Looking eastward, you can see the results of another strategy for slum removal: the high-rise public housing projects built during the 1950s and 1960s as part of Baltimore's urban renewal program. Lexington Terrace (south of I-170) and the George P. Murphy homes (on the north side) represent an attempt at meeting the needs of Baltimore's black population on the near west side (*sites 5 and 6*). But these projects eventually became towering slums.

Today, the nearby neighborhoods are 99 percent black. Average income is slightly more than half of that for the metropolitan area as a whole, and approximately 3 of every 10 households have incomes below the poverty level. The area's suburban era is long forgotten, as residents confront the stark realities of urban poverty.

Rowhouses by the Block or by the Neighborhood

As builders like Keelty gained capital from their successful small-scale developments, they frequently proceeded to larger enterprises with upgraded versions of the earlier house designs, seeking a slightly more affluent buyer. Keelty targeted the Poplar Grove section by Edmondson Avenue and Poplar Grove Street for development. Farther west in the city's 1888 annex and well served by suburban streetcar lines, it seemed the perfect location to build entire blocks of rowhouses.

The rowhouses on the 2700 and 2800 blocks of Harlem Avenue were built a block at a time and were advertised in 1912 for $1,350 to $1,400 (*site 7*). Their fronts of iron-spot brick with upper bay windows were set directly on the street, as the earlier westside Keelty rowhouses had been. But Keelty's 1916 rows—in the 2700 and 2800 blocks of Riggs Avenue and the 1000 and 1100 blocks of Dukeland, just to

A plastering crew working on a Keelty family project, *ca.* 1920. Standing with his hands folded in the center is the plastering contractor, Gideon Sauter, who lived in Catonsville. The dwelling, located on Edmondson Avenue near Kingston Road, was the home of Patrick Keelty, brother and business associate of James Keelty. The man standing on the right with the black hat may be Patrick Keelty. Note the two black laborers, standing apart on the left, who served as hod carriers.

the north—suggest a shift to a new suburban style (*sites 8 and 9*). Set back from the street with small yards and stone porch fronts, these buildings offered amenities that might appeal to those seeking new housing on the urban fringe.

The end of World War I produced a record housing boom, and developers like Keelty expanded their operations to meet the new demands. Keelty looked westward to the hill beyond Poplar Grove across the Edmondson Avenue bridge over the Gwynns Falls, an area inhabited by only 97 people in 1910 (*site 10*). Systematically acquiring large tracts of land in the late 1910s and early 1920s, Keelty set out to develop an entire neighborhood along Edmondson Avenue. By 1930, the hillside population had surged to 8,991, the majority settling in Keelty-built rowhouses. The gracefully arched bridge, completed in 1910 to replace a wooden trestle structure, became the gateway to this next era in suburban rowhouse living.

Evolution of the Rowhouse

Housing at the bottom of the hill, near the intersection of Edmondson Avenue and Hilton Street, is a veritable museum of the rowhouse adaptations developers experimented with in efforts to capture the new suburban market. For example, the areaway-type house built about 1910 is evident on the north side of the 3300 block of Edmondson Avenue (*site 11*). Narrow spaces between the rear rooms of every two houses provided air and sunlight to the middle rooms, which formerly had no windows. These houses were still only 10 to 12 feet wide, but they boasted a depth of 45 feet and fronts with porches and upper bay windows.

Across the street, on the south side of the same block, pairs of duplex rowhouses have narrow alleys extending the entire length of every other house to allow for windows along the outside wall of each (*site 12*). Two blocks south, in the 300 and 400 blocks of Hilton Street, houses built in the late 1910s by Judd Stevens represented a particularly fine version of the duplex, with bay windows on the narrow open side affording ample light to the center rooms (*site 13*). These houses were promoted as overlooking the new Gwynns Falls Park, whose valley was considered a natural buffer from older parts of the city.

About 1915, the designation of Gwynns Falls Park as one of the stream valley parks in the city's new park system, following the recommendations of the noted Frederick Law Olmsted landscape design firm, brought strollers to the millrace path.

Construction on the Edmondson Avenue bridge, looking west, 1909. The new, higher bridge portion had been completed on the right, while the old, lower span was still in use on the left. Beyond are two of the few houses on the hill at the time; one belonged to William Linthicum.

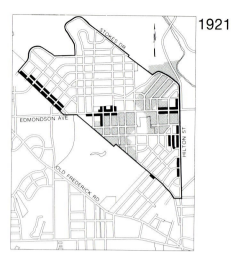

1921

Development of the Edmondson Area

Development of the Edmondson area, 1921–1941. The street network is shown as it existed in 1980.

LEGEND:

▨ Keelty Properties

▬ Housing

— Limit of Study Area

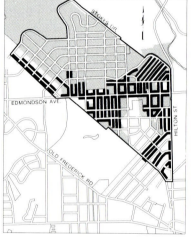

1931

Edmondson Avenue Area (in bold) on Baltimore's West Side

1941

(Source: Baltimore City Tax Records. Street network as of 1982.)

Traffic along Edmondson Avenue straddles the double tracks of the streetcar line in this view looking west from the vicinity of Hilton Street, 1954. Rowhouses on the right are typical Keelty Company daylights, built in the early 1920s. Beyond them stand two community institutions, the Edgewood movie theater (now the Olivet Baptist Church) and St. Bernardine's Roman Catholic Church.

But the daylight rowhouse was the most popular style built by Keelty from the 1920s onward. A distinctive advance in rowhouse design, there are examples of it in the 3400 block of Edmondson, which begins as standard rows and ends as daylights (*site 14*), the 600 block of Grantley (*site 15*), and most of the other cross streets up the Edmondson Avenue hill. For other Keelty daylight houses of this era, see the 300 and 400 blocks of Lyndhurst Street and Normandy Avenue (*site 16*).

The daylight (sometimes called "sunlight") house had at least one outside window in each room. The design eliminated the need for the narrow areaway by creating wider fronts and shallower depths—typically 20 to 22 feet wide and 35 feet deep. Upstairs,

each of the three or four bedrooms had at least one window. Downstairs, an entry hall with stairs and spacious living room occupied the front, and the dining room and kitchen both had windows to the rear.

For the buyer, the daylight rowhouse meant a spacious, pleasant house at a modest cost that made homeownership possible for middle-income people. For the developer, the slight decrease in density (two of the newer rowhouse fronts were as wide as three conventional rowhouses) was offset by economies of rowhouse construction: shared walls, common utility lines, and simultaneous erection.

Between 1920 and 1940, homeownership along Edmondson Avenue stood substantially above 50 percent, thanks to moderate prices and easy terms. For example, Robert Lansinger, a postal worker, made a $100 down payment on a $3,650 purchase price for a house in the 4000 block of West Franklin Street in 1922.

As consistent as the housing styles in Keelty's new developments was the social homogeneity of the new community, one very significant product of the streetcar/auto era. Residents were a vanguard of Baltimore's growing class of moderate-income white people seeking housing opportunities on the city's suburban edge. They were predominantly young families who had moved from older areas of the city, primarily on the west side. All were white and most had white-collar or blue-collar, middle-level occupations. Very few women worked outside the home.

In a new neighborhood with few other institutions, churches provided important centers for community activity and identity for a population approximately evenly divided between Catholics and Protestants. During the 1920s, St. Bernardine's Roman Catholic Church at 3812 Edmondson Avenue was built by James Keelty (*site 17*). Several Protestant churches, including the nearby Christ Edmondson United Methodist Church and All Saints Lutheran Church—now Mount Olive Holy Evangelistic Church —were also established to serve the religious and social needs of the new community (*sites 18 and 19*).

Keelty daylight rowhouses reached the apex of their appeal on the west side when, in the late 1920s and early 1930s, he began to develop Wildwood along the ridgetop Wildwood Parkway off Edmondson Avenue. Billed as "English type," these dwellings represented an upgraded form of the basic daylight box. Houses in the 600 block along the west side are a good example; see also the 600 block of nearby Augusta Avenue (*sites 20 and 21*). They were distinguished from the earlier houses primarily by slightly more spacious dimensions (some were 22 by 37 feet, with an additional half-story in a gabled attic); quality features such as slate roofs, copper spouting, tile porches, and fireplaces; architectural variation— gabled roofs, red Tudor brickwork; and architectural variety within the row.

Keelty ads for Wildwood evoked the suburban ideal of a natural setting with urban conveniences:

"Baltimore's newest suburban development," they boasted, was "splendidly convenient to the cars [streetcars], churches of various denominations, schools, stores and banks, and but a quarter hour's drive to the city." Yet the development enjoyed the benefits of nearby parkland and a ridgetop location— "standing on the front porch of these homes you can see all over the city."

The Great Depression curbed Keelty's development of Wildwood, while World War II interrupted further construction. In the late 1930s, he built more modest versions, such as the narrower English-style houses in the 700 and 800 blocks of Mt. Holly Street and the 3800 block of Cranston Avenue (*sites 22 and 23*).

After World War II, Keelty again responded to a booming housing market by developing extensive land holdings to the north and west of Wildwood, by then building in the popular colonial style, involving only modest architectural adaptation of the basic daylight floor plan. Rowhouses along Flowerton, from Woodington to Walnut, illustrate this era in the builder's development (*site 24*).

The First Regional Shopping Center

The housing boom after World War II also brought the Edmondson Village Shopping Center, along the 4400 and 4500 blocks of Edmondson Avenue—claimed to be the first regional suburban shopping center of harmonious design on the East Coast when it was erected in 1947 (*site 25*). The center provided the large Edmondson Avenue section with the commercial core it had long lacked, and Edmondson Village quickly gained acceptance as the entire neighborhood's name.

The new shopping center opened on May 7, 1947, occupying the site of the former Edward Austin Jenkins estate, "Hunting Ridge," a pre–Revolutionary War mansion with a commanding view of the Baltimore area. Developers for the center were Jacob and Joseph Meyerhoff. Joseph had come to the United States in 1906 with his Russian-Jewish parents. In the 1920s and 1930s he built housing in northeast and northwest Baltimore. Joined by his brother Jacob ("Jack"), the two turned to large-scale residential development in the Dundalk–Essex area after World

Christmas lights at the
Edmondson Village
Shopping Center, 1958

Two mothers walk their children across the intersection of Poplar Grove and Franklin Streets, September 1950. In the background, along Edmondson Avenue, are an Arundel ice cream store and Ludwig's drugstore. Within a very few years, the area made a near-total racial changeover.

War II. Edmondson Village was their first shopping center, though later Joseph built the Westview and Eastpoint centers under a separate company.

The most striking aspect of Edmondson Village Shopping Center was its handsome Williamsburg architecture. The red brick colonial village motif was enhanced by such architectural variations as irregular roof lines, bay and dormer windows, and gables, which masked the actual regularity of the straight strip design. Notable, too, was its provision for cars, a clear sign of changing times. The center was set back from Edmondson Avenue to allow for parking lots in front, depressed below street level to maximize the view from the avenue.

When the center opened, it boasted an anchor department store (Hochschild Kohn), 29 shops and stores, and a clubhouse for community organizations

and activities. In 1949, recreational functions were enhanced by the opening of a large movie theater and bowling alley below. The addition in 1956 of a Hecht branch department store across the street contributed to the regional appeal of the center, even though the store did not conform to the village's architectural style.

Residents of the area from the 1950s have fond memories of the Edmondson Village Center and its role in the neighborhood. Most often remembered are the monkeys in the windows of the Hess shoe store, the fascination of children who came there to buy shoes or get their hair cut, and the lights that outlined the shops at Christmas time, drawing crowds from far and wide. Ads stressed the aspirations of the center to regional prominence, as when the third-anniversary flyer in 1950 claimed that "Baltimoreans make it a point of pride to bring out-of-town visitors to Edmondson Village, a landmark to Baltimore progress." The center provided the entire community with a place to shop, but it was also a focal point, a meeting place, a town square.

Blockbusting: Housing Push and Pull in the 1950s and 1960s

In retrospect, the 1950s represented the culmination of the rowhouse version of suburbia. In 1954, the James Keelty Company abruptly sold off its remaining undeveloped tracts in Edmondson Village and concentrated on rowhouse and detached-house developments in the Baltimore County suburbs of Catonsville and Towson.

The 1950s also brought a dramatic challenge to the way of life the older rowhouse suburbs had engendered as insulated and secure havens from the racial and social diversity of the metropolis. The 1954 U.S. Supreme Court ruling that segregated schools were unconstitutional—followed quickly by the Baltimore School Board's decision to integrate the city's schools—was only one of many challenges to the old pattern of race relations.

In Baltimore, extreme housing pressures had been building in areas of black settlement, and by the early 1950s, the residential color line had moved a full mile west of the wartime Fulton Avenue boundary to reach Poplar Grove, just across the Edmondson Avenue bridge from Keelty's hillside developments. To people in the Edmondson Village area, however, it was conventional wisdom that blacks would never cross the bridge; natural and social boundaries had always felt secure, and housing integration was not an alternative whites were willing to consider.

The 1950s also brought unprecedented suburban expansion for white Baltimoreans, with new houses and apartments rapidly filling up the remaining tracts within the city limits, then leapfrogging into the metropolitan counties beyond, just as the Keelty Company had done. If white rowhouse dwellers were feeling the push of the urban population, they were also attracted by the pull of the metropolitan frontier, where detached housing set the new suburban standard.

About 1955, the first black settlers crossed the Gwynns Falls valley to settle in the southeastern corner of the Edmondson area near the Baltimore Street Bridge, some six blocks south of the corner of Edmondson and Hilton (*site 26*). What ensued was panicked white flight, fueled by systematic blockbusting by real estate speculators. In the words of one white resident: "When the [black] people started moving into the neighborhood, they did come in, literally, block by block. I can recall when they came across the . . . bridge, everybody was very upset; they said, 'Oh my God, they're over the bridge now; our street will be next.'"

By 1960, the area immediately south of Edmondson Avenue had changed from its 1950 racial composition of more than 99 percent white to 62 percent black. In 1970, the same area was 92 percent black. North of Edmondson Avenue, the racial line remained virtually intact in 1960, with a population 99 percent white. But during the early years of the 1960s, population there also changed drastically, and the section was 97 percent black by 1970.

Blockbusting preyed equally on white racial fears and black housing needs to reap a profit for blockbusters. Typically, they offered premium prices to the first whites to sell, often specifically alluding to the prospect of potential racial change in the area and to the threat of lowered property values for those not wise enough to see the handwriting on the wall. Having secured the first house by such means, blockbusters quickly installed black tenants in the house— sometimes renters, sometimes buyers. After sowing the seeds of racial change, the blockbuster then proceeded to reap the harvest by purchasing the remaining houses, often at prices below market value.

These tactics were extremely effective. As one area resident remembers, "It was gradual—then a rush. . . . A lot of people said they would never sell their houses to blacks, and they were the first ones to do it." Another recalls:

The only thing that people kept secret was whether they were going to be one of the first sellers—everybody would say, "Well, if I move, I'm not going to sell to blacks, I'm only going to sell to whites"—they would tell this to their neighbors, because they didn't want to be thought of as contributing to the problem. But, of course, there wasn't anybody but the blacks who were going to buy the houses, so everybody did sell to blacks in the end.

A white homeowner reflects on the way in which blockbusting divided family and friends from one another:

If you were depending on a certain number of neighbors to stick it out so you'd have white neighbors, forget it! Even my dear uncle. . . . Guess when we found out he was moving? The day the moving van pulled up! This was right next door, and he never told us one word about it.

Having little prior experience with blacks, sheltered in a totally white suburban environment, and apparently feeling quite vulnerable to the economic threat represented by blockbusting tactics, whites fled the settled environs of their neighborhood in panic proportions. In doing so, they repeated a long established pattern: Rather than accommodate to racial change, they joined what some of them called "the exodus." As one white former resident observed: "They saw a very secure world changing very drastically, and they couldn't accept it. This was distasteful, and in some respects, it was forced down their throats, and they felt they had no choice, I guess."

Some new black residents could not help feeling that the reason had been racism, pure and simple. As one said, "They were friendly people, but they were prejudiced; they didn't want to live where colored people did. . . . They don't have to say it. . . . They didn't tell you [why]; they just moved."

While the new black settlers undoubtedly benefited from the housing opportunity, they usually did so at a steep price—the blockbuster's profit. In 1969, after racial turnover in the Edmondson area was virtually complete, an interracial fair housing coalition, whose members called themselves The Activists, began picketing and other protest activities against the Morris Goldseker Company outside its West Franklin Street offices downtown.

The Goldseker firm had played a major role in real estate transactions on Edmondson Avenue during the racial change process, operating through a variety of fronts. The Activists presented evidence that the average markup for house sales in the Edmondson area had been double the increase in a comparable Baltimore neighborhood where blockbusting had not occurred. For example, their studies found that Goldseker-related companies in the section north of Edmondson Avenue purchased houses for an average of $7,320 and then sold them immediately for an average of $12,387, a markup of $5,067 (69 percent). This difference they called the black tax, and they felt the conclusion was clear: "The dollar in the hands of the white man buys more than the dollar in the hands of the black man."

Black Suburban Pioneers

Racial change, which had begun in 1955 in the area's southeast corner, reached the area's northwest boundary, beyond Wildwood Parkway, by 1965. In 1970, the two census tracts primarily composing the community were 94 percent black.

Despite the destabilizing and exploitative conditions under which blacks gained new housing and the unsettling pace of racial change, the community of black pioneer settlers achieved remarkably high rates of residential stability and ownership. For example, homeownership rates in the area stood at 58 percent in 1970 and at 64 percent in 1980. Such rates represented considerable achievement under the circumstances; undoubtedly, they also represented some measure of real economic strain.

In terms of social and economic status, black pioneer settlers actually resembled the area's former white residents more than they differed from them. For many, Edmondson Village afforded blacks the same promise of the suburban dream that had brought whites to the area: improved housing opportunity, more space, and a more secure neighborhood. As one resident said, "When I moved to this neighborhood, I said, 'Gee, it's so nice and clean'—it was just a perfect place, and convenient to everything. I walked around the neighborhood and saw all the beautiful houses, and Edmondson Village [Shopping Center] was so nice, and I just couldn't believe it— it seemed that it was just like a little colonial town." High prices and shaky finance mechanisms created burdens but, as one resident put it, blacks had little

Young residents pose outside the newly repainted recreation building in the Lyndhurst section of Edmondson Village, 1985.

choice if they wanted new housing opportunities: "When you've been down and out, you know they [the speculators] are having a field day, but that's what you want, and you're going to pay that. It's a dream you want to come true, so you will pay."

However, this aging rowhouse district would not afford the newer residents the same suburban dream it had their white predecessors. The reality was that a segregated dual housing market made it less likely that the new black community could maintain the middle-income character of the previous white community. While the average income of new black residents was not substantially lower than the average for the whites who had left, frequently the job status of blacks was less advantageous, and the prospects for advancement less strong. Moreover, there was a proportionally smaller pool of potential new settlers of similar status.

Unquestionably, a slow but steady decline in the socioeconomic status of community residents occurred during the 1960s and 1970s. In 1960, black settlers in the neighborhood had average incomes only slightly below the level of their white neighbors. Ten years later, when the area had completely changed racially, black Edmondson Village residents had incomes 9 percent below the metropolitan average and, by 1980 (the last year for which figures are available), median income had slipped 20 percent below the metro figures.

A Shopping Center Declines, a Church Is Reborn

The changing status of the Edmondson Village Shopping Center might be viewed as a symbol of some of the hopes and frustrations of the black settlers, as well as an index of the changing prospects of the community. When black pioneers began to patronize the center in the late 1950s and early 1960s, it was still in its heyday, and as such was a major attraction to settlement in the area. But a racially changing neighborhood and rapid suburbanization in the metropolitan area combined to doom the center and its service to the community.

In 1958, Joseph Meyerhoff's Westview Shopping Center was completed two miles west, at the inter-

section of Route 40 and the new circumferential Baltimore Beltway, the suburb's new main street (*site 27*). Hochschild's, Edmondson Village's first department store, closed in 1974, and Hecht's closed five years later (23 years after it was built), confirming the common perception that the center was declining dramatically. The former was still vacant in 1990; the latter has been renovated as the Westside Skills Center.

By the mid 1970s, the shopping center was owned by an absentee landlord (Harry Weinberg's Honolulu Limited) with no apparent interest in revitalization. Until recently, concerted community organizing has had little success in improving the center, but in 1987 a local firm, JHP Realty, leased the center and initiated a series of renovations.

Why did the Edmondson center decline? Current residents tend to blame the owner and the merchants, the latter because they cut back on the quality of merchandise and the level of service when the clientele became increasingly black. Others note such economic factors as the decreased buying power of the new residents, combined with competition from outer suburban centers. Still others see it as a symbol of negative changes in the community as a whole, an area whose housing stock has begun to show signs of age and deterioration, and whose social and economic status has shown some erosion in recent years.

If the decline of the center is a symbol of the new community's disappointments, St. Bernardine's Roman Catholic Church offers a counterexample. It is one of the few neighborhood institutions to make the transition from a predominantly white to a predominantly black constituency. When new black residents first attended the church, they were met with coldness and hostility. In 1975, however, after most of the congregation's white members had left the area and the church's future was very much in doubt, two young priests—one white and the other black— were assigned to reach out to the black community.

The results were dramatic. Not only was the worship style adapted to the traditions of a black congregation, but the church became a center for local social and political programs. Today, neighborhood participation in the church is high, and St. Bernardine's is one of a number of community-building institutions in Edmondson Village.

The Suburbs Today

Along Route 40, a mile west of the Edmondson Village Shopping Center, past rowhouse and detached-house developments dating from the 1910s through the 1950s, the 1918 boundary separates Baltimore City and Baltimore County as political jurisdictions (*site 28*). Although the line is invisible, in recent decades it has divided an increasingly black city from a predominantly white county. In 1970, for instance, Baltimore City's black population constituted 46 percent of the total, while across this line, in Baltimore County, the comparable percentage was 3 percent. By 1980, the black percentage of the city population was 55 percent; for the county, it was 8 percent.

The Baltimore Beltway and Westview Shopping Center serve as the western terminus of this chapter. This section of the beltway was completed in 1959. Westview opened the preceding year, boasting a central mall design then considered innovative. In recent years, the mall has been renovated and enclosed in an effort to help the center remain competitive with newer shopping malls serving developing suburbs beyond the beltway.

Many of the earlier restrictions on black settlement have changed, both in law and in practice, and the traumatic blockbusting that occurred in Edmondson Village during the 1950s and 1960s has not been repeated on any comparable scale. Some formerly exclusively white areas, on both sides of the city/county line, have been integrated without necessarily producing white flight. Still, the legacy of blockbusting and white flight remains part of Baltimore's social reality. Black settlement in formerly all-white suburban neighborhoods continues to pose the question whether the result will be integration or eventual resegregation.

Meanwhile, the suburban fringe has pushed far to the west, across the Patapsco River into rapidly expanding sections of Howard and Carroll Counties, doubling the distance from the city center reached by the 1950s and 1960s in the Westview area. Many of these areas tend to be relatively affluent and predominantly white preserves. Thus, in spite of some change, the traditional pattern of new suburbs as havens, older urban areas as resegregated and secondhand suburbs repeats itself in the push and pull of the contemporary metropolis.

Acknowledgment: The author wishes to acknowledge the support afforded by colleagues in the American Studies Department at the University of Maryland Baltimore County and the generous cooperation of the residents of Edmondson Village, past and present.

The shops and leisure-time
activities of Harborplace contrast with the new financial
offices that rise above it.

Chapter 11 A View from Federal Hill

DAVID HARVEY

An' they hide their faces,
An' they hide their eyes,
'Cos the city's dyin'
An' they don' know why;
Oh! Baltimore!
Man it's hard, jus livin'
Jus livin'.
—Randy Newman

A city center, it has been said, is a great book of time and history. The view of Baltimore from Federal Hill (*site 1*) is an impressive introduction to that book and conveys a powerful image of what the city is about. But we have to learn to read all the signs of the landscape.

Certain things stand out in a city. A medieval European city immediately signals that religion and aristocracy were the chief sources of power by the way cathedrals and castles dominate. The United States struggled long and hard to get rid of aristocratic privilege, but Baltimore's downtown skyline says that a financial aristocracy is alive and well. As you look down on the city from Federal Hill, banks and financial institutions tower over everything else,

proclaiming in glass, brick, and concrete that they hold the reins of power.

The Federal Building (*site 2*), buried in the midst of all these financial institutions, signals a system of governance that is, as Mark Twain once put it, "the best that money can buy." City Hall (*site 3*), attractive and classical though it may be, is neither centrally located nor conspicuous enough to suggest it has more than a marginal role to play in determining the city's fate. As for churches, they can be seen only when you look across the densely packed rowhouses of ethnic and working-class East Baltimore. God, it seems, has meaning for the working class; mammon is fully in control downtown.

The other image that stands out is the importance of water, of Chesapeake Bay, which formed Baltimore's commercial lifeline to the world and became the nexus for much of its now declining manufacturing industry. Signs of those connections abound: the Domino Sugar plant (*site 4*), grain elevators, the chemical plant, and oil tanks that line the edge of the bay, as it opens out from Federal Hill toward the Bethlehem Steel plant at Sparrows Point (*site 5*), and the Dundalk Marine Terminal (*site 6*), still one of the most important ports of entry on the East Coast of the United States.

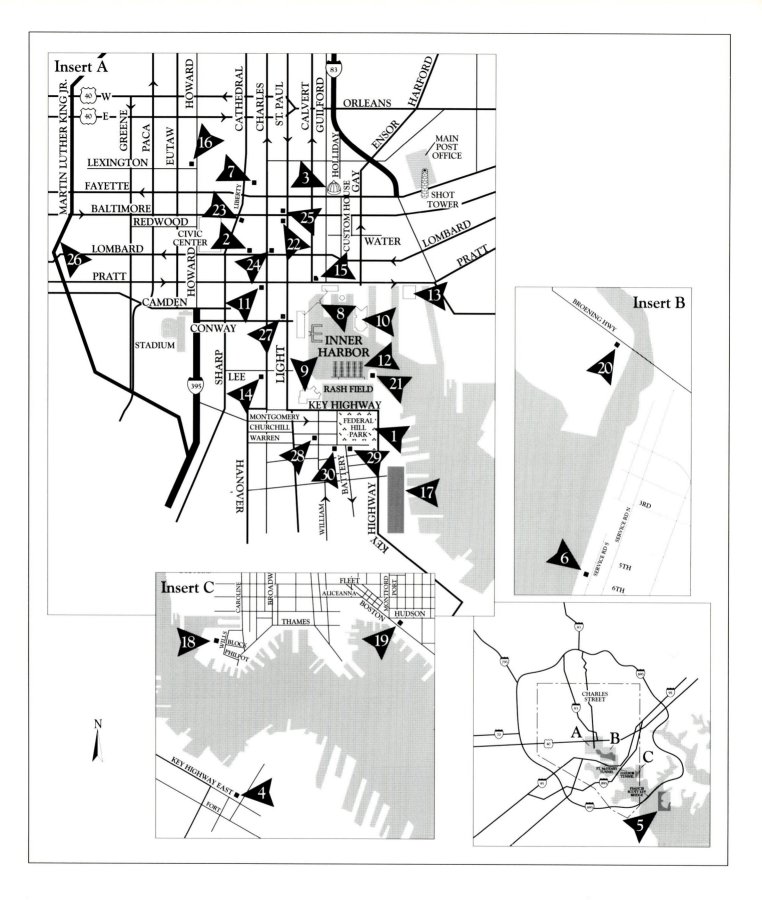

Italic type indicates original building site or function.

* indicates original building is not extant.

1. Federal Hill

2. The Federal Building

3. City Hall

4. Domino Sugar plant

5. Bethlehem Steel plant, Sparrows Point

6. Dundalk Marine Terminal

7. Charles Center

8. Pavilions at Harborplace

9. Maryland Science Center

10. National Aquarium

11. Convention Center

12. Marina at Inner Harbor

13. Power Plant at Inner Harbor

14. Harbor Court

15. Gallery at Inner Harbor

16. *Hutzler's Palace*

17. *Bethlehem Steel shipyards*

*18. Allied Chemical plant

19. American Can Company

20. Western Electric plant

21. Rusty Scupper at Inner Harbor

22. Maryland National Bank

23. Mercantile Safe Deposit and Trust Company

24. First National Bank

25. *Merritt Commercial Savings and Loan*, now Citibank

26. Martin Luther King Boulevard

27. Hyatt-Regency Hotel

28. 820 Churchill Place, condominium

29. *Shofer Furniture Warehouse*; called The Paper Mill by developers; now Federal Park Condominium

30. *Southern High School*, now Harbor View

Baltimore harbor in 1930s

Downtown and the Inner Harbor, from Federal Hill, 1966.
The Maryland National Bank
Building dominates the center,
illustrating the power and authority of financial institutions
compared to those of politics,
symbolized by the less conspicuous Federal Building on
the left and the dome of City
Hall on the right.

Downtown and the Inner Harbor from Federal Hill, 1988.
The Federal Building and
City Hall are engulfed by the
mass of buildings given over
to financial functions and the
pavilions of Harborplace, a
center of leisure and consumerism sprawled around the
Inner Harbor edge.

Nor is it hard to imagine that the Inner Harbor, now important as a tourist attraction and leisure park, was once the main port of entry to the city. Indeed, those functions were preserved there until shortly after World War II.

Though the view from Federal Hill tells us much about the city, it cannot tell us how what we see came into being. How was Baltimore built? Who decided that it should be a tourist mecca rather than an industrial city? Why do the buildings look the way they do, and to what traditions are they monuments?

Charles Center

Most of the downtown skyline has been in place since 1970 or so, though a transitional period dates to the mid 1950s. By then, the boom in production and trade that had powered Baltimore's economy dur-

ing World War II had begun to fade. Strong currents of suburbanization, both of industry and of population (see Chapter 10), particularly the more affluent whites, the immigration of poor rural African Americans from the South, and the shift of port functions to deep water down the bay left Baltimore's downtown and inner city in a parlous state.

The formation of the Greater Baltimore Committee (GBC), an association of local business leaders, in 1956 marked a turning point. The committee recognized that downtown deterioration threatened the future of business in the city and that it was politically dangerous for any ruling elite to abandon the symbolic and political center of the metropolitan region to an underclass of impoverished blacks and marginalized whites.

The committee developed a plan and then pres-

The Mies van der Rohe building, One Charles Center, centerpiece of Baltimore's first attempts at downtown revitalization, 1988.

Tour boats, the converted Power Plant, and Scarlett Place, captured in a view from the pavilions of the Inner Harbor redevelopment.

vestment, Charles Center (*site 7*) was essentially completed by the late 1960s. Modernist in design (its Mies van der Rohe building is considered a classic), Charles Center houses office workers and financial or governmental institutions in somewhat arid modern buildings punctuated by bleak open public spaces.

The city, it was argued, would receive two main benefits from such development: The increase in employment would help the city's economy, and the increase in the tax base would provide the city with more resources to meet the needs of its poor. Unfortunately, from the beginning, Charles Center was conceived and built as a property development scheme of direct benefit to corporate and finance capital. The city as a whole received very little benefit from it. Much of the new downtown employment, particularly in skilled and well-paying jobs, went to residents of the suburbs. The jobs created for city residents were either in temporary construction or low-paying services.

Moreover, Charles Center was so heavily subsidized that it was a drain on, rather than a benefit to, the city's tax base. This was particularly true before an upward revaluation in 1975, a year after it was revealed that tax assessments in Charles Center were lower than they had been before redevelopment.

The Inner Harbor

With the completion of Charles Center in the late 1960s, downtown realtors and business leaders turned their attention to the Inner Harbor. Plans were laid to extend development to the decaying waterfront of derelict piers and crumbling warehouses, marks of Baltimore's once significant water trade now rendered obsolete by the trucks that rolled across the expanding network of federally subsidized highways.

There were few takers for developing this zone until the early 1970s. And it took a basic shift in orientation and philosophy to bring about this new and most recent phase of construction.

Baltimore, like many cities in the 1960s, was racked by race riots and civil strife. Concentrated in the abandoned and decayed inner cities, this breakdown in civil order focused on racial discrimination in job and housing markets, unemployment, and the

sured city government into pursuing a downtown urban renewal project that would revive property development and corporate power in the downtown core. Federal urban renewal funds were available, Mayor Thomas D'Alesandro was persuaded, and the Greater Baltimore Committee/Charles Center Management Corporation was formed to promote and organize the renewal. This was the first of a succession of quasi-public agencies, dominated by corporate and business interests and outside any democratic control, that were to shape downtown renewal efforts over the next 20 years.

After nearly $40 million in public expenditures, which attracted a further $145 million of private in-

The postmodernism of Scarlett Place, with its preserved
nineteenth-century seed
warehouse on its lefthand corner and its attempt to simulate
a Mediterranean-style hilltop
village, contrasts with the
austere modernism of Mies
van der Rohe.

Baltimore riots in 1968, following the assassination of
Dr. Martin Luther King, Jr.,
resulted in significant property damage in several of the
city's neighborhoods. The
riots dramatically enacted the
deep racial tensions of the city
and represented the first time
since the railroad riots of 1877
that the National Guard was
summoned to Baltimore to
enforce state power.

disempowerment and impoverishment of much of
the city's African-American population. Investment
in the inner city seemed neither safe nor profitable.
The urban spectacles that drew the crowds downtown were race riots, antiwar demonstrations, and
all manner of countercultural events.

The riots and burnings that gutted areas of Gay
Street and North Avenue in the wake of the assassination of Dr. Martin Luther King, Jr., in April 1968,
left six people dead, some 5,000 arrested, massive
property damage, and streets patrolled by the military. In 1970, a day-long skirmish between youths
and the police at the city's flower mart—an annual
event promoted by Baltimore's elite since 1911—
indicated that anger was common to disempowered
blacks and discontented white youths.

On October 25, 1973, a group of women representing Baltimore's elite placed a plaque at the Washington Monument to commemorate the end of the
flower mart. At the time it seemed a fitting symbol of
the lack of confidence and social malaise that inhib-
ited any investment in the city's future. The business
climate in downtown Baltimore could not have been
less propitious.

It was precisely in this context that many in the city
sought for some way to restore a sense of civic pride,
some way to bring the city together as a working
community, some way to overcome the siege men-
tality with which investors and the citizenry viewed
the inner city and its downtown spaces. The coalition
that was to form was much broader than the Greater
Baltimore Committee. It included church and civil
rights leaders, distressed that the riots generated as
much self-inflicted pain as social redress for those
doing the rioting; academics and professionals, including downtown lawyers, suddenly made aware of

Where the Jobs Have Gone

The recession of 1980–1983 brought a powerful wave of job losses to the Baltimore region, as illustrated in this list of cutbacks in manufacturing and retail establishments from 1980 through 1985. The list is adapted from a chart appearing in the *Baltimore Sun*, March 21, 1985. Companies marked with an asterisk have shut down operations completely.

Company	Type of business	Number of jobs lost
*Acme Markets	Grocery chain	1,200
*Airco Welding	Cored wire	150
*Allied Chemical	Chromium	145
Bethlehem Steel	Steel	7,000
*Bethlehem Steel Shipyard	Ship repair	1,500
*Brager-Gutman	Retail stores	180
*Cooks United	Discount stores	220
Esskay	Meat packing	240
General Electric	Electrical products	550
General Motors	Auto parts and distribution	247
*Korvette's	Department stores	350
*Maryland Glass	Glass	325
*Maryland Shipping & Drydock	Ship repair	1,500
Max Rubins	Apparel	225
*Misty Harbor Raincoat	Rainwear	210
*Pantry Pride	Grocery chain	4,000
*Plus Discount Stores	Discount stores	150
*Two Guys	Discount stores	500
Vectra	Fiber and yarn	600
*Western Electric	Electrical products	3,500

the wretched living conditions of the majority of the city's population; city officials who had long striven to build a better sense of community; and downtown business leaders who saw their investments threatened.

In this climate, the idea of a city fair that would build on neighborhood traditions but would celebrate a common purpose began to take shape. In 1970, when the first fair was held, the fear of violence was great. But 340,000 people came during the weekend of the fair in peaceable fashion, proving that disparate neighborhoods and communities could come together around a common project.

"A city reborn through a fair of neighbors," trumpeted Baltimore's newspapers. A Department of Housing and Urban Development report in 1981 recommended the fair to other urban governments in these terms: "Spawned by the necessity to arrest the fear and disuse of downtown areas caused by the civic unrest of the late 1960s, the Baltimore City Fair was originated by individuals in city government who seized upon the idea of a country fair in the city as a way to promote urban redevelopment."

By 1973, the fair was attended by nearly 2 million people. It had abandoned its location in the secure heart of Charles Center and moved to the edge of the Inner Harbor. In so doing, it suggested an entirely different set of uses to which that site could be put. The city fair proved that large numbers of people could be attracted downtown without having a riot. It also helped Baltimore rediscover the ancient Roman formula of bread and circuses as a means of masking social problems and controlling discontent.

The story of the Inner Harbor's construction is one of a steady erosion of the aims of the coalition that set it in motion and its capture by the narrower forces of commercialism, property development, and financial power. Two events had particular significance. The first was the election of a strong-willed and authoritarian mayor, William Donald Schaefer, in 1971.

Schaefer had grown up in Baltimore's Democratic party machine politics, and he was everything a machine politician should be. He believed strongly in a partnership of business and private enterprise for furthering the city's development and in an elaborate and often ruthless politics of social control over the city's neighborhoods. To offend the mayor was to risk retribution; to play along with him meant patronage and access to city services.

The second event was the recession of 1973–1975, which brought a massive wave of plant closures and deindustrialization to the Baltimore region. Unemployment surged. The prognosis for the city's economic future was bleak. In 1973, after President Nixon announced that the urban crisis was over, Baltimore faced the beginning of the end of large-scale federal programs to assist cities with their problems.

Budgetary cutbacks in the Reagan years were the highwater mark of federal government withdrawal from its commitment to help the nation's cities. The recession of 1981–1983—along with sharper foreign competition from Japan, Western Europe, and a host of newly industrializing countries—added to the city's difficulties. The list of plant closures and layoffs grew daily more threatening. A new international division of labor was coming into being, with manufacturing plants moved to cheap-labor locations overseas and basic U.S. industries like steel falling behind Japan and South Korea in world markets. Baltimore now had to find its way in a hostile and highly competitive world.

The turn to tourism, the creation of an image of Baltimore as a sophisticated place to live, the razzle-dazzle of downtown, and the commercial "hype" of Harborplace (*site 8*) have to be seen as Mayor Schaefer's (and the GBC's) distinctive solution to that problem. With the crowds pouring in, it was a short step to commercializing the city fair, first by adding all manner of ethnic festivals, concerts, and spectacular events—for example, the visit of the "tall ships" during the 1976 bicentennial celebration—to draw even more people downtown.

Then, having proved the existence of a market, the next step was to institutionalize a permanent commercial circus through the construction of Harborplace, the Maryland Science Center (*site 9*), the National Aquarium (*site 10*), the Convention Center (*site 11*), a marina (*site 12*), and innumerable hotels, shopping malls, and pleasure citadels of all kinds. The strategy did not even have to be consciously thought out, it was such an obvious thing to try.

This thrust had the additional virtue of projecting a new persona for the city. The "armpit of the East" had been the out-of-town image of Baltimore in the 1960s. But by transforming the entertainment spectacle into a permanent image, it became possible to use it to lure in developer capital, financial services, and entertainment industries—all big growth sectors in the U.S. economy during the 1970s and 1980s.

The imaging of Baltimore itself became important. The mayor, the media, and civic leaders set out on a binge of civic boosterism that would brook no criticism. When excessive cancer rates were reported in a neighborhood long exposed to chemical wastes, the mayor criticized those who did the reporting because they had sullied the city's image. When an impoverished population took advantage of a heavy snowstorm in 1978 to loot city stores, the mayor accused them of creating unemployment because they had damaged the city's image. So pervasive did the campaign become that when someone dreamed up the catchy slogan "Think pink," the mayor had downtown sidewalks painted pink.

Image building of this sort had definite rewards. The mayor, designated the best mayor in America by *Esquire* in 1984, appeared more and more to be the savior of a city, a magician who had made Renaissance City emerge phoenixlike out of the ashes of the civil strife of the 1960s. Twice featured in *Time*, Baltimore's Inner Harbor began to gain national and even international recognition as an example of urban revitalization. In November 1987, even the *London Sunday Times* bought the idea, lock, stock, and barrel:

Baltimore, despite soaring unemployment, boldly turned its derelict harbor into a playground. Tourists meant shopping, catering and transport, this in turn meant construction, distribution, manufacturing— leading to more jobs, more residents, more activity. The decay of old Baltimore slowed, halted, then turned back. The harbor area is now among America's top tourist draws and urban unemployment is falling fast.

If people could live on images alone, Baltimore's populace would have been rich indeed.

After 15 years as mayor, Schaefer was elected governor in 1986. Only then could another tale of

Gay Street: Baltimore Then and Now

The statistics that follow appeared in the *Baltimore Sun* on April 4, 1988. They were compiled from surveys commissioned by the Baltimore Urban Renewal and Housing Agency in 1966 and by the *Baltimore Sun* in April 1988, and are reprinted with permission.

	1966	1988
Economic Percentages		
Adult unemployment rate	7	19
Households receiving welfare	28	30
Households with incomes under $10,000 (1988 dollars)	41	47
Households with incomes over $20,000 (1988 dollars)	16	18
Adults who are high school graduates	10	49
Households in which at least one person owns a car	23	36
Percentage employed as laborers	43	8
Percentage doing clerical work	1	30
Household and Family Structure		
Median household size	2.9	1.9
Percentage of adults retired	13	30
Percentage of population under 18 years of age	45	34
Percentage of households with children that contain a male adult	56	43
Percentage of one-person households	16	31
Percentage of households with five or more people	30	12
The Neighborhood		
Most commonly cited "good" aspect	people	people
Most common complaint	housing	drugs, crime
Percentage of residents who are renters	85	78
Percentage of adults who have lived in neighborhood 10 or more years	48	60
Percentage who think neighborhood is getting better	N.A.	14

Baltimore be freely told. *Baltimore 2000*, a report commissioned by the Goldseker Foundation in 1987, summed up Baltimore this way:

Over the last twenty-five years, Baltimore has lost a fifth of its population, more than half of its white population, and a hard to enumerate but very large proportion of its middle class, white and black. It has lost more than ten per cent of its jobs since 1970, and those that remain are increasingly held by commuters. By 1985, the city's median household income was just over half that of surrounding counties and the needs of its poor for services were far more than the city's eroded tax base could support.

There was plenty of "rot beneath the glitter," as one consultant to the report put it. The depth of that rot can perhaps best be illustrated by the rapid rise in the city's status to that of fifth-worst-off city in the nation, according to a 1984 congressional estimate. The city was ranked next to last among the nation's 15 largest cities in the proportion of 20- to 24-year-olds who had completed high school, in part reflecting the more than 15 percent decline in municipal spending on education between 1974 and 1982.

Impoverishment in inner-city neighborhoods increased. "Of the officially designated neighborhoods in the city," wrote Marc Levine in an article in *Urban Affairs*, "210 (75.8 percent) experienced increases in the percentage of their residents living below the poverty line between 1970 and 1980," while almost 90 percent of the city's predominantly African-American neighborhoods saw their poverty rates rise. A *Baltimore Sun* survey of the Gay Street neighborhood, scene of some of the worst rioting in 1968, showed little change in conditions of impoverishment between 1966 and 1988. Yet the city's expenditures on social services for the poor fell by an astounding 45 percent in real terms over the 1974–1982 period.

These facts cannot be seen from Federal Hill, but they belie the image of affluence and fun that the Inner Harbor conveys. Nor can we see the more than 40,000 families that wait patiently for access to public housing and the many others suffering from housing deprivation.

We cannot see the 45 percent of the population

Strolling along the dockside at Harborplace.

over age 16 who either do not or cannot enter the job market, the desperate plight of female-headed households, the record number of teenage pregnancies, the severe problems of infant mortality that put some neighborhoods on a par with Mexico or Venezuela, the problems of rats, high cancer rates, and a resurgence of tuberculosis and lead poisoning. The conditions of grinding poverty in the city do not in any way appear to have been assuaged by all that massive downtown redevelopment.

This failure of the downtown redevelopment to make any substantial dent in the city's social and economic problems is all the more shocking when the vast public subsidy is taken into account. According to a U.S. Civil Rights Commission report of 1983, the first phase of the Inner Harbor development (costing $270 million) was 90 percent funded from the pub-

lic treasury "either in infrastructure, business subsidies, or loans/grants." Yet the management of the project remained entirely in corporate hands.

Where did the benefits of all this public investment go? There is no easy answer to that question, but some tentative conclusions can be drawn. First, most of the development so far has been hugely profitable to those who undertook it, with a few signal exceptions, such as the conversion of the old Baltimore Gas and Electric Company power plant into the Six Flags Power Plant entertainment center (*site 13*).

Second, though not as seriously undertaxed as in the early 1970s, present tax flows barely match public expenditures on the Inner Harbor. Indeed, a recent internal study suggested that Baltimore spends $17 million a year more on servicing the downtown and Inner Harbor than it gets back in tax revenues.

Third, the Renaissance has indeed brought jobs to the city, but most are low-paying jobs (janitors, hotel staff, service workers). Those who hold well-paid managerial jobs, such as the six directors of T. Rowe Price—a dynamic Baltimore money fund that grew rapidly in the 1980s—each of whom gets more than $600,000 a year, tend to live in the suburbs. Some middle-level managers stay downtown and create a demand for gentrified housing and condominiums.

Fourth, and perhaps most problematic, the redevelopment has certainly brought money into the city through a rapid growth of the convention and tourist trades. But there is no guarantee that the money stays in Baltimore. Much of it flows out again, either as profits to firms or payments for goods from Europe, Hong Kong, South Korea, Japan, England, or elsewhere. Spending money at Benetton or Laura Ashley does not stimulate the Baltimore economy. Evidence is hard to find, but the Inner Harbor may function simply as a harbor—a transaction point for money flowing from and to the rest of the world.

Baltimore's urban elite have struggled to make a new city. Powerless to prevent deindustrialization and recession, they have tried to create a profitable growth machine that has focused on tourism, leisure, and conspicuous consumption as an antidote to falling profits and urban decline. In limited ways, the strategy has worked—though mainly for them. By putting Baltimore on the map and by creating a prideful image of place and community, they have to some degree secured the political compliance of the majority. This can be measured by Mayor Schaefer's reelection victories of 1979 and 1983, in which community activists lost heavily to machine politicians.

The close public–private partnership forged between City Hall and dominant corporate power helped turn Baltimore into an entrepreneurial city that fared rather better in a highly competitive world than some of its rivals, cities like Detroit, Newark, Cleveland, or even Pittsburgh. Yet such victories may prove pyrrhic. Excess investment in shopping malls, entertainment facilities, high-priced condos, office space, convention centers, and sports stadiums throughout urban America spells trouble for some cities—and Baltimore may or may not be one.

The failure of the Six Flags Power Plant amuse-ment park in the Inner Harbor and the difficulties encountered selling high-priced condos in Harbor Court (*site 14*) are warning signals. And there are signs that the city is robbing Peter to pay Paul in the downtown commercial redevelopment stakes. James Rouse's Gallery (*site 15*), a three-story shopping mall at Harborplace, is a success, but Hutzler's Palace (*site 16*) four blocks away on Howard Street has had to close its doors.

Several festival marketplaces in other cities (Norfolk, Toledo, Flint, and even New York's South Street Seaport) are awash in red ink. Houston, Dallas, Atlanta, and Denver experienced overinvestment in hotels and office space in the 1970s, with catastrophic effects on the financial health of local banks and savings and loans. There is no reason to think that Baltimore is immune. There are already signs that the tourist trade is leveling off (according to Baltimore Office of Promotion and Tourism data), while employment in financial services took some hard knocks in the wake of the stock market crash of October 1987.

Furthermore, a serious social danger attaches to creating an island of affluence and power in the midst of a sea of impoverishment, disempowerment, and decay. Like the city fair, the Inner Harbor functions as a sophisticated mask. It invites us to participate in a spectacle, to enjoy a festive circus that celebrates the coming together of people and commodities. Like any mask, it can beguile and distract in engaging ways, but at some point we want to know what lies behind it. If the mask cracks or is violently torn off, the terrible face of Baltimore's impoverishment may appear.

The Lost Treasures of Chesapeake Bay

Turn your back on all the downtown glitter and look down the long reach of the Chesapeake Bay, and you will see another, far less glamorous Baltimore. The landscape reflects the change from manufacturing to service industry and the growing influence of foreign capital in the Baltimore economy.

Along with this has come harder times for Baltimore workers. Total employment in the metropolitan region has remained fairly constant since 1970, but the average wage has declined substantially. Employment has shifted radically from blue-collar jobs (many in relatively high-paying unionized industries sprawling around the edge of the bay) to white-collar occupations (many in low-paying and insecure service jobs, often held by women, and concentrated downtown). Where family incomes have risen, it is nearly always because more women have entered the workforce.

For example, at the foot of Federal Hill, on the eastern side, you can see the abandoned Bethlehem Steel Corporation shipyard (*site 17*), once a thriving centerpiece of Baltimore industry that employed some 1,500 blue-collar workers, many of whom lived in South Baltimore. The yard was closed in 1983, put out of business by foreign competition, particularly from the Far East, and world recession, in spite of wage concessions and give-backs by the workers.

To the chagrin of even South Baltimore gentrifiers, the yard was bought by a developer who proposed to convert the site into a marina, a repair yard for pleasure boats, a large office and commercial complex, and more than 1,500 expensive condos with two 29-story towers that would block views of the harbor. The Coalition of Peninsula Organizations protested loudly and won some concessions, but they lost the battle for the site. A zoning change from industrial uses to residential and commercial uses was approved in 1985.

But the developers went bankrupt, and the project's most recent $100 million incarnation, Harbor Keys, is funded by a consortium of investors from Singapore, Malaysia, Hong Kong, and Australia, all brokered by the Bangkok Bank of Thailand, which financed the purchase of the site. This means that jobs lost in the region through competition from the Far East allow capital abroad to return to dominate Baltimore.

The closure of the Allied Chemical plant (*site 18*) directly across the Inner Harbor is another sign of lost industrial power. A gray-striped eyesore, it was the last barrier to continuous condos and conversions on the northern side of the harbor from downtown through Fells Point to Canton. Developers would like to build condos here too if a way can be found to get the poisonous chromates out of the soil underneath.

The list of plant closures and industrial loss grows

longer as we look down the harbor's edge—the American Can Company at Fells Point (*site 19*), the Western Electric plant on Broening Highway (*site 20*) that eliminated 3,500 jobs in 1984, and the host of abandoned warehouses and rotting piers that testify to Baltimore's decline from a once-powerful port and manufacturing city.

Even with the costly modernization projects recently undertaken with taxpayer dollars, the port of Baltimore is barely competitive as a major seaport on the East Coast. But the price has been tighter labor contracts and rapidly falling employment for Baltimore workers. The death of a union picket in 1985 in a struggle to stop the use of nonunion labor may signal a return to a bitter era of labor relations. The International Longshoreman's Association, once a powerful voice in Baltimore's labor movement, now has to balance a struggle to improve wages and working conditions against the kind of concessions demanded to keep Baltimore competitive with Norfolk, Charleston, and other ports. The difficulty of dredging the Bay and disposing of the soil, the long journey up the Bay, and the canalization of the Mississippi–Tennessee river system also threaten the viability of the port.

We should be careful not to romanticize the lost era of powerful industry and commerce and the strong traditions and labor culture it nurtured. Many of the traditional industries (including the port before containerization) were onerous and dangerous. The division in the labor force between relatively affluent white male workers and the less skilled, less powerful women and African Americans was always a barrier to efforts to improve the lot of working people. Moreover, the economy was heavily involved in the exploitation of Third World resources and labor and was largely dependent on defense contracts. The Domino Sugar plant reminds us, for example, of the strong connection between Baltimore and Havana that had Baltimore businessmen rooting for Fulgencio Batista and against Fidel Castro precisely because of the cheap sugar produced by wretchedly paid Cuban sugarcane cutters. The Cuban revolution forced a major shift in Baltimore's trade. Interestingly enough, Domino Sugar has recently been sold to a British company (Tate and Lyle), illustrating

The Rusty Scupper Restaurant provides a foreground to Scarlett Place.

once again how vulnerable Baltimore's industry is to international forces.

The Rusty Scupper, a restaurant at the foot of Federal Hill (*site 21*), is another reminder of the negative aspects of international trade. Permission to build the Rusty Scupper was held up by local protests because the developer was a subsidiary of Nestlé, a Swiss corporation accused in the early 1980s of the deaths of thousands of babies in the Third World by marketing its infant formula as a substitute for breast feeding. The Rusty Scupper opened only after Nestlé agreed to change its practices in the face of widespread international protest.

Military contracts have always been an important source of employment in the Baltimore region. Steel and shipbuilding were heavily favored in World War II, but military expenditures in recent years have focused on more high-tech materials for which Baltimore was not so well positioned. It was the loss of military contracts that put the final nail in the coffin of the Bethlehem shipyard.

Some of the region's most thriving firms, such as Martin Marietta and Westinghouse, depend heavily on defense contracts. This fact of Baltimore's existence has not changed, despite efforts by local peace activists to focus attention on the waste of such expenditures relative to the social needs of the city. It should be possible, they argue, to convert industries producing instruments of death and destruction into activities that serve more human and benign social purposes.

For most visitors, Baltimore's dependence on military production and its connection with the exploitation of Third World labor are the least visible aspects of a view from Federal Hill. Stroll along the Inner Harbor or climb to the top of Federal Hill, and you are more likely to notice how pretty the sight is and to appreciate it as a place of entertainment and diversion. But whether or not you care to consider it, the landscape of the center city is a great book of time and history, proclaiming in glass, brick, and concrete who holds the reins of power.

Baltimore's Banks

The Citibank Building, formerly the Merritt Tower, home of the ill-fated Merritt Commercial Savings and Loan that went into state conservatorship during the savings and loan crisis of 1985.

Banks and financial institutions dominate the downtown skyline. There are no huge corporate headquarters in Baltimore of the sort we would encounter in Pittsburgh or Cincinnati because Baltimore is a branch manufacturing city run by financiers rather than industrialists. Only one of the Fortune 500 largest manufacturing companies has its headquarters here. It has been like that since the turn of the century when many local industrialists sold out to the trusts and cartels that were forming at the time.

Bethlehem Steel, General Motors, Westinghouse, and the now-departed Western Electric play a small role in what happens in Baltimore, because corporations with branch plants are usually less concerned about the effects of plant closure and less involved with local education, cultural facilities, and the like. In contrast, local banks and financial institutions are much more interested in property development than they are in employment and education.

Historically, the governance of Baltimore has been heavily influenced by a small group of local banks. As recently as 1968, a congressional report depicted Baltimore as one of the most monopolistically organized cities in the United States with respect to its financial structure. The Maryland National Bank (*site 22*), together with the Mercantile Safe Deposit and Trust Company (*site 23*) and the First National Bank (*site 24*), decided what the city was to be about and who was to run it.

A list of directors of these institutions reads like a Who's Who of Baltimore's elite. It includes members of the media and educational institutions (e.g., Johns Hopkins), and leaders of the city's cultural and business life. It was in the Maryland National Bank building that Mayor Schaefer waited for the result of his final mayoral election.

Consider, then, the two buildings that form the pinnacle of the downtown skyline. A venerable old Baltimore institution, the Maryland National Bank lies at the center; beside it rises, like an upraised finger, the newer and more

formidable-looking building owned by Citibank (*site 25*), a recent interloper from out of state.

A prime funder of real estate speculation and blockbusting in the 1960s, Maryland National persisted in its lack of concern for mortgage financing for low- to moderate-income inner-city neighborhoods, a recent study showed. The effect has been to promote the deterioration of housing conditions for the less well off, and so prepare the way for more urban development and gentrification. At the same time, Maryland National was using the deposits of Baltimore residents to invest in South Africa. Only after an intense campaign by an activist group called the Maryland Alliance for Responsible Investment did Maryland National agree to pull out of South Africa and promise $50 million, over a five-year period, for financing inner-city housing.

The Citibank Building was begun in the early 1980s as the prestigious headquarters of the Merritt Commercial Savings and Loan Association, a fast-growing financial institution that rivaled another savings and loan, Old Court, in competing for deposits and in undertaking spectacular ventures. Caught in the shifting sands of interest-rate fluctuations and recession, Maryland's state-insured savings and loan industry came crashing down in the late spring of 1985 because Merritt, Old Court, and several other savings and loan institutions had engaged in shady deals and made preposterous unsecured loans.

The Maryland Deposit Insurance Corporation, which is supposed to guarantee customer deposits, went bankrupt, forcing the state government into a crisis that took two years to resolve. Depositors could not gain access to their funds, and the flamboyant philanthropist Jeffrey Levitt, head of Old Court, ended up in jail for bilking his S & L of millions. Both Merritt and Old Court were put into state conservatorship. Merritt was eventually sold to Citibank, an out-of-state bank that appropriated Merritt's building for its own use and gained access to a Baltimore market long monopolized by local banks.

This opening up of Baltimore's financial market to out-of-state banks marked the end of local control. In 1983, for example, the largest bank in Ireland acquired a stake in First Maryland, the second-largest bank in the state with assets of $6.1 billion, and plans a total takeover. Breaking the local financial monopoly opens Baltimore even further to the chill winds of competition for money capital, which these days flashes around the world in the twinkling of an eye. Thus, the local economy becomes much more vulnerable to the whims and insecurities of international finance.

Bank Control of Baltimore

Until the recent deregulation, a few Baltimore banks controlled much of the economic activity in the Baltimore region. The concentration of banking power, documented for 1968 in the congressional Wright–Patman Report, showed the statistics that follow.

Bank	Percentage of bank trust assets in the region[a]	Number of companies on the boards of which bank directors had positions	Number of companies in which bank held more than 5 percent of the stock
Mercantile Safe Deposit and Trust Company	63.38	196	213
Equitable Trust Company	13.85	137	53
Maryland National Bank	13.51	86	13
First National Bank of Maryland	5.28	213	56
Union Trust Company	3.66	74	55

[a] Bank trust assets are investment funds, such as pension money, administered by the bank on behalf of others.

The Maryland Science Center, designed like a fortress, without windows, guards the southern approach to the Inner Harbor from potential rioting by neighborhood residents.

The western edge of the Inner Harbor with the Maryland Science Center on the left, Harbor Court towers rising behind, and the Hyatt-Regency Hotel to the right.

The Harbor Court tower block, 1988

Redevelopment in the Inner Harbor

Maryland Science Center

Four sites in Baltimore's Inner Harbor may help explain what the redevelopment process has been about. The Maryland Science Center, which opened in 1976, was one of the first buildings planned there. It looks like a fortress. It has no entrance facing the community or even the street. The building was designed in the wake of the 1968 riots, at a time when a substantial African-American population inhabited the close-by community of Sharp–Leadenhall. The fortress design is deliberate; it is designed to keep out social unrest and minimize property damage.

The Maryland Science Center functions as a kind of strategic outpost, now rendered largely irrelevant by the gentrification of South Baltimore, at the south end of the Inner Harbor. Another example of strategic building is Martin Luther King Boulevard (*site 26*). Besides relieving traffic congestion downtown, it creates an easily patrolled line of defense between the mass of downtown buildings and the low-income and largely African-American communities of West Baltimore.

Hyatt-Regency Hotel

The shimmering, glass-fronted Hyatt-Regency Hotel (*site 27*), costing $35 million, was almost entirely financed by a $10 million federal subsidy in the form of an Urban Development Action Grant, plus loans that the city secured. The owners, the Pritzker and Hyatt interests, put up only $500,000. They took no risks and ended up with a $35 million hotel. Holiday Inn and other hotel chains in the city protested that the arrangement was unfair. Since Urban Development Action Grants were originally set up to help cities deal with problems of urban distress, their diversion into this project was justified in terms of employment and tax-base benefits. But the benefit and subsidy to the developers was enormous compared to the numbers of relatively low-paid service jobs created and a tax benefit that barely kept pace with public costs.

Harbor Court

Harbor Court is another example of a public subsidy for private gain. In 1984, the city transferred one of the prime pieces of development property on the East Coast to David Murdock, a California developer. Mayor Schaefer agreed (over oysters at Lexington Market, some say) to sell the land at a net loss of $500,000 in return for a promise that Murdock would help redevelop the predominantly black retailing district around Lexington Market.

Murdock took the property, erected an $85 million building, then sold condos in it for up to $1 million each—in a city with a huge waiting list for public housing. In 1986, Murdock withdrew from the Lexington Mall development proposal with no penalty, leaving the city with nothing except a supposedly improved tax base and an ugly tower to block the view.

Harborplace Pavilions

The pavilions of Harborplace, built by James Rouse, were the subject of considerable controversy. Rouse was originally offered the option to convert the long-abandoned Baltimore Gas and Electric Company power plant at the harbor's edge into a pavilion, but he refused. He wanted to use the public land at the strategic corner of the Inner Harbor. The city agreed but was legally obligated to put the proposed transfer of the land to a public referendum. Opposition was strong, especially from South Baltimore residents, who felt the waterfront and their access to it would be lost to private control. They also feared the impact of the development on this traditional working-class community, which had long lived and worked in South Baltimore. But the referendum passed.

Rouse's project opened in the summer of 1980 and was an instant commercial and popular success. It became the crown jewel of Baltimore's Renaissance, supposedly drawing in more visitors than Disney World.

The rate of return per square foot of rental space is reputed to be one of the highest in the United States, yet the

tax benefit to the city is relatively modest, given the public expenditures required. Much of the attraction and charm of Harborplace comes from the people who mass there and provide the spectacle—the same crowd that pays for the overpriced goods and services that generate such fabulous financial returns for private and corporate business.

South Baltimore

The Inner Harbor has had a substantial impact on areas immediately surrounding it, such as the streets in South Baltimore behind Federal Hill. A glance down the western side of the hill shows a solidly gentrified community with its sundecks, newly cleaned brick exteriors, and shuttered windows. The ubiquitous coach lamps, a symbol of the new urban gentry that lives here, march street by street into South Baltimore.

An African-American neighborhood church has been converted into condos (*site 28*), as was the old Shofer Warehouse (*site 29*). Developers call it the Paper Mill—a reflection of its earlier use—perhaps to make the price of $300,000 (and up) per unit a bit more palatable. Housing prices have shot up from the $10,000 level common in the early 1970s to well over $100,000 for a refurbished row-house in the late 1980s.

The effect has been to increase local tax assessments and property tax burdens (from $300 to $2,000 a year, in some cases), pushing poor people out and making way for speculators and developers. The displacement of local residents sparked local resistance, and the Coalition of Peninsula Organizations led the way in trying to rescue the neighborhood, in spite of (then) Mayor Schaefer's opposition. But with no more employment in the shipyards, South Baltimore has become vulnerable to the inflow of young professionals seeking a safe neighborhood close to downtown office jobs.

City Hall's part in that transition can be seen most clearly in its role in the conversion of the old Southern High School (*site 30*), on the southwest corner of Federal Hill Park, into condos. Now called Harbor View, this building is one of many memorials to an undemocratic system of

The old Southern High School converted into the condominiums of Harbor View with the help of the "shadow government" of city trustees.

A neighborhood church, once a place of worship for African Americans in South Baltimore, now converted to condominiums.

Shofer Warehouse, once an old paper mill, has been converted to condominiums.

city governance that has allowed the City Council's control over city expenditures to be superseded by the formation of what became known as a shadow government.

In the 1970s, Mayor Schaefer designated two trustees to administer all federal loans and grants to private developers. As repayments from developers came in, the trustees built up a $200 million development bank, entirely under the mayor's control, that could be used as a revolving fund to promote further private development. One such project was the conversion of Southern High School by the Jolly Company, which acted as developer and builder. The company put up no money of its own, but borrowed everything it needed from the trustee fund. When the company failed to make interest payments on the loan they had taken to purchase the site, the city foreclosed. But the company continued with the lucrative business of building conversion at a price it had set as a developer.

The city ultimately managed to sell off the condos without too much loss, but Jolly the builder profited most handsomely from the conversion at public expense from an operation with no risk. In fact, none of the agencies responsible for the downtown and Inner Harbor redevelopment were accountable to anyone but themselves, even though they were awash with public funds. In 1980, a reporter from the *Baltimore Sun*, C. Frazier Smith, exposed the whole structure of shadow governance, including several quasi-public agencies (the Charles Center Management Corporation was the first) that controlled public funds for largely private purposes.

The issue, most agreed, was not corruption of the ordinary sort but circumvention of the democratic processes of government and of public accountability for the use of public money. The mayor argued, with some justification, that the trustee system was the only way he could bypass the conservatism of Baltimore banks. He wound up the trustee system as banking became more open and competitive in the mid 1980s, but other quasi-public corporations, still unaccountable to the City Council, have not been touched and have remained the vital center of Baltimore's so-called public–private partnership.

Federal Park Condos, after conversion from the warehouse.

The coach lamps of gentrifiers, marching into South Baltimore behind Federal Hill, leaving the formstone houses as a sign of long-standing residency.

Afterword

What conclusions can we draw from the histories and interviews in this book? First, many Baltimoreans have improved their working and social conditions through their own efforts to organize and take control of their lives. In contrast to the late nineteenth century, a union wage has provided many families with enough income to finance a house and enjoy a variety of material goods and services. Unions also have improved the health and safety of industrial workers and their families. Labor's organizing efforts have contributed to workers' self-respect and the respect afforded them by employers and politicians.

Second, while it is obvious to anyone who travels through the city that gains for African-American Baltimoreans have been limited in recent decades, chapters in this book detail how the ongoing struggles for civil rights and economic equality have resulted in better conditions for many. As a result of desegregation and affirmative action, Baltimore's African-American population has had greater access to stores, restaurants, public facilities, housing, and educational and job opportunities than at any point in the city's past. Prominent public positions have been held by black men and women, including the office of mayor. African Americans have served as executive officers of unions, as teachers and administrators in the public schools, and in positions of responsibility in city government. In the steel industry and on the waterfront, as well as in other industries and trades, blacks have held jobs once exclusively held by whites.

Women also have experienced gains as a result of their own efforts. The fight for woman's suffrage and the women's and gay rights movements have enlarged the sphere of women's civic participation, heightened the respect afforded women, and increased the resources available to them. Such women as Mary Elizabeth Garrett no longer are excluded from managing a business enterprise or denied access to higher education solely on the basis of gender. Increasingly, women who work outside the home work in jobs traditionally held by white men. Unions are beginning to recognize that working women are an important force to organize; in the Amalgamated Clothing Workers, for example, women are in positions of leadership. And as several chapters illustrate, women have played an essential role in neighborhood organizing.

These achievements for workers, African Americans, and women indicate that there have indeed been positive changes in Baltimore. The accounts presented here clearly point to cooperation among workers, neighbors, and neighborhoods and the formation of worker, community, and civil rights organizations as essential to progress. But cooperation and organization have not been the only factors. To succeed, Baltimoreans have had to play an active role in the direction of communities and industries and to challenge the power of corporations, banks, developers, and unsympathetic politicians. From the first to the final chapter in this book, the need to exert control over those whose primary concern is profit has been made clear. From the early history of the Baltimore and Ohio Railroad, we can see that once private investors gained control of an industry, the interests of the public are usually ignored. African Americans were only able to claim their fundamental rights as citizens when they used the vote and the courts to their advantage. Today, unless community residents and ordinary citizens take charge of future downtown development, banks and developers will continue to set the priorities for growth that mainly benefit out-of-town interests and the wealthy.

Corporations, banks, and developers have enormous power and resources, so it is not surprising that people do not challenge them easily and that when they do, successes are limited. Residents of Fells Point and neighboring Canton are still fighting to retain parts of their neighborhood for community use, to maintain the culture and fabric of the neighborhood, and to limit the transformation of abandoned warehouses into upscale condominiums and office buildings. Sometimes struggles are lost when owners of industries, impatient with citizen challenges, simply leave town, taking their capital and resources elsewhere. Workers in the garment industry, for example, won improvements in working conditions when they unionized, but the garment and textile workers of Hampden–Woodberry lost their jobs when industries abandoned the city in search of cheaper nonunion labor. Steelworkers in Sparrows Point saw their community destroyed when it no longer served company interests, and the union has had to fight simply to maintain a few gains from the past now that the steel industry is battling foreign competition with cutbacks.

Residential segregation and blockbusting may no longer be legal, but the city is still segregated; residents still must watch out for banks that use "red-lining" in city neighborhoods. The desegregation of schools and public facilities, however desirable, has not led to equality of economic opportunity for the African-American population. Relatively well-paid jobs have left the city, the quality of education for the largely black school population has eroded, and the low-skill service sector has offered inadequate wages. The economic outlook for both Baltimore's black and white populations has become increasingly grim.

To suggest that an alternative future for Baltimore can be achieved if ordinary citizens direct the decision-making process in their workplaces and communities is perhaps audacious. Success would dramatically shift the alignment of power, forcing those who currently wield power to relinquish it. And as the chapters in this book illustrate, no one gives up power without a struggle. But this is the only way to redress inequality and injustice, both in Baltimore and in the nation.

We find it encouraging to note that when ordinary Baltimoreans have taken charge of a project—whether in the workplace or in their communities—they have accomplished a great deal. In 1934, Baltimore's seamen impressed federal authorities with their efficiency in distributing unemployment assistance for white and black seamen on the waterfront. Hiring practices of seamen's worker councils were recognized as fairer than management's. In the garment industry, the Amalgamated Clothing Workers streamlined the production process and increased profitability in the industry. Community activists Lucille Gorham and Betty Hyatt have demonstrated the feasibility of community control of the design and development of housing for low- and middle-income families. Beryl Williams has shown the way an educator can design and implement alternative approaches to education.

Finally, we are inspired by the many principled Baltimoreans who appeared in this book and by their persistence in trying to improve their city. Though many of them have achieved, at best, only partial victories, Baltimoreans continue to work for positive changes in their lives. Baltimore needs that kind of energy. And the histories in this book tell us that there is no better way to mobilize that energy than to give Baltimoreans the opportunity to direct their own future. A strategy that would give ordinary citizens decision-making power over economic and community development would foster positive change in the city. Imagine the possibilities.

Bibliography

Sources for Baltimore History

This bibliography provides a brief overview of some of the primary and secondary sources available for further research on Baltimore's history. It emphasizes social history, especially community history. Although the bibliography is by no means complete, many of the sources direct interested readers to additional material.

Following this introduction are separate bibliographies for each chapter in the book. In addition to listing where each author got his or her information, these also provide further leads to source material for Baltimore history.

Anyone interested in pursuing local historical research would do well to browse through the catalogues and stacks of local libraries. Especially rich collections of materials are available at the Maryland Room of the Enoch Pratt Free Library and the Albin O. Kuhn Library and Gallery at the University of Maryland Baltimore County.

Primary Sources

Several published guides to archival collections and other records are available for the study of Baltimore history. These include the following:

Baltimore History Network. *Baltimore's Past: A Directory of Historical Sources*. Baltimore: Baltimore History Network, 1989.

Cox, Richard J., and Larry Sullivan, eds. *Guide to the Research Collections of the Maryland Historical Society*. Baltimore: Maryland Historical Society, 1981.

Cox, Richard J., and Patricia M. Vanorny. "The Records of a City: Baltimore and Its Historical Sources." *Maryland Historical Magazine* 70, no. 3 (Fall 1975): 286–310.

Gertler, John T., ed. *The Records of Baltimore's Private Organizations: A Guide to Archival Research*. New York: Garland, 1981.

Pedley, Avril M., comp. *Manuscript Collections of the Maryland Historical Society*. Baltimore: Maryland Historical Society, 1968.

Porter, Glenn, and William H. Mulligan, Jr. *Working Papers from the Regional Economic History Research Center*, vol. 4, nos. 1 and 2, *Baltimore History*. Wilmington: Eleutherian Mills–Hagley Foundation, 1981.

Additional Primary Sources

Census materials, available for individual households in manuscript form on microfilm for 1790 through 1910 (except 1890) and compiled for enumeration districts and other local jurisdictions in published form for 1790 through 1980, can be found at the Enoch Pratt Free Library, the Albin O. Kuhn Library and Gallery at the University of Maryland Baltimore County, the Maryland State Archives, and the Maryland Historical Society.

Local newspapers, from the eighteenth century to the present, are available at the Enoch Pratt Free Library, the Maryland State Archives, and the Maryland Historical Society, as well as other repositories. Literally hundreds of newspapers are available, not only the main dailies but also the *Afro-American*, several immigrant newspapers, labor papers, and local community papers. The Maryland Newspaper Project is currently preparing a bibliography of the titles and locations of the publicly accessible newspaper runs held in Maryland; this should be available in 1991. Many are also listed in *Newspapers in Maryland Libraries: A Union List*, compiled by Eleanore O. Hofstetter and Marcella S. Eustis (Baltimore: Maryland State Department of Education, 1977).

Oral history collections are housed at the Maryland Historical Society and in the special collections of the Langsdale Library of the University of Baltimore. The historical society collection includes the McKelden–Jackson Project interviews, focusing on the civil rights movement in Baltimore, as well as a number of interviews emphasizing the immigrant experience. The University of Baltimore holds the collection of the Baltimore Neighborhood Heritage Project, which includes more than 300 interviews with longtime residents of the neighborhoods of Highlandtown, Old West Baltimore, South Baltimore, Hampden–Woodberry, Old Park Heights, and Little Italy.

Vertical files on hundreds of local subjects can be located in the Maryland Room of the Enoch Pratt Free Library and at the Maryland Historical Society. The historical society also includes the very useful Dielman–Hayward biography files.

Secondary Sources

An excellent overview of secondary literature available on Baltimore history is Richard M. Cox, "Understanding the Monumental City: A Bibliographical Essay on Baltimore History," *Maryland Historical Magazine* 77, no. 1 (Spring 1982): 70–111.

This is supplemented by bibliographies on Maryland history appearing in the following issues of the *Maryland Historical Magazine*: Fall 1982, Fall 1983, Spring 1987, and Summer 1989. See also the comprehensive "Bibliographic Essay," in Robert J. Brugger, *Maryland: A Middle Temperament, 1634–1980* (Baltimore: Johns Hopkins University Press in association with the Maryland Historical Society, 1988), 711–769.

The single best source of well-documented articles on Baltimore history is the *Maryland Historical Magazine*. Hundreds of articles that relate to local history have appeared in this journal since it started publishing in 1906. Recently, four issues have been devoted exclusively to articles on the city's history: Fall 1976, September 1979, March 1982, and Summer 1989.

In recent years, a number of neighborhood and community histories have been written for the general public. These include the following:

Dorsey, John. *Mount Vernon Place: An Anecdotal Essay with Sixty-six Illustrations*. Baltimore: Maclay and Associates, 1983.

Farrell, Michael. *Who Made All the Streetcars Go? The Story of Rail Transit in Baltimore*. Baltimore: Baltimore RHS Publications, 1973.

Freeman, Roland L. *The Arabbers of Baltimore*. Centreville, Md.: Tidewater Publishers, 1989.

Harvey, Bill. *"The People Is Grass": A History of Hampden–Woodberry, 1802–1945*. Baltimore: Della Press, 1988.

Keith, Robert. *Baltimore Harbor: A Picture History*. Baltimore: Ocean World Publishing, 1982.

Kelly, Jacques. *Peabody Heights to Charles Village: The Historic Development of a Baltimore Community*. Baltimore: Equitable Trust Bank, 1976.

Lewand, Karen. *North Baltimore: From Estate to Development*, pt. 1 of *Baltimore Neighborhoods: A Community Book*, ed. D. Randall Beirne. Baltimore: University of Baltimore, 1989.

Miller, Mark. *Mount Washington, a Baltimore Suburb: A History Revealed through Pictures and Narrative*. Baltimore: GBS Publishers, 1980.

Nash, Lenora Heilig, Laurence N. Krause, and R. C. Monk, eds. *Baltimore: A Living Renaissance*. Baltimore: Historic Baltimore Society, 1982.

Rehbein, Leslie, and Kate E. Peterson, eds. *Beyond the White Marble Steps: A Look at Baltimore Neighborhoods*. Baltimore: Citizens Planning and Housing Association, 1979.

Rukert, Norman. *Federal Hill: A Baltimore National Historic District*. Baltimore: Bodine and Associates, 1980.

———. *The Fells Point Story*. Baltimore: Bodine and Associates, 1976.

———. *Historic Canton: Baltimore's Industrial Heartland and Its People*. Baltimore: Bodine and Associates, 1980.

———. *The Port: Pride of Baltimore*. Baltimore: Bodine and Associates, 1982.

Sandler, Gilbert. *The Neighborhood: The Story of Baltimore's Little Italy*. Baltimore: Bodine and Associates, 1974.

Shivers, Frank, Jr. *Bolton Hill: Baltimore Classic*. Baltimore: Equitable Trust Company, 1978.

Waesche, James. *Crowning the Gravelly Hill: A History of the Roland Park-Guilford-Homeland District*. Baltimore: Maclay and Associates, 1987.

Several collections of historical prints and photographs of the city have also been published, including the following:

Baltimore: A Picture History. Commentary by Francis F. Beirne and Carleton Jones. Baltimore: Bodine and Associates and Maclay and Associates, 1982.

Bodine's Baltimore: Forty-six Years in the Life of a City. Photographs by A. Aubrey Bodine. Commentary by Wilbur Harvey Hunter. Baltimore: Bodine and Associates, 1973.

Dürr, W. T., ed. *Baltimore People, Baltimore Places*. Baltimore: University of Baltimore, 1981.

Kelly, Jacques. *Bygone Baltimore*. Baltimore: Donning, 1982.

———. *The Pratt Library Album: Baltimore Neighborhoods in Focus*. Baltimore: Enoch Pratt Free Library, 1986.

Warren, Marion E., and Mame Warren, eds. *Baltimore When She Was What She Used to Be*. Baltimore: Johns Hopkins University Press, 1983.

While Baltimore remains an underresearched city, several academic and scholarly books, among other publications, have appeared recently, helping us put together a fuller picture of the city's past. Among these are the following:

Argersinger, Jo Ann E. *Toward a New Deal in Baltimore: People and Government in the Great Depression.* Chapel Hill: University of North Carolina Press, 1988.

Bilhartz, Terry. *Urban Religion and the Second Great Awakening: Church and Society in Early National Baltimore.* Rutherford, N.J.: Fairleigh Dickinson University Press, 1986.

Browne, Gary. *Baltimore in the Nation, 1789–1861.* Chapel Hill: University of North Carolina Press, 1980.

Brugger, Robert. *Maryland: A Middle Temperament, 1634–1980.* Baltimore: Johns Hopkins University Press, 1988.

Crooks, James. *Politics and Progress: The Rise of Urban Progressivism in Baltimore, 1895–1911.* Baton Rouge: Louisiana State University Press, 1968.

Fee, Elizabeth. *Disease and Discovery: A History of the Johns Hopkins School of Hygiene and Public Health, 1916–1939.* Baltimore: Johns Hopkins University Press, 1987.

Fields, Barbara. *Slavery and Freedom on the Middle Ground: Maryland during the Nineteenth Century.* New Haven: Yale University Press, 1985.

Gardner, Bettye Jane. "Free Blacks in Baltimore, 1800–1860." Ph.D. dissertation, George Washington University, 1974.

Graham, Leroy. *Baltimore, the Nineteenth Century Black Capital.* Washington, D.C.: University Press of America, 1982.

Harvey, A. McGehee, Gert H. Briegler, Susan L. Abrams, and Victor A. McKusick. *A Model of Its Kind: A Centennial History of Medicine at Johns Hopkins.* Baltimore: Johns Hopkins University Press, 1989.

Kahn, Philip, Jr. *A Stitch in Time: The Four Seasons of Baltimore's Needle Trades.* Baltimore: Maryland Historical Society, 1989.

Neverdon-Morton, Cynthia. *Afro-American Women of the South and the Advancement of the Race, 1895–1925.* Knoxville: University of Tennessee Press, 1989.

Olson, Sherry H. *Baltimore: The Building of an American City.* Baltimore: Johns Hopkins University Press, 1980.

Paul, William. "The Shadow of Equality: The Negro in Baltimore, 1864–1911." Ph.D. dissertation, University of Wisconsin, 1972.

Reutter, Mark. *Sparrows Point: Making Steel—The Rise and Ruin of America's Industrial Might.* New York: Summit Books, 1988.

Steffen, Charles. *The Mechanics of Baltimore: Workers and Politics in the Age of Revolution, 1763–1812.* Urbana: University of Illinois Press, 1984.

Szanton, Peter. *Baltimore 2000: A Choice of Futures.* Baltimore: Morris Goldseker Foundation of Maryland, 1986.

Thomas, Bettye Collier. "The Baltimore Black Community, 1865–1910." Ph.D. dissertation, George Washington University, 1974.

Watson, Denton. *Lion in the Lobby: Clarence Mitchell, Jr.'s Struggle for the Passage of Civil Rights Laws.* New York: William Morrow, 1990.

Chapter Sources

Chapter 1

Baltimore Sun, September 21 and 25, 1877; October 16, 1877; and *Baltimore News American*, September 15, 1877.

Baltimore Sun. "Recalls Thrilling Features of Riot Nearly 50 Years Ago," June 6, 1927.

Brecher, Jeremy. *Strike!* Boston: South End Press, 1972.

Bruce, Robert V. *Year of Violence.* Indianapolis: Bobbs-Merrill, 1959.

Foner, Philip S. *History of the Labor Movement in the United States*, vol. 4. New York: International Publishers, 1947.

Johnson, Gerald W., Frank R. Kent, H. L. Mencken, and Hamilton Owens. *The Sunpapers of Baltimore.* New York: Knopf, 1937.

Kent, Frank Richardson. *The Story of Maryland Politics.* Baltimore: Thomas and Evans, 1911.

Licht, Walter. *Working for the Railroad: The Organization of Work in the Nineteenth Century.* Princeton: Princeton University Press, 1983.

Wallock, Leonard. "The B & O 'Monopoly' and the Baltimore Crowd: Patterns of Crowd Participation in the Riots of 1877." Master's thesis, Columbia University, 1974.

Yearley, Clifton K., Jr. "The Baltimore and Ohio Railroad Strike of 1877." *Maryland Historical Magazine* 61, no. 3 (September 1956): 188–211.

Chapter 2

Catton, William B. "John W. Garrett of the Baltimore and Ohio: A Study in Seaport and Railroad Competition, 1820–1874." Ph.D. dissertation, Northwestern University, 1959.

Chesney, Alan M. *The Johns Hopkins Hospital and the Johns Hopkins University School of Medicine: A Chronicle.* Baltimore: Johns Hopkins University Press, 1943.

City Atlas of Baltimore, Maryland and Environs. Philadelphia: G. M. Hopkins, 1876.

Dehler, Katherine. "Mount Vernon Place and the Turn of the Century: A Vignette of the Garrett Family." *Maryland Historical Magazine* 69, no. 3 (1974): 279–292.

Dobkin, Marjorie Housepian, ed. *The Making of a Feminist: Early Journals and Letters of M. Carey Thomas.* Kent, Ohio: Kent State University Press, 1979.

Dorsey, John. *Mount Vernon Place: An Anecdotal Essay*

with Sixty-six Illustrations. Baltimore: Maclay and Associates, 1983.

Ely, Richard T. *The Labor Movement in America*. New York: Crowell, 1886.

Finch, Edith. *Carey Thomas of Bryn Mawr*. New York: Harper & Bros., 1947.

Hungerford, Edward. *The Story of the Baltimore and Ohio Railroad*. 2 vols. New York and London: Putnam's, 1928.

McCall, Nancy. "The Savvy Strategies of the First Campaign for Hopkins Medicine." *Hopkins Medical News* 8, no. 6 (Fall 1984): 2–5.

"Mary Elizabeth Garrett, 1854–1915: Philanthropist" and "Martha Carey Thomas, 1857–1935: Feminist and Pioneer Educator." In *Notable Maryland Women*, ed. Winifred G. Holmes. Cambridge, Md.: Tidewater Publishers, 1977.

Rossiter, Margaret. *Women Scientists in America: Struggles and Strategies to 1940*. Baltimore: Johns Hopkins University Press, 1982.

Waesche, James F. *Crowning the Gravelly Hill: A History of the Roland Park-Guilford-Homeland District*. Baltimore: Maclay and Associates, 1987.

Worley, William S. "J. C. Nichols and the Origins of the Planned Residential Community in the United States, 1903–1930." Ph.D. dissertation, University of Kansas, 1986.

Chapter 3

Arnold, Joseph L. "Suburban Growth and Municipal Annexation in Baltimore, 1745–1918." *Maryland Historical Magazine* 73, no. 2 (Summer 1978): 109–128.

Baltimore Labor Leader. Issued by Baltimore Federation of Labor, 1901–1919.

Baltimore Neighborhood Heritage Project Oral History Collection, Hampden–Woodberry interviews. University of Baltimore, 1979–1981.

Baltimore Sun. Various years.

Beirne, Daniel Randall. "Steadfast Americans: Residential Stability among Workers in Baltimore, 1880–1930." Ph.D. dissertation, University of Maryland, 1976.

———. "Hampden–Woodberry: The Mill Village in an Urban Setting." *Maryland Historical Magazine* 77, no. 1 (March 1982): 6–26.

Brooks, Neal, and Eric Rockel. *A History of Baltimore County*. Towson, Md.: Friends of the Towson Library, 1979.

Bullock, James G., Jr. *A Brief History of the Textile Manufacturing Mills along Jones Falls*. Baltimore: Mount Vernon Mills, 1970.

Hare, Jean, ed. *Hampden–Woodberry*. Baltimore: The Hampden Bicentennial Committee [1976].

Maryland Bureau of Industrial Statistics. *Annual Report*. Baltimore, various years.

Memories. A film about Hampden–Woodberry. Baltimore

Neighborhood Heritage Project, University of Baltimore, 1983.

Otey, Elizabeth. *The Cotton Mill Workers on Jones Falls*. Pamphlet no. 1. Baltimore: Christian Social Justice Fund, 1924.

Chapter 4

Baltimore Sun. "The Royal Theater and Its Big-Name Performers," October 1, 1972.

Callcott, George H. *Maryland and America, 1940–1980*. Baltimore: Johns Hopkins University Press, 1985.

Callcott, Margaret Law. *The Negro in Maryland Politics, 1870–1912*. Baltimore: Johns Hopkins University Press, 1969.

Calloway, Cab, and Bryant Rollins. *Of Minnie the Moocher and Me*. New York: Harper & Row, 1976.

Diner, Hasia. *In the Almost Promised Land: American Jews and Blacks, 1915–1935*. Westport, Conn.: Greenwood Press, 1977.

Groves, Paul A., and Edward K. Muller. "The Evolution of Black Residential Areas in Late-Nineteenth-Century Cities." *Journal of Historical Geography* 1, no. 2 (April 1975): 169–191.

Hawkins, Mason Albert. "Frederick Douglass High School: A Seventeen-Year Period Survey." Ph.D. dissertation, University of Pennsylvania, 1933.

Johnson, Charles S. "Negroes at Work in Baltimore, Maryland." *Opportunity: A Journal of Negro Life* 1, no. 6 (June 1923): 12–19.

Kemp, Janet E. *Housing Conditions in Baltimore*. Baltimore: Federated Charities, 1907.

McKeldin–Jackson Oral History Collection. Maryland Historical Society, June–August 1976.

Mencken, H. L. "The Lynching Psychosis." *Baltimore Evening Sun*, March 28, 1932.

Neverdon-Morton, Cynthia. "Black Housing Patterns in Baltimore City, 1885–1953." *Maryland Historian* 16, no. 1 (Spring/Summer 1985): 25–39.

Olson, Sherry H. *Baltimore: The Building of an American City*. Baltimore: Johns Hopkins University Press, 1980.

Power, Garrett. "Apartheid Baltimore Style: The Residential Segregation Ordinances of 1910–1913." *Maryland Law Review* 42, no. 2 (November 1983): 289–328.

Reid, Ira. *The Negro Community of Baltimore: A Summary Report of a Social Study Conducted for the Baltimore Urban League through the Department of Research, National Urban League*. Baltimore, 1935.

Ryon, Roderick N. "Old West Baltimore." *Maryland Historical Magazine* 77, no. 1 (March 1982): 54–69.

Toward Equality: Baltimore's Progress Report Since World War II for Negroes in Maryland. Baltimore: Sidney Hollander Foundation, 1960.

White, John C. "Jazz Greats Played at the Royal." *Baltimore Evening Sun*, February 3, 1971.

Chapter 5

Amalgamated Clothing Workers of America Papers. Martin P. Catherwood Library of the New York School of Industrial and Labor Relations, Cornell University.

Argersinger, Jo Ann E. *Toward a New Deal in Baltimore: People and Government in the Great Depression.* Chapel Hill: University of North Carolina Press, 1988.

Baltimore Sun. 1914–1916; 1920–1922; 1928–1940. Especially useful for accounts of specific strikes and description of economic conditions in the garment industry.

Barron, Sara. Oral history interview by Barbara Wertheimer, June 4, 1976. New York State School of Industrial and Labor Relations Library, New York City Division of Cornell University.

Carpenter, Jesse Thomas. *Competition and Collective Bargaining in the Needle Trades, 1910–1967.* Ithaca: Cornell University Press, 1972.

Fraser, Steve. "Dress Rehearsal for the New Deal: Shop-Floor Insurgents, Political Elites, and Industrial Democracy in the Amalgamated Clothing Workers." In *Working-Class America: Essays on Labor, Community, and American Society,* ed. Michael H. Frisch and Daniel J. Walkowitz. Urbana: University of Illinois Press, 1983.

Hardy, Jack. *The Clothing Workers: A Study of the Conditions and Struggles in the Needle Trades.* New York: International Publishers, 1935.

Hollander, Jacob H. *Report of the Hearing of Strikers from the Shoeneman Shops in Connection with an Investigation of Conditions in the Clothing Industry Held at City Hall.* Baltimore, 1932.

——— . *Report to Honorable Howard W. Jackson on Working Conditions in the Garment Industry.* Baltimore, 1932.

Imberman, Abraham. *Report on Men's Clothing Industry.* Sponsored by the Works Progress Administration. Baltimore: State Planning Commission, 1936.

Jensen, Joan M., and Sue Davidson, eds. *A Needle, A Bobbin, A Strike: Women Needleworkers in America.* Philadelphia: Temple University Press, 1984.

Josephson, Matthew. *Sidney Hillman: Statesman of American Labor.* New York: Doubleday, 1952.

Kahn, Philip, Jr. *A Stitch in Time: The Four Seasons of Baltimore's Needle Trades.* Baltimore: The Maryland Historical Society, 1989.

Levine, Louis. *The Women's Garment Workers.* New York: Arno Press, 1969; reprint of 1924 ed.

Schaefer, Robert J. "Educational Activities of the Garment Unions, 1890–1948." Ph.D. dissertation, Columbia University, 1951.

Seidman, Joel. *The Needle Trades.* New York: Farrar & Rinehart, 1942.

Stolberg, Benjamin. *Tailors Progress: The Story of a Famous Union and the Man Who Made It.* New York: Doubleday, Doran, 1944.

Taylor Society. *Scientific Management in American Society,* ed. H. S. Person. New York: Easton Hive Publishing, 1972; facsimile of 1929 edition.

Tax, Meredith. *The Rising of the Women: Feminist Solidarity and Class Conflict, 1880–1917.* New York: Monthly Review Press, 1980.

Willett, Mabel Hurd. *The Employment of Women in the Clothing Trade.* New York: AMS Press, 1968; reprint of 1902 edition.

Zaretz, Charles Elbert. *The Amalgamated Clothing Workers of America: A Study in Progressive Trade Unionism.* New York: Ancon Publishing, 1934.

Chapter 6

Baltimore Federation of Labor. *Illustrated History of the Baltimore Federation of Labor.* Baltimore, 1900.

Baltimore Typographers Union, Local 12, Minutes, 1886–1917. University of Baltimore, Baltimore, Maryland.

Beirne, D. Randall. "Late Nineteenth Century Industrial Communities in Baltimore." *Maryland Historian* 11, no. 1 (Spring 1980): 39–49.

Bricklayers Union, Local 1, Minutes, 1886–1917. Bricklayers and Allied Craftsmen Union No. 1 of Maryland, Towson, Maryland.

Bruchey, Eleanor S. *The Business Elite in Baltimore, 1880–1914.* New York: Arno Press, 1976. Reprint of Johns Hopkins University dissertation, 1967.

The Critic (Baltimore), 1888–1893.

Fink, Leon. *Workingmen's Democracy: The Knights of Labor and American Politics.* Urbana: University of Illinois Press, 1983.

Labor Leader (Baltimore), 1910–1911.

Maryland Bureau of Industrial Statistics (known variously as Bureau of Industrial Statistics and Information, Bureau of Statistics and Information of Maryland, and State Board of Labor and Statistics). Annual and biennial reports, 1887–1918.

Montgomery, David. *The Fall of the House of Labor: The Workplace, the State, and American Labor Activism, 1865–1925.* Cambridge: Cambridge University Press, 1987.

——— . *Workers' Control in America: Studies in the History of Work, Technology, and Labor Struggles.* Cambridge: Cambridge University Press, 1979.

Noble, David F. *America by Design: Science, Technology, and the Rise of Corporate Capitalism.* New York: Knopf, 1977.

Ryon, Roderick N. "Baltimore Workers and Industrial Decision-Making, 1890–1917." *Journal of Southern History* 51, no. 4 (November 1985): 565–580.

Chapter 7

Bernard, Richard M. "A Portrait of Baltimore in 1880: Economic and Occupational Patterns in an Early American

City." *Maryland Historical Magazine* 69, no. 4 (Winter 1974): 341–360.

"Census of Deptford Hundred or Fells Point, 1776." *Maryland Historical Magazine* 25, no. 3 (September 1930): 271–275.

Douglass, Frederick. *My Bondage and My Freedom.* New York: Dover Publications, 1969.

"Fells Point." Vertical files. Maryland Room, Enoch Pratt Free Library, Baltimore.

Fells Point Gazette. December 1977–December 1986.

Foner, Philip S., and Ronald L. Lewis. *The Black Worker: A Documentary from Colonial Times to the Present*, vol. 1, *The Black Worker to 1869.* Philadelphia: Temple University Press, 1978.

Garitee, Jerome. *The Republic's Private Navy: An American Privateering Business as Practiced by Baltimore during the War of 1812.* Middletown, Conn.: Wesleyan University Press for Mystic Seaport, 1977.

Hirschfeld, Charles. *Baltimore, 1870–1900: Studies in Social History.* Baltimore: The Johns Hopkins Press, 1941.

Hollowak, Thomas. "The Emergence of a Baltimore Polonia." Manuscript.

Kemp, Janet. *Housing Conditions in Baltimore.* Baltimore: Federated Charities, 1907.

Louis Sauer Associates. *Fells Point Land Use Recommendations: Final Report.* Philadelphia, March 1977.

———. *Fells Point Urban Design Guide: Final Report.* Philadelphia, December 1976.

Obenauer, Marie L. *Working Hours, Earnings and Duration of Employment of Women Workers in Selected Industries of Maryland and of California.* Bulletin no. 96, U.S. Bureau of Labor. Washington, D.C.: Government Printing Office, 1911.

Olson, Sherry. *Baltimore: The Building of an American City.* Baltimore: Johns Hopkins University Press, 1980.

Planning and Urban Design Section, Baltimore Department of Housing and Community Development. *West Fells Point Development Guidelines.* Baltimore, 1985.

Robinson, James. *The Baltimore Directory for 1804.* Baltimore, 1804.

Shopes, Linda. "The Can Makers of Baltimore, 1870–1900." Manuscript.

———. "Women Cannery Workers in Baltimore, 1880–1945." Manuscript.

Steffen, Charles. *The Mechanics of Baltimore: Workers and Politics in the Age of Revolution, 1763–1812.* Urbana: University of Illinois Press, 1984.

———. "Who Owns the Waterfront: Property Relations in Fells Point, Baltimore, 1783." *Urbanism Past and Present* 8, no. 1 (1983): 12–17.

Stickle, Douglas F. "Death and Class in Baltimore: The Yellow Fever Epidemic of 1800." *Maryland Historical Magazine* 74, no. 3 (September 1979): 282–299.

Thomas, Bettye C. "A Nineteenth Century Black Operated Shipyard, 1866–1884: Reflections upon Its Inception and Ownership." *Journal of Negro History* 59, no. 1 (January 1974): 1–12.

U.S. Bureau of the Census. *1970 Census of Population and Housing, Census Tracts, Baltimore, Md. SMSA.* Washington, D.C.: Government Printing Office, April 1972.

———. *1980 Census of Population and Housing, Census Tracts, Baltimore, Md. SMSA.* Washington, D.C.: Government Printing Office, July 1983.

Weeks, Thomas. *Third Biennial Report of the Bureau of Industrial Statistics and Information of Maryland, 1888–1889.* Baltimore, 1890.

Wheeler, William Bruce. "The Baltimore Jeffersonians, 1788–1800: A Profile of Intra-Factional Conflict." *Maryland Historical Magazine* 66, no. 2 (Summer 1970): 153–168.

Chapter 8

Argersinger, Jo Ann E. *Toward a New Deal in Baltimore: People and Government in the Great Depression.* Chapel Hill: University of North Carolina Press, 1988.

Avnet, I. Duke. "Pat Whalen." *Phylon: The Atlantic University Review of Race and Culture.* Reprint, n.d., 249–254.

Baltimore Sun. March 20–May 31, 1936; October 13, 1936; February 6, 1937.

Bernstein, Irving. *Turbulent Years: A History of the American Worker, 1933–1941.* Boston: Houghton Mifflin, 1969.

De Caux, Len. *Labor Radical: From the Wobblies to CIO.* Boston: Beacon Press, 1970.

Nelson, Bruce. *Workers on the Waterfront: Seamen, Longshoremen, and Unionism in the 1930s.* Urbana: University of Illinois Press, 1988.

Raskin, Bernard. *On a True Course: The Story of the National Maritime Union AFL-CIO.* Washington, D.C.: Merkle Press, 1967.

Rubin, Charles. *The Log of Rubin the Sailor.* New York: International Publishers, 1973.

Chapter 9

"Bethlehem Steel," "Dundalk," "Sparrows Point," and "United Steelworkers of America." Vertical files. Maryland Room, Enoch Pratt Free Library, Baltimore.

Brody, David. *Steelworkers in America: The Nonunion Era.* New York: Harper & Row, 1960.

Green, James R. *The World of the Worker: Labor in Twentieth-Century America.* New York: Hill and Wang, 1980.

Reutter, Mark. *Sparrows Point: Making Steel—The Rise and Ruin of American Industrial Might.* New York: Summit Books, 1988.

Ryon, Roderick N. "An Ambiguous Legacy, Baltimore Blacks and the CIO, 1936–1941." *Journal of Negro History* 65, no. 1 (Winter 1980): 18–33.

Chapter 10

Erickson, Rodney A., and Marylynn Gentry. "Suburban Nucleations." *Geographical Review* 75, no. 1 (1985): 19–31.

Hayward, Mary Ellen. "Urban Vernacular Architecture in Nineteenth-Century Baltimore." *Winterthur Portfolio* 16 (1981): 33–63.

Hirsch, Arnold. *Making the Second Ghetto: Race and Housing in Chicago.* Cambridge: Cambridge University Press, 1983.

Jackson, Kenneth. *Crabgrass Frontier: The Suburbanization of the United States.* New York: Oxford University Press, 1985.

Olson, Sherry. *Baltimore: The Building of an American City.* Baltimore: Johns Hopkins University Press, 1980.

Orser, W. Edward. "The Making of a Baltimore Townhouse Community: The Edmondson Avenue Area, 1915–1945." *Maryland Historical Magazine* 80, no. 3 (Fall 1985): 203–227.

———. "Racial Change in Retrospect: White Perceptions of Stability and Mobility in Edmondson Village, 1910–1980." *International Journal of Oral History* 5, no. 1 (February 1984): 36–58.

———. "Second-Hand Suburbs: Black Pioneers in Baltimore's Edmondson Village, 1955–1980." *Journal of Urban History* 16, no. 3 (May 1990): 227–262.

Power, Garrett. "Apartheid Baltimore Style: The Residential Segregation Ordinances of 1910–1913." *Maryland Law Review* 42, no. 2 (November 1983): 289–328.

"Rowhouse: A Baltimore Style of Living." Exhibition at the Peale Museum, Baltimore City Life Museums, 1981–1990. Barry Dressel, chief curator; Mary Ellen Hayward, exhibition curator; Jane Webb Smith, field curator; Robert Weis, decorative arts curator.

U.S. Bureau of the Census. Tract Data for the Baltimore SMSA (Standard Metropolitan Statistical Area), 1930–1980.

Chapter 11

Berkowitz, B. "Economic Development Really Works: Baltimore, Maryland." In *Urban Economic Development,* ed. R. D. Bingham and J. P. Blair. Sage Urban Affairs Annual, no. 27. Beverly Hills, Calif: Sage, 1984.

———. "Rejoinder to Levine." *Journal of Urban Affairs* 9, no. 2 (1987): 125–132.

Garland, E. "The End of Baltimore as a Blue-Collar Town." *Baltimore Magazine* (December 1980): 53–60.

Levine, Marc. "Downtown Redevelopment as an Urban Growth Strategy: A Critical Appraisal of the Baltimore Renaissance." *Journal of Urban Affairs* 9, no. 2 (1987): 103–123.

Lyall, K. *A Bicycle Built for Two: Public/Private Partnership in Baltimore's Renaissance.* Washington, D.C.: Committee for Economic Development, 1980.

Stoker, Robert P. "Baltimore: A Self-Evaluating City?" In *The Politics of Urban Development,* ed. C. N. Stone and H. T. Sanders. Lawrence: University of Kansas Press, 1987.

Szanton, Peter. *Baltimore 2000: A Choice of Futures.* Baltimore: Morris Goldseker Foundation of Maryland, 1986.

Photo Sources

Afro-American Company of Baltimore: 64, 71, 189; Amalgamated Clothing Workers of America Records, Labor-Management Documentation Center, Cornell University: ii (detail), 80, 87, 92, 94, 97, 99; American Social History Project: xx, 7 (top), 9, 10 (top & bottom).

B & O Railroad Museum: 4 (top & bottom); Baltimore City Department of Transportation: 217; Baltimore Museum of Industry: 47 (bottom), 83, 106 (bottom), 107; Baltimore Neighborhood Heritage Project Collection, Langsdale Library, University of Baltimore: 38 (detail), 40 (top), 41, 45 (Jean Hare), 46, 51, 136 (top); Baltimore Steelworkers History Project: 176 (bottom), 177, 186, 191; *The Baltimore Sun*: 168, 169, 171, 173, 235; Bryn Mawr College Archives: 28; Bryn Mawr School Archives: 29.

Mrs. Florine Camper: 76; Art Cohen: 55, 147, 150, 152, 194, 198, 200.

Eleutherian Mills Library, Hagley Foundation: 174, 176 (top), 182 (top & bottom), 183 (top & bottom), 250–51 (detail); Enoch Pratt Free Library: 13, 16, 25, 31, 40 (bottom), 43, 44, 47 (top), 100, 112, 123, 214.

Ferdinand Hamburger, Jr. Archives of The Johns Hopkins University: 77; David Harvey: 226, 231, 232, 233, 234, 239, 242–43, 244, 246 (top & bottom), 247, 248 (top, middle, & bottom), 249 (top & bottom); Sirkka Holm: 188, 196.

Jewish Historical Society of Maryland, Inc.: 84, 89.

Jacques S. Kelly: 52–53, 59, 74, 136 (bottom), 202, 210, 215, 219, 220.

Maryland Historical Society: 3, 19, 78–79 (detail), 85, 105, 106 (top); Maryland Institute of Art, Equitable Photographic Survey: 139 (Peggy Fox), 140 (Peggy Fox), 207 (David Lavine), 209 (David Lavine); Maryland State Archives, Robert G. Merrick Archives of Maryland Historical Photographs: 34 (MdHRG1477-4905); George Meyers: 192; Office of Barbara Mikulski: 148; Juanita Jackson Mitchell: 56, 68, 69.

The National Portrait Gallery, Smithsonian Institution: 124 (detail/portrait attributed to Elisha Hammond).

W. Edward Orser: 223.

The Peale Museum, Baltimore City Life Museums: vi (detail) (The A. Aubrey Bodine Photographic Collection), 23, 36, 60 (top & bottom), 62 (Bodine Collection), 65, 66, 90, 102, 110, 113, 120 (Bodine Collection), 127 (Bodine Collection), 129, 134–35, 156–57 (Bodine Collection), 162 (Bodine Collection), 184 (Bodine Collection), 229, 230 (Bodine Collection); Photography Collections, Albin O. Kuhn Library & Gallery, University of Maryland Baltimore County: 130 (top/#3528, bottom/#835), 131 (top/#854, bottom/#2058); Amelia B. Pully-Pruitt: 67.

Charlotte Cannon Rhines: 109, 111, 142.

St. Bernardine's Roman Catholic Church: 206; Christian Penn Sauter: 212–13; Smithsonian Institution: 15 (photo #49652, detail), 22 (photo #49764), 26 (photo #49652); Special Collections and Archives, Rutgers University Libraries: 154, 158, 159 (top & bottom), 161, 163.

George Vorth: 185.

Beverly and Jack Wilgus: 7 (bottom); Beryl Warner Williams: 144.

About the Contributors

Jo Ann E. Argersinger is the Associate Vice-President for Academic Affairs and a member of the History Department at the University of Maryland Baltimore County campus. She is completing a study of garment workers and the Amalgamated Clothing Workers and has published a book entitled *Toward a New Deal in Baltimore: People and Government in the Great Depression* (1988).

Elizabeth Fee is Associate Professor of Health Policy and Management at the Johns Hopkins University School of Hygiene and Public Health. She is currently writing a book about the history and politics of public health in Baltimore. She is the author of *Disease and Discovery* (1987), editor of *Women and Health* (1983), coeditor with Daniel M. Fox of *AIDS: The Burdens of History* (1988), and coeditor with Roy M. Acheson of *A History of Education in Public Health: Health that Mocks the Doctors' Rules* (1991).

Sylvia Gillett is Associate Professor of English at Dundalk Community College. She is also a freelance writer, who has published numerous poems, short stories, articles, and reviews.

Eric Hallengren, a Baltimore resident for most of his life, teaches English at the New Community College of Baltimore. He has been active in progressive political activities since 1967.

Bill Harvey, a native of Hampden, lives in Baltimore and writes on local labor issues. He has published *"The People* Is *Grass": A History of Hampden-Woodberry, 1802–1945* (1988).

David Harvey teaches at Oxford University. He was previously a faculty member in the Department of Geography and Environmental Engineering at Johns Hopkins University. His books include *Social Justice and the City* (1973), *The Limits to Capital* (1984), and *The Condition of Postmodernity* (1989).

Donna Poggi Keck has lived in Baltimore for 25 years and has been active in antiwar, women's liberation, and community issues. She currently works for the city's Department of Housing and Community Development, where she is developing affordable housing for low-income and homeless families and individuals.

Karen Olson teaches history and anthropology at Dundalk Community College. In 1965 and 1966 she was a staff member in the Atlanta office of the Student Non-Violent Coordinating Committee (SNCC).

W. Edward Orser is Associate Professor and Chairperson of the Department of American Studies at the University of Maryland Baltimore County. He has directed students in a series of community studies projects on Baltimore's west side, including Irvington, Gwynns Falls and Leakin Parks, Catonsville (with Joseph Arnold), and Woodlawn. His research on the dynamics of racial change in Edmondson Village has appeared in the *International Journal of Oral History, Maryland Historical Magazine,* and *Journal of Urban History.*

Irene Reville is a socialist feminist who works as a social worker and is the mother of a three-year-old daughter.

Roderick Ryon teaches labor history at Towson State University. His articles on women, African Americans, and labor have appeared in the *Maryland Historical Magazine, Journal of Southern History,* and *Journal of Negro History.* He is at work on a book about residential neighborhoods on Baltimore's west side.

Linda Shopes is an associate historian with the Pennsylvania Historical and Museum Commission. Previously she taught for many years at the University of Maryland Baltimore County. She has worked and written widely in the areas of oral and public history.

James Sizemore is a freelance humorous illustrator and writer. He teaches the history of cartooning at a Baltimore area university and playwriting to elementary and middle-school children at Center Stage.

Andrea Kidd Taylor currently works as an industrial hygienist and occupational health policy consultant for the International Union, United Automobile, Aerospace, and Agricultural Implement Workers of American (UAW) in Detroit. She has a doctorate of public health from the Johns Hopkins University School of Hygiene and Public Health in Baltimore. While in Baltimore, Taylor held the offices of vice-president and treasurer of the African-American Women's Caucus, a community-based organization that addresses a broad range of social and political issues affecting women of color in the United States and other countries around the globe.

Linda Zeidman teaches economics and history at Essex Community College. She was coproducer and director of the Baltimore Steelworkers History Project film, "One Voice," about the history of Locals 2609 and 2610, United Steelworkers of America, funded by the National Endowment for the Humanities.

Index